Architectures of Revolt

In the series *Urban Life, Landscape, and Policy*, edited by David Stradling, Larry Bennett, and Davarian Baldwin. Founding editor, Zane L. Miller.

Maureen Donaghy, *Democratizing Urban Development: Community Organizations for Housing across the United States and Brazil*

Maureen A. Flanagan, *Constructing the Patriarchal City: Gender and the Built Environments of London, Dublin, Toronto, and Chicago, 1870s into the 1940s*

Harold L. Platt, *Sinking Chicago: Climate Change and the Remaking of a Flood-Prone Environment*

Pamela Wilcox, Francis T. Cullen, and Ben Feldmeyer, *Communities and Crime: An Enduring American Challenge*

J. Mark Souther, *Believing in Cleveland: Managing Decline in "The Best Location in the Nation"*

Nathanael Lauster, *The Death and Life of the Single-Family House: Lessons from Vancouver on Building a Livable City*

Aaron Cowan, *A Nice Place to Visit: Tourism and Urban Revitalization in the Postwar Rustbelt*

Carolyn Gallaher, *The Politics of Staying Put: Condo Conversion and Tenant Right-to-Buy in Washington, DC*

Evrick Brown and Timothy Shortell, eds., *Walking in Cities: Quotidian Mobility as Urban Theory, Method, and Practice*

Michael T. Maly and Heather Dalmage, *Vanishing Eden: White Construction of Memory, Meaning, and Identity in a Racially Changing City*

Harold L. Platt, *Building the Urban Environment: Visions of the Organic City in the United States, Europe, and Latin America*

Kristin M. Szylvian, *The Mutual Housing Experiment: New Deal Communities for the Urban Middle Class*

Kathryn Wilson, *Ethnic Renewal in Philadelphia's Chinatown: Space, Place, and Struggle*

Robert Gioielli, *Environmental Activism and the Urban Crisis: Baltimore, St. Louis, Chicago*

Robert B. Fairbanks, *The War on Slums in the Southwest: Public Housing and Slum Clearance in Texas, Arizona, and New Mexico, 1936–1965*

Carlton Wade Basmajian, *Atlanta Unbound: Enabling Sprawl through Policy and Planning*

A list of additional titles in this series appears at the back of this book

EDITED BY MARK SHIEL

Architectures of Revolt

The Cinematic City circa 1968

TEMPLE UNIVERSITY PRESS
Philadelphia • Rome • Tokyo

TEMPLE UNIVERSITY PRESS
Philadelphia, Pennsylvania 19122
www.temple.edu/tempress

Copyright © 2018 by Temple University—Of The Commonwealth System of
  Higher Education
All rights reserved
Published 2018

Cover photos from the film *El grito* (Leobardo López Arretche, Centro
Universitario de Estudios Cinematográficos, UNAM, México, 1970).
Copyright © 1970 by Universidad Nacional Autónoma de México. Used with
permission of the Universidad Nacional Autónoma de México.

Library of Congress Cataloging-in-Publication Data

Names: Shiel, Mark, editor.
Title: Architectures of revolt : the cinematic city circa 1968 / edited by
  Mark Shiel.
Description: Philadelphia : Temple University Press, 2018. | Series: Urban
  life, landscape and policy | Includes index.
Identifiers: LCCN 2017052255 (print) | LCCN 2017059926 (ebook) | ISBN
  9781439910054 (E-book) | ISBN 9781439910030 (hardback : alk. paper) | ISBN
  9781439910047 (paper : alk. paper)
Subjects: LCSH: Cities and towns in motion pictures. | City planning. |
  Motion pictures—History—20th century. | BISAC: PERFORMING ARTS /
  Film & Video / History & Criticism. | ARCHITECTURE / Urban & Land
  Use Planning.
Classification: LCC PN1995.9.C513 (ebook) | LCC PN1995.9.C513 A73 2018
  (print) | DDC 791.43/621732—dc23
LC record available at https://lccn.loc.gov/2017052255

9 8 7 6 5 4 3 2 1

This book is dedicated with love to Alyce, Anouk, and Adam.

Contents

List of Illustrations		ix
Acknowledgments		xi
Introduction: Cinema, Architecture, and Cities circa 1968 • Mark Shiel		1
1	The *Cinétracts*, *Détournement*, and Social Space in Paris • Jennifer Stob	35
2	Milan, the Cine City of 1968: Metamorphosis and Identity • Gaetana Marrone	66
3	Inextinguishable Fire—or How to Make a Film in Berlin in 1968 • Andrew J. Webber	91
4	Slouching toward Chicago in Search of Peace and Love: *Medium Cool* and Chicago 1968 • Jon Lewis	112
5	New York, 1968 • Stanley Corkin	141
6	"It's a Big Garage." Cinematic Images of Los Angeles circa 1968 • Mark Shiel	164
7	Cinema and the Mexico City of 1968 • Jesse Lerner	189
8	Tokyo 1969: Revolutionary Image-Thieves in the Disintegrating City • Stephen Barber	212
Contributors		229
Film Title Index		231
Subject Index		235

Illustrations

I.1	Walter Cronkite broadcasts for CBS from Hue, Vietnam, during the Tet Offensive	6
I.2	Demonstrators protest charges against Jane Jacobs	23
I.3	Entrance of the École des beaux-arts, Paris	24
1.1	Selected frames from *Cinétract 004* showing CRS riot police	49
1.2	Selected frames from *Cinétract 003* commemorating the death of Gilles Tautin	50
1.3	Selected frames from *Cinétract 018* showing a pro-Gaullist demonstration and anti-establishment graffiti	52
1.4	Selected frames from *Filmtract 015* calling on the viewer to "regardez les choses en face"	54
2.1	The Guest and the mother in the garden of the Milanese villa in *Teorema*	72
2.2	The father and industrialist walks through the desert in *Teorema*	77
2.3	Tiresias and Antigone walk past dead bodies in the streets of Milan in *I cannibali*	80
2.4	Antigone is questioned by military police in *I cannibali*	84
3.1	Barbed wire protects the modernist office building of Axel Springer publishers in Berlin	94
3.2	The burning of skin in *NOT Extinguishable Fire*	100
3.3	Burning vans outside the Springer building in *Break the Power of the Manipulators*	106
4.1	Harold in Chicago's Grant Park in *Medium Cool*	116
4.2	The squalor of Little Appalachia in Chicago in *Medium Cool*	121
4.3	Kids on the street in Bronzeville in *Medium Cool*	125

4.4	White college students supporting Senator Robert Kennedy near the beginning of *Medium Cool*, and the Democratic National Convention later in the film	128
4.5	Location footage of real demonstrations and riots in Chicago from *Medium Cool*	129
5.1	The architecture of Columbia University in *Columbia Revolt*	147
5.2	The built environment of Manhattan in *Midnight Cowboy*	148
5.3	Two locations from *Columbia Revolt*	152
5.4	Selected New York locations in *Greetings*	156
6.1	"Diary of the French Revolt," cover story in the *Los Angeles Free Press*	166
6.2	*Demonstration, Century Plaza, 1967*	171
6.3	Contra Costa College standing in for a Los Angeles university in *Zabriskie Point*	173
6.4	The Sunset Strip re-created in studio and shot on location in *Riot on the Sunset Strip*	175
6.5	The heavily commercialized streetscapes of Los Angeles in *Model Shop*	179
7.1	Front cover of the official *Mexico 68* magazine, no. 31	198
7.2	Student life and student demonstrations in Mexico City as seen in *El Grito*	200
7.3	The prelude, events, and aftermath of the military massacre of demonstrators as depicted in *El Grito*	202
8.1	The fragmented urban space of Tokyo in *Funeral Parade of Roses*	221
8.2	The performative space of Tokyo's Shinjuku district in *Diary of a Shinjuku Thief*	223
8.3	Street riots at the Shinjuku train station at night near the end of *Diary of a Shinjuku Thief*	224

Acknowledgments

This book has been several years in gestation, so I welcome the opportunity to finally record my profound gratitude to Zane Miller, David Stradling, and Stanley Corkin, all of the University of Cincinnati, for first approaching me with the idea of publishing an edited collection on 1968 in cinema and urban history, and then for proposing the book to Temple University Press. The first seeds of the book's content came from a panel on the subject that I organized and chaired at the Society for Cinema and Media Studies conference in Philadelphia in 2008, and to which Ruben Gallo, Jon Lewis, and Jennifer Stob made fascinating contributions. Mick Gusinde-Duffy, who was then senior acquisitions editor at Temple University Press, welcomed the book proposal and saw it through its initial stages, and since then the project has been expertly managed by Temple's editor-in-chief, Aaron Javsicas, to whom I'm also deeply grateful. Other Temple University Press staff helped chaperone the book through various maneuvers—thanks, therefore, to Gary Kramer, Micah Kleit, Nikki Miller, Katie Wertz, and Sara Cohen. The manuscript and my editing of it benefited from the wisdom and insight of Temple's two anonymous readers, and from in-depth commentary and critique from Larry Bennett of De Paul University, Chicago. My home institution, the Department of Film Studies at King's College London, provided valuable support of my research for the project and an always-stimulating intellectual environment, in which discussion often turned toward '68— thank you especially to Rosalind Galt, Belen Vidal, and Michele Pierson, and, in other departments at King's, to Patrick Ffrench and David Treece. Parts of the arguments I make in my contributions to this book were tested out in lectures and conference presentations at several institutions, so I'm grateful to the colleagues who invited me to speak and the audiences who gave me useful feedback: thanks to Rebecca Farnum and Clare Herrick for the opportunity to address the Human Geography Seminar at King's; to Adrian Parr, Jana Braziel, and Stanley Corkin at the Taft Research Center of the University of Cincinnati; to Mark Quigley and Jan-Christopher Horak at the University of California Los Angeles Film and Television Archive, and to Berit Hummel at the Center for Metropolitan Studies of the Technische Universität Berlin. The various contributors to the book have shown great commitment and tenacity during its long evolution, for which I owe them warm thanks in addition to my admiration of their scholarship.

Architectures of Revolt

Introduction

Cinema, Architecture, and Cities circa 1968

MARK SHIEL

The histories of cinema and of the city have been closely intertwined for over one hundred years. However, at few precise moments in time has their intertwining been more evident than in 1968, a year that witnessed political revolutions and a revolutionary cinematic engagement, both of which relied upon interacting with and using the city in new ways. As the various chapters in this book detail in city-specific case studies, from Paris, Berlin, Milan, and Chicago to New York, Los Angeles, Mexico City, and Tokyo, activists and filmmakers took to the streets, commandeered buildings and spaces, and sought to remake the urban landscape as an expression of utopian longing or as a dystopian critique of the established order.

Fifty years later, this book seeks to explore the degree to which the real events of political revolt in the urban landscape in 1968 drove change in the nature and attitudes of filmmakers and architects alike. On the one hand, they required filmmakers to reinvent their ways of making motion pictures because of the distinctive technical and artistic challenges of shooting on location in real urban environments, while encouraging many to rethink the line between filmmaker and activist. On the other hand, architects were forced to critically reflect on the role of their profession in creating or failing to solve the problems of the built environment that were such a prominent root cause of unrest, and this self-reflexive thinking prompted an opening of architecture to greater influence from other arts and to a reenvisioning of architecture as another kind of representation.

Cinema, Contestation, and the Built Environment

The films discussed in this book cover a range from avant-garde and agitprop to mainstream narrative feature films, all sharing a focus on the city and, often, particular streets and buildings, as places of political contestation, and often violence, which the medium of cinema was uniquely equipped to capture. Equally, the various contributors investigate the ways in which cinematic representations of the city circa 1968 revealed and exposed to scrutiny processes endemic in all modern city growth but that were seemingly exaggerated then, including rationalist architecture and planning, the increasing encroachment of systems of control and observation by the state and corporate powers, and the increasing interpenetration of the urban landscape, media, and consumption. These important themes, which recur throughout the book, demonstrate that cinema's close interest in the built environment circa 1968 not only implicated the discipline of architecture but also that of urban planning—two fields that are not identical but that refer to overlapping micro and macro spatial scales, building and city, respectively, and are often taught and institutionally organized together in education, in professional practice, and in government and policy. In this Introduction, I will begin to enumerate some of the rich variety of filmmaking that 1968 inspired and the urban and architectural issues cinema of that era examined, while thinking through some of the key disciplinary issues raised by considering film and the built environment together. Identification of the broad questions at stake in the book will then lead me to highlight the important additions to knowledge and debate made by the contributing authors in the subsequent chapters.

The book is founded on the idea that this was a unique moment of parallel and intertwined contestations. For example, cinema was thrown into turmoil by the decision of the government of Charles de Gaulle to fire Henri Langlois, the much-admired director of the Cinémathèque française, in a move seen by filmmakers as dangerous state interference in cultural affairs. Filmmakers soon after shut down the Cannes Film Festival in sympathy with protesting students in Paris; censorship regimes in the United States and other countries were weakened; there was a precipitous (if temporary) decline in the power of industrial cinemas such as Hollywood, matched by a rise in interaction between narrative fiction film, experimental film, and documentary film; and there was an explosion of politically agitational filming across Europe, North and South America, Japan, and Southeast Asia. This was a moment of exceptional tension, competition, and conflict at the box office, for financing, distribution, audiences, and critical attention, as the various kinds of cinema articulated different ideological positions, different models of what film and film culture should be and, often, with a particular concern for marginal and oppressed social groups. Paramount was a clash between declining industrial, studio-based, genre-based, entertainment-oriented, profit-driven cinema (often known as "classical" cinema), and emergent new waves and undergrounds, usually low budget, thriving on low production values with strongly realist or abstract visual style, or new combinations of the two, and new utopian thinking (the high point of cinematic "modernism").[1]

This moment of turmoil also entailed an overhaul of critical and intellectual thinking about cinema, playing a decisive role in the very formation of the discipline of film studies (as well as media studies and mass communications), especially by encouraging interpretations of film in terms of ideology and ideology critique, and the proliferation of a rich canvas of Marxist, structuralist, semiotic, psychoanalytic, feminist, and post-structuralist analyses—to point to just one foundational example, the publication of Christian Metz's *Essais sur la signification au cinéma* (1968).[2] The culmination of a longer evolution and growth of art cinema and political film that had dominated the international scene since World War II in the aftermath of fascism and accompanying a decline of European empires, 1968 became a high-water mark in the history of *engagé* film culture—reflected in the Paris-based journal *Cahiers du cinéma* or New York's *Cineaste*—and especially among an outraged and burgeoning student generation in the major metropolises of advanced industrial nations. For example, Thomas Elsaesser has recently explained the decisive influence on his subsequent career of his experience as a young film critic living in Paris for much of 1968, from which he gained the belief "that the cinema was worth devoting one's life to," while Francesco Casetti in his comprehensive *Theories of Cinema, 1945–1995* privileges 1968 for "the perception of art as a particular battlefield, rather than as a mere extension of the battles fought inside society . . . a movement from cinema towards politics."[3]

Likewise, both the practice and study of architecture were overturned by the political turmoil of the day, as contestations in the streets radicalized large numbers of professional architects, and faculty and students at schools of architecture and urban planning, by demonstrating the role of certain kinds of utilitarian architecture in alienating young people and minorities, and in aiding and abetting the repressive agendas of the state and capitalist powers. Planning and construction continued apace on iconic late modernist buildings such as the World Trade Center (1966–1973) and Tour Montparnasse (1969–1973). But leftist vanguards such as the Internationale Situationniste and Lotta Continua insisted that any successful change in the social, political, and economic status quo would require, as a fundamental ingredient, a redefinition of the physical and ethical character of cities. Architectural avant-gardes such as the London-based Archigram and the Florence-based Superstudio modeled futuristic urban utopias, and architectural historians and theorists such as Peter Cook, Reyner Banham, Aldo Rossi, Manfredo Tafuri, Denise Scott Brown, and Robert Venturi entered into intense, and often antagonistic, debates on the best future direction for buildings and urban planning. Interventions into these debates often prominently featured critiques of Le Corbusier or Mies van der Rohe and hypotheses on the emergence of postmodernism.[4]

The clash in architecture also often involved open conflict between government and/or private owners of buildings and land, intent on real estate development and supported by the military and/or police, and various oppositional groups, including racial minorities, bohemians, New Leftists, feminists, homosexuals, local residents, neighborhood activists, architectural preservationists, and especially the poor and the marginal in society, who were more often displaced by grand urban projects than others. In conflicts between these forces, land use, architecture and design, construction and environmental impact, and public access to and use of urban space were all at issue, while in terms of architectural history and preservation the conflict opposed modernist, rationalist, and functionalist planning and design to older styles and structures (e.g., ancient, folk, arts and crafts, art nouveau, art deco, beaux-arts, neoclassical) as significant parts of innumerable cities were subject to actual or proposed destruction to make way for new development.

Hence, a special—arguably unique—moment of intense experimentation and critique was evident in both cinema and architecture circa 1968, and the two were closely intertwined. Filmmakers engaged more directly than ever before in self-conscious examination of the built environment through rendering it on film, and often with an awareness of architectural debates of the day. And architects, who were often also cinephiles, reflected on the mass mediation of their profession and the cities it produced. Developments in the two fields of endeavor were not always exactly simultaneous: the chapters in this book take into account, and explore, the different timing of key events in film and architecture in and around 1968, and from one city to another. But, in a variety of cities worldwide, both film and architecture were gripped by self-conscious reflection on their raison d'être as much as by innovative making and creating. Forming the heart of the book, this exceptional conjuncture is central to its exploration of the two fields and of the historical moment of "1968." Indeed, it is an aim of this book also to make the case that the significance of 1968 as an historical moment continues to merit and reward documentation and analysis and ought to be actively remembered. The book will do this by honing in on key events of the era, and their representation, on the ground or at a grassroots level in specific urban contexts that were the scene of both planned and spontaneous revolt, seeking to rematerialize those events in space and time.[5]

1968 as a Revolutionary Moment

As a starting point, we have to ask ourselves why 1968 can be claimed as a revolutionary moment in the first place, a question around which a voluminous literature has developed in many countries and languages in the past fifty years. (See Figure I.1.) First, it surely has to do with that year's particular density of turning points: in January, the Tet offensive against U.S. forces launched by Vietcong and North Vietnamese troops; in February, the French government's incendiary decision to fire the director of the Cinémathèque française, Henri Langlois; in March, the outbreak of student protest on the suburban campus of the University of Paris at Nanterre; in April, the assassination of Martin Luther King Jr. in Memphis, Tennessee (an event that prompted a two-day delay in that year's Academy Awards ceremony); in May, the paralysis of central Paris by student occupations and street violence; in June, the assassination of U.S. presidential contender Senator Robert Kennedy in Los Angeles; in August, the Soviet invasion of Czechoslovakia; and so on. Second, 1968 stems from broader and long-term factors in the twenty-three years after World War II, too large to detail here but, briefly, including the postwar baby boom and new political and cultural importance of young people; rapid economic expansion in North America and Europe, as well as parts of Latin America and Asia, before recession in 1969 presaged the profound economic crises of the following decade; the objective expansion of technocracy and consumer capitalism as well as critiques of them; resistance to colonialism and imperialism in the Third World (the Vietnam War in particular); resistance to repressive state apparatuses by grassroots protest movements, fueling an intersection between extraparliamentary political activism and new political and cultural theories on the left of the political spectrum (i.e., the New Left, aided by the new prominence and size of youth populations in higher education); and attempts by leftists to connect protest by disaffected members of the white middle class with protest and resistance by colonized peoples, racial minorities, and the working class.

Figure I.1 CBS television news anchor Walter Cronkite broadcasts from Hue, Vietnam, during the Tet Offensive, February 1968 (CBS Photo Archive/Getty Images)

With respect to the specificities of urban life, other explanatory factors must also be reckoned with. These included the crisis of inner cities in the face of ongoing rapid and widespread suburbanization; an emerging sense of globalization given not only the ubiquity of trains, automobiles, and telephones but the increasing affordability of jet travel; the proliferation of media and media awareness (cinema, television, the mainstream and underground press, and rock music); mass media reporting of urban unrest from Paris and Prague to Chicago and Tokyo; the emergence of computing and other new technologies in everyday life; and the first photographs of Earth from outer space produced by the Apollo 8 mission in December 1968. Those photos, the geographer Denis Cosgrove has explained, were "the very first photos of Earth taken from space by human observers" and they "forced humans to acknowledge the bounds of life and the need to share a small, fragile globe."[6] In this book, all of these transformations of the quotidian come together powerfully, for example, in Jon Lewis's analysis of *Medium Cool* (Haskell Wexler, 1969), one of most notable feature-length films of a specific urban conflict of the day—the riots that overshadowed the Democratic National Convention in Chicago in August 1968, seen in Wexler's film through the eyes of a TV cameraman.

There is, of course, a large and substantial literature on the history and meaning of 1968 and the larger era known as the sixties from Ronald Fraser's *1968: A Student Generation in Revolt* (1988) to Kristin Ross's *May 1968 and Its Afterlives* (2002) and Sherman et al.'s *The Long 1968: Revisions and New Perspectives* (2013), to name just three titles.[7] Each of these has a different geographic emphasis or methodology, but all are cultural and political histories and involve not only documentation of the events of 1968 but reflection on their legacy for subsequent generations. This book aims to do some of the same kind of work, while also arguing that histories of 1968 have not yet sufficiently taken account of the specific roles played in the confrontations and crises of that era by film and by architecture. Seeking to add this new dimension to the history of the era and its distinctive political controversies and social movements, I hope this book will be taken as evidence that considering film and architecture in 1968 alongside each other is not only appropriate but necessary given that the era's political activism, to a great extent, grew out of a reconsideration of the relationship between reality and representation in urban space.

It is also important to admit a certain complexity in the chronological definition of "1968" because it is an undeniable fact that many important events in architecture and film happened a few years before or after 1968 as such, even though we can still say that 1968 retains preeminent historical importance. Events unfolded at a different pace in each city—hence the title of this book refers to "circa" rather than "in" 1968. That was the most important year in every respect in Paris but, for example, in San Francisco the "death of hippie" was already declared in 1967 while in New York 1969 and 1970 were the biggest years for mass political protest. In China, the Cultural Revolution led by Mao Tse-tung was inaugurated in 1966 and ran until 1973 but was arguably at its height in 1967 and 1968, exerting a profound influence on many elements of the Far Left worldwide.⁸ In Italy, as Gaetana Marrone explains in her essay in this book, Pier Paolo Pasolini's film *Teorema* (1968) articulated growing social and political unrest in that year in Milan, but some of the most interesting political cinema from that country and city emerged in the even more intense atmosphere that took hold after the Piazza Fontana bombing in December 1969. Therefore, one also has to be precise about the chronology in cinema. For example, many histories of Hollywood cinema of "the sixties" highlight 1967 as the year in which the old-fashioned hegemony of the major studios was broken by Arthur Penn's revisionist gangster film *Bonnie and Clyde* (1967) and Mike Nichols's study of suburban youth alienation *The Graduate* (1967). Other historians, however, make a case for Penn's earlier *The Chase* (1966) as the beginning of the paradigm shift to the so-called New Hollywood, while still others point to Dennis Hopper's *Easy Rider* (1969). All agree that 1968 was a definite turning point in the era's relaxation of film censorship because of the inauguration in October that year of the so-called ratings system of the film industry–governing Motion Picture Association of America. Still others note that year for the publication of Andrew Sarris's highly influential *The American Cinema: Directors and Directions* (1968), for its pioneering popularizing in English of the idea of the movie director as an *auteur*.⁹

Meanwhile, in architecture, for example, Robert Venturi published his seminal *Complexity and Contradiction in Architecture* in 1966, but it was in the fall of 1968 that he and Denise Scott Brown taught the groundbreaking architecture studio at Yale that would result in their book *Learning from Las Vegas* in 1972.¹⁰ As I will explain further below, many historians of architecture acknowledge 1968 as a turning point, including Alexander Tzonis and Liane Lefaivre, Harry Francis Mallgrave, Anthony Vidler, and K. Michael Hays, all of whom pinpoint that year. It was not necessarily the one year in that era that saw the most signature buildings completed, but many paradigmatic structures were being built or in planning (e.g., the aforementioned World Trade Center and Tour Montparnasse) and some major buildings had been completed a couple of years before but took a little while to become a focus of attention—for example, as Andrew Webber explains in his essay in this volume, the Springer Building corporate media headquarters in Berlin, completed in 1965, became one of the key sites of student protest in 1968. Some of the most important protests of the year arose directly in response to actual architectural interventions in real communities—for example, Columbia University's plans for construction of a gymnasium in nearby Morningside Park, which sparked the student occupation of that university of April–May 1968. And several of the year's most notable films placed architectural critique at their center—see, for example, Chris Marker's *The Sixth Side of the Pentagon* (1968), which anatomically dissects that building's gargantuan size and symbolic power while presenting the tens of thousands of demonstrators who massed around its walls on October 21, 1967, as a kind of spectacular architectural intervention.

Besides buildings, major events also took place in architectural education and theory: for example, students stormed and effectively closed the Milan Triennale architectural exhibition; the BBC first broadcast the series of radio talks by Reyner Banham that would become his famous book *Los Angeles: The Architecture of the Four Ecologies* (1971); and architectural journals such as *l'Architecture d'aujourd'hui* in France and *Casabella* in Italy published polemics and became deeply involved in the political controversies of the day.[11] Manfredo Tafuri moved to Venice to take up a new post as professor in the Institute of Architectural History, publishing *Teorie e storia dell'architettura* (1968), followed at the beginning of 1969 by his famous militant Marxist essay in sympathy with student strikes and occupations, "Per una critica dell'ideologia architettonica" in the new political journal *Contropiano*.[12] Nineteen sixty-eight was also something of a high point in experimentation by architects with the potential for cinema and cinema-related technologies: for example, in Charles and Ray Eames' tour de force filmic exploration of microscopic and interplanetary spatial scales in *Powers of Ten* (1968), in Robert Venturi and Denise Scott Brown's use of an automobile-mounted camera to film the Las Vegas Strip, and in Rem Koolhaas's decision to relocate from the Netherlands to London where he added to his early filmmaking training by studying at the Architectural Association and began to develop the especially cinematic approach to architecture that would underpin his subsequent fame.[13]

Reviewing the Literature

In insisting on the specificity of 1968, one of the aims of this book is to add to the rich range of literature on cinema and the city that has proliferated increasingly in the past twenty years, produced and used by scholars and students in a variety of fields including history of art and architecture, social and political history, urban planning and urban design, sociology, and cultural geography.

A significant number of valuable anthologies of scholarly essays present close analyses of the multiple aspects of the cinema-city relationship from the late nineteenth century to the present day, and in an international array of cities, from David Clarke's *The Cinematic City* (1997) to Yomi Braester and James Tweedie's *Cinema at the City's Edge: Film and Urban Networks in East*

Asia (2010).¹⁴ There has also been a growing number of monographs addressing the cinema-city relationship from a broad historical or philosophical point of view—for example, James Donald's *Imagining the Modern City* (1999)—and there have been several cinema histories of individual cities or geographically distinct groups of cities, including Paula Massood's *Black City Cinema: African American Urban Experiences in Film* (2003), Charlotte Brunsdon's *London in Cinema: The Cinematic City since 1945* (2007), and Lawrence Webb's *The Cinema of Urban Crisis: Seventies Film and the Reinvention of the City* (2015).¹⁵ It is a premise of this book that as the cinema-and-the-city field matures, there is a need for further studies that document and examine interconnections between geographically dispersed cities at very precise turning points in history. This book seeks not to examine cinema and the city in general, nor cinema and the city in one particular place, but the ways in which more or less simultaneous events and representations across a network of cities were part of a crisis that was globally distributed but temporally concentrated. Hence, this book aims to strike a somewhat new balance between geographic range and historical depth, recognizing that cities are important both for their individual existence and their interaction through an intensified form of what geographers call "comparative urbanism" transposed to film studies.¹⁶ The edited collection is arguably an especially appropriate response to the methodological challenge of addressing in one book the diverse conditions and histories of urbanization and cinema in geographically far-flung locales, and the historical and ongoing inseparability of urbanization and globalization is surely one of the factors that explains the large number of edited books on cinema and the city.¹⁷

It seems to me, however, that the cinematic connection with cities has been more extensively explored by scholars than has the relationship of cinema and architecture, although the latter field is also rich and most books on cinema and urban history, or cinema and urbanization, discuss architecture to some extent. Certain studies seem positioned fairly squarely between film studies and the other two fields—for example, Linda Krause and Patrice Petro's edited collection *Global Cities: Cinema, Architecture, and Urbanism in a Digital Age* (2003) and Pamela Robertson Wojcik's monograph *The Apartment Plot: Urban Living in American Film and Popular Culture, 1945–1975* (2010).¹⁸ Some studies are especially concerned with historical contexts while others foreground techniques of representing architecture in films (real buildings shot on location or imagined ones created through studio-based mise en scène). Some studies emphasize formal and experiential homologies between the two (a building as a kind of narrative to the visitor or user moving through it, the ability of a film to map the particularities of a building's structures and spaces, the visual and acoustic character of both) and others deal with the ramifications of moving image culture and technology for current architectural practice and training (e.g., architectural computer-aided design or virtual reality walk throughs as screen-based media). Examples of such studies range from Donald Albrecht's *Designing Dreams: Modern Architecture in the Movies* (2000) and Giuliana Bruno's *Atlas of Emotion: Journeys in Art, Architecture, and Film* (2002) to François Penz and Andong Lu's *Urban Cinematics: Understanding Urban Phenomena through the Moving Image* (2011) and Richard Koeck's *Cine-scapes: Cinematic Spaces in Architecture and Cities* (2013).[19]

In addition to Wojcik's book on apartments in cinema, particular building types are the focus of Merrill Schleier's monograph *Skyscraper Cinema: Architecture and Gender in American Film* (2009) and David B. Clarke and Marcus A. Doel's *Moving Pictures/Stopping Places: Hotels and Motels on Film* (2009).[20] In addition to Albrecht, several other titles focus on interwar cinema and modernist architecture—the era of art deco and streamlined moderne design having been particularly influential on set design in France and the United States, while others point to the special importance of Weimar Germany's expressionist and New Objectivity movements as film-architecture points of contact.[21] Another cluster of books can be identified for their primary preoccupation with broad histories of cinematic set design and production design—most recently, Lucy Fischer's edited volume *Art Direction and Production Design* (2015)—although the degree to which they discuss architecture and architectural practice proper varies considerably.[22]

This book aims to add to the many valuable insights this rich literature has provided, while pushing in three directions whose combination will distinguish it from existing work: first, and distinctively, in focusing on 1968, it examines the architectural environment at the very end of the era of architectural history generally described as "modern," concentrating not on that tendency's artistic high points but drawing attention to its collapse and deconstruction, and the battering of its critical reputation in the turn toward postmodernism; second, in emphasizing the importance of actual contestation in real public and private buildings and urban places, it avoids discussion of movie sets almost entirely; and, third, where much of the existing literature examines how architecture in cinema reveals ideologies of class, race, or gender over long periods of time, by linking architecture and revolt this book implies that the built environment, like cinema, is especially interesting and revealing at times when ideological struggle breaks out in the massing of bodies in peaceful protest and the confrontation of forces prepared for, and sometimes using, violence.

Surprisingly few books have been published in English that deal extensively with events in architecture in 1968, although most histories of modern and contemporary architecture, and of architectural theory, do acknowledge that 1968 was a key turning point in its effects. In the epilogue to his anthology *Modern Architectural Theory: A Historical Survey, 1673–1968* (2005), Mallgrave identifies it with "a genuine architectural crisis of colossal magnitude," although he withholds judgment of its net effect, declaring open-endedly "whether one looks at the year as the beginning of the end of modern theory or simply as a period of retrenchment and critical reassessment, it cannot be disputed that architectural theory would never again be the same. A new (or old) direction had to be found."[23] While Mallgrave suggests that architecture felt the effects of 1968 mainly "psychologically," Tzonis and Lefaivre give it more weight in *Architecture in Europe since 1968: Memory and Invention* (1992):

> In no other major political upheaval had architecture occupied such a privileged position. In the manifestos of Spring '68, from Berkeley to Berlin, from Paris to Prague, architecture became a central focus. In the varying degrees of sophistication or apocalyptic ecstasy typical of the period, architecture was used to attack the establishment in order to exemplify the poverty, pain, and pollution of the modern machine civilization, or it was held up as the sensuous, visionary, utopian "alternative" worth fighting for.[24]

For Tzonis and Lefaivre, indeed, 1968 was also important because architecture had not played such an important role in the French, American, or Russian revolutions before it. Barry Bergdoll and Alice Thomine likewise contend that May 1968 had concrete implications for architecture in France, in forcing a wholesale reorganization of architectural education, especially as a result of the student occupation of the École des beaux-arts, "the locus of entrenched academicism, which by 1968 translated as a kind of modernist orthodoxy, and the reaction against it took the form of embracing historical research, a new respect for the city, and a rejuvenated interest in a critical historical approach to the modern movement."[25] Bernard Tschumi has claimed that the two key consequences were an increase in the importance of architectural theory relative to practice and a much greater freedom among theorists and practicing architects to think across boundaries from architecture into "the arts, philosophy, literary criticism."[26] K. Michael Hays has similarly pointed to a qualitatively new theoretical and technical self-reflexivity in the profession, chief among which was the realization that "architecture theory is a practice of mediation" and as such was newly opened to Marxism, semiotics, psychoanalysis, formalism, phenomenology, and post-structuralism, "rewriting systems of thought assumed to be properly extrinsic or irrelevant into architecture's own idiolect."[27]

The Importance of the City in 1968

The reenergizing of architecture by 1968 appears to have been matched by an intensified sense of the importance and distinctive textures of the city. One of the best photojournalistic accounts of May 1968 in Paris—Philippe Labro's *Les barricades de mai* (1968)—expresses this lyrically: "This is Paris, the Paris of violence and enthusiasm, this is the street, with its horrors and surprises, its strangeness, its ugliness, its poetry, its immutable aspect which children wreak havoc with nevertheless. This is the capital of consumption, which is becoming, in the space of a few nights, the capital of contestation."[28] The geographer David Harvey is adamant that urban protest in 1968 must be seen as a reaction to a post–World War II reconfiguration of space in which city centers were deprioritized: "in the same way that the Haussmanization of Paris had a role in explaining the dynamics of the Paris Commune, so the soulless qualities of suburban living played a role in the dramatic protest movements of 1968 in the USA."[29] That year the dynamism of urban life was powerfully evoked by Norman Mailer in his electrifying account of the national conventions of the Republican Party and the Democratic Party, *Miami and the Siege of Chicago* (1968). In his distinctively brash tone, and with more than a hint of nostalgia, Mailer argued for the uniqueness of the latter city, contrasting it with New York, a world capital, Los Angeles, "a constellation of plastic," and Philadelphia, Baltimore, and Washington "wink[ing] like dull diamonds in the smog":

> But Chicago is a great American city. Perhaps it is the last of the great American cities. . . . the urbanites here were . . . simple, strong, warm-spirited, sly, rough, compassionate, jostling, tricky, and extraordinarily good-natured because they had sex in their pockets, muscles on their back, hot eats around the corner, neighborhoods which dripped with the sauce of local legend, and real city architecture, brownstones with different windows on every floor, vistas for miles of red-brick and two-family wood-frame houses with balconies and porches, runty stunted trees rich as farmland in their promise of tenderness the first city evenings of spring, streets where kids played stick-ball and roller-hockey, lots of smoke and twilight. The clangor of the late

nineteenth century, the very hope of greed, was in these streets. London one hundred years ago could not have looked much better.[30]

And yet Mailer clearly had a sense of the susceptibility of the city to destruction, alluding to American conservatives' "visions of future Vietnams in our own cities."[31] If the textures and dynamism—indeed, violence—of cities were to the fore circa 1968, it is also the case that the war in Vietnam, and other wars in former colonies, created a heightened awareness of the opposition of urban and rural space and in some contexts a perceived threat to the city from the countryside. This was partly because of the agrarian bases, or sheer underdevelopment, of many so-called Third World economies, but it was also due to a proliferation of theories of mass protest and revolutionary war centered in rural space.

The most widely read of these, Regis Debray's *Revolution in the Revolution?* (1967), argued for the validity and importance of power struggles across Latin America waged by the disenfranchised outside cities—peasants in Colombia, miners in Bolivia—and the inspirational models of Fidel Castro's overthrow of the Batista regime in Cuba and Vietnamese resistance to French and U.S. forces.[32] As Debray described it, such movements were underpinned by long and careful persuasion and mobilization of the rural population first, followed much later by attacks on cities from outside. Here he evoked Castro and Che Guevara's small, secretive, highly committed cadres of paramilitaries hidden in the Sierra Maestra mountains and rarely descending to the cities for fear of entrapment or assassination:

> The "fist," however well-armed it may be, must consult the head before making a move. The "head"—the leadership—is in the capital. After all, isn't that where the political life of the country is concentrated—the leaders of other parties, the press, Congress, the ministries, the post offices—in sum, the organs of central power? After all, isn't that the centre of concentration of the industrial proletariat, the factories, the trade unions, the university, in a word, the vital forces of the population? The norms of democratic centralism require the commander of the guerilla front ... must sooner or later descend to the city.[33]

Slightly later, and especially *after* the protests and attempted revolutionary actions of 1968, which were met by often brutal repressive violence and which disillusioned many leftists, interest in the "urban guerilla" became more pronounced. In a 1969 book of that name, Martin Oppenheimer traced the historical roles of the countryside and the city in progressive political revolt, from the Middle Ages through Fanon, Mao, Lenin, and Rosa Luxemburg, arguing that one of the key questions for leftist political organizers had always been "is the lever for social change to be the peasantry or the urban working class?"[34] Oppenheimer analyzed various types, or degrees, of urban revolt, from marches and general strikes to terrorist groups and armed insurrection, evoking the situations of "the black guerilla" and the "inter-urban guerilla" by quoting the House Un-American Activities Committee report *Guerilla Warfare Advocates in the US* (1968), which described a possible future in that committee's typically apocalyptic tone: "The new concept is lightning campaigns conducted in highly sensitive urban communities.... It dislocates the organs of harmony and order and reduces central power to the level of a helpless, sprawling octopus... Violence and terror will spread like a firestorm."[35]

Oppenheimer ultimately rejected what he characterized as the suicidal strategy of the urban guerilla, calling instead for nonviolent revolution with guerilla-like organization and commitment, but his analysis nonetheless tellingly and not unsympathetically traced the cycle of protest and repression that led many to greater and greater degrees of radicalization. In his autobiography *Underground* (2009), Mark Rudd, who was one of the leaders of the Columbia University student protests of April–May 1968, charted such a narrative in his own evolution from typical college freshman to chairman of Columbia's chapter of the national organization Students for a Democratic Society (SDS) and, later, membership in the armed revolutionary underground movement known as the Weathermen (also often referred to as Weatherman or the Weather Underground Organization). While tracing an arc from mass public protest to clandestine actions by small revolutionary cells, Rudd also emphasizes another distinctive spatial issue prominent in many cities at that time—that is, tension between the university and the city. Although many important universities, especially in the United States, have small-town or rural settings, Columbia University's distinctive setting, embedded in but also aloof from the surroundings of Harlem, gave its buildings an especially charged meaning. Rudd describes his impression of the place when he first enrolled there as a freshman in 1965:

> Columbia was built on one of the highest points in Manhattan, first called Harlem Heights and later Morningside Heights. An early battle of the Revolutionary War, in which the Americans finally proved themselves, had taken place here. Morningside Heights looked out over Harlem, a vast valley of apartment buildings, mostly walk-up tenements, extending miles to the east and north, at the time the largest black ghetto in the United States. Columbia University was set atop the

Heights. At the loftiest point on the campus, the central visual focus, loomed the monumental Low Library, the seat of the university's administration, immodestly modeled after the Roman Pantheon, its enormous columns and huge rotunda the symbol of imperial power.[36]

Although Rudd's account grounds Columbia University in New York City, he also points to many connections between that school's occupation and those in other far-flung places. The comparative urbanism principle organizing this book is intended to reflect a new sense of connectedness between cities at this time. The principle is evident in the book's range, dealing with a mixture of primary and secondary cities on three continents, with histories of different lengths, significant geographic, demographic, and architectural differences, varying types of demolition and construction in the built environment, varying degrees of political radicalization and mass protest, and different amounts and kinds of film production, whether industrial or avant-garde.[37] And yet the intention is to also underline a commonality of experience in keeping with the plentiful evidence that exists that one of the key ways in which 1968 differed from earlier revolutionary moments was in the rapid or even instantaneous manner in which news, ideas, and images were communicated from one city to the other, even across great distances.

In his almost-live analysis of the French student movement of May 1968, *Obsolete Communism: The Left-Wing Alternative* (1968), Daniel Cohn-Bendit begins with an evocation of revolt spreading in this way in a section titled "From Berkeley to Berlin":

> A spectre is haunting Europe—the spectre of student revolt. All the powers of old Europe have entered into a holy alliance to exorcize this spectre: Pope and Central Committee, [German Chancellor] Kiesinger and De Gaulle, French Communists and German police-spies. But now it has become world-wide: Berkeley, Berlin, Tokyo, Madrid, Warsaw—the student rebellion is spreading like wildfire, and authorities everywhere are frantically asking themselves what has hit them.[38]

Cohn-Bendit's tracing of the gathering pace of revolt, from what he sees as its origin in Berkeley, to Berlin, then Strasbourg, Nantes, Clermont-Ferrand, Nanterre, Paris, and Rome, is surely one of the most powerful statements of urban interconnectedness during the global events of 1968. This is a key feature of later historical accounts as well, such as George Katsiaficas's *The Imagination of the New Left: A Global Analysis of 1968* (1987) and Jeremy Suri's *The Global Revolutions of 1968* (2007). It is also a key theme of many of the essays in this book—notably, for example, Stephen Barber's analysis of political filmmaking in Tokyo's Shinjuku district, where the neighborhood and its representation were profoundly, often violently, shaped by the international avant-garde and U.S. foreign policy in Asia.[39]

Other evidence of this new interconnectedness is abundant, too. For example, the third published bulletin of the leftist film collective known as the États généraux du cinéma, published in October 1968, contained an article entitled "Paris-Mexico, un même combat." This explained that the Mexican government's recent massacre of protesting students at the Plaza de las Tres Culturas in Mexico City "demonstrates the latent fascist character of the regime" of Diaz Ordaz, while the bulletin's back pages listed the latest militant films in exhibition in Paris, including titles from Caracas, Montevideo, Chicago, and New York.[40] The rapid growth of networks devoted to counter-information was known to the authorities, of course—Gassert and Klimke quote the executive secretary of the U.S. State Department's Inter-Agency Youth Committee, who opined, "What happens in New York is known overnight in Paris and Manila. The speeches of [German student leader] Rudi Dutschke are in the hands of [New York student leader] Mark Rudd faster than you can seem to get your mail delivered."[41] However, the linking of cities also took artistic form—for example, on September 25, 1968, the Gruppo 1999 performance group mounted a "Projectual Happening" in Florence, in which three large-scale film images were projected on the Ponte Vecchio, showing an astronaut in space, animated geometric shapes, and an aerial view of a freeway interchange in Los Angeles.[42]

1968 and Cinema

By stitching together international cinema connections in a concentrated moment in time, I hope this book will add to our understanding of 1960s cinema in general, an era that scholars, students, and aficionados continue to return to as one of the richest in motion picture history. Broad cultural histories of "the sixties" have been published on many areas of cultural practice—recently, for example, Elissa Auther and Adam Lerner's *West of Center: Art and the Counterculture Experiment in America, 1965–1977* (2012), and Timothy Scott Brown and Andrew Lison's *The Global Sixties in Sound and Vision: Media, Counterculture, Revolt* (2014).[43] Studies of 1960s cinema are also numerous and generally concerned with charting in broad terms the impact of the era's dramatic social changes on filmmaking and film audiences, as well as its many notable technical and film industry innovations—in American cinema, for example, Paul Monaco's *The Sixties, 1960–1969* (2001).[44] Some studies take a more thematically concentrated approach, as Angelo Restivo does, for example, in his insightful study *The Cinema of Economic Miracles: Visuality and Modernization in the Italian Art Film* (2002), which is largely an examination of the related images of the body and the city in Michelangelo Antonioni and Pier Paolo Pasolini.[45]

Film histories zooming in on 1968 are relatively rare—Sylvia Harvey's *May '68 and Film Culture* (1978) and Margaret Atack's *May '68 in French Fiction and Film* (1999) are the two notable examples and both are about the special case of France.[46] On the other hand, two notable surveys of 1960s cinema by veterans of that era point to its international variety, albeit evaluating it in different ways. Peter Cowie's *Revolution! The Explosion of World Cinema in the Sixties* (2004), while colorful, sounds skeptical notes about the revolutionary movements of the era, devoting a short chapter to 1968, in which he discusses Milos Forman, Volker Schlondorff, Bernardo Bertolucci, and Richard Lester, as well as the Cannes Film Festival, but concludes: "The world did not end in the wake of May 1968—although for just about twenty-four hours some of us trapped in Cannes thought that the earth might indeed halt on its axis . . . Plus ça change. . . . For many, the decade throbbed with new-found liberty—in fashion, in music, in art, even, to some extent, in politics. For others, it was a time of levity, when speculation was skin deep."[47] By contrast, Geoffrey Nowell-Smith's *Making Waves: New Cinemas of the 1960s* (2007)—a book that covers much of the same cinema history but with more political nuance—takes the more progressive view that "the liberationist narrative is still convincing as a means of understanding the 1960s as they happened."[48]

While Cowie and Nowell-Smith focus mainly on feature films, and especially art cinema, the most consciously and insistently political history of 1960s cinema must be David James's *Allegories of Cinema: American Film in the Sixties* (1989), which is not so international in scope but presents a compelling Marxist account of underground film, political documentary, and independent feature filmmaking with an admiration of the era's integration of "previously unaccommodated and disenfranchised groups" in a distinctive "flowering of participatory social life."[49] Indeed, James appears almost entirely distrustful of Hollywood and other industrial cinemas and skeptical even of the politics of European art cinema—a characteristic also of his more recent and very geographically specific *The Most Typical Avant-Garde: History and Geography of Minor Cinemas in Los Angeles* (2005), large parts of which are also about the 1960s.[50]

It is an important lesson of James's analysis that not all artistically innovative or socially progressive films of the era were engaged consistently or in depth with urban environments. For example, in the films of Michael Snow,

Paul Sharits, and Hollis Frampton, the "pure film" approach of "structural film" from 1967 to 1974 was precisely marked by a flight from narrative, genre, figuration, and representation, or, as James puts it, a "determinate negation" of cinema's photographic basis and real-world events.[51] Meanwhile, the widespread popularity of American road movies meant that mainstream cinema audiences often spent much of their time watching romantic imagery of countryside and wilderness—most famously, in *Easy Rider* (1969), which begins amid the steel and concrete of Los Angeles International Airport but then quickly proceeds to the desert.

Nonetheless, it is a premise of this book, supported by much of the literature on cinematic cities, that most cinema of the late 1960s *was* concerned with the urban condition (even *Easy Rider*, in a negative sense), and much filmmaking had architectural programs in mind.[52] In Italy, for example, the architectural journal *Casabella* carried frequent bulletins from the Strum Group of artists and activists calling for a reorganization of the built environment, social housing, and antiauthoritarian systems of education and social regulation, backed up and publicized by documentary filmmaking as part of "an autonomous system of counter-information to back and promote class development and to oppose the mystification of capitalistic 'culture.'"[53] The most important analogous organization in the United States context was surely the Newsreel collective of activist filmmakers that first emerged in New York before setting up branches in San Francisco, Los Angeles, and other cities. One of the subjects of Stanley Corkin's essay in this book, Newsreel was just one of many highly active and influential networks of urban political documentarists—also in this book, for example, Jennifer Stob examines the Parisian Cinétracts group and Jesse Lerner studies Mexico City's "superocheros" movement, all of which viewed filmmaking as an inseparable aspect of political praxis.

Alongside agitprop documentary film, another important trend was the political radicalization of filmmakers working in narrative fiction film, either veterans of established film industries or students aspiring to work in them. Marc Raymond has recently brought to light the little known but intriguing case of Martin Scorsese's role in supervising production of the seventy-five minute documentary feature film *Street Scenes* (1970) made by the New York Cinetracts Collective in May that year as a record of protests against the bombing of Cambodia and U.S. National Guard killings of four students at Kent State University in Ohio.[54] The most influential case, however, was surely the États généraux du cinéma, an organization of film professionals and film students closely linked to major Parisian film schools—the Institut des hautes études cinématographiques and the École technique de photographie et cinématographie. The founding of the États généraux followed the spontaneous closing down of the Cannes Film Festival of May 13–19, 1968, by directors, actors, and film critics outraged by the police repression of students in Paris—an action that involved many of the most celebrated filmmakers of the era, including Jean-Luc Godard, Alain Resnais, François Truffaut, Carlos Saura, Louis Malle, Roman Polanski, and Monica Vitti.[55] Indeed, the États généraux not only called for more politically conscious filmmaking, especially the documentation of protests and police actions but for new networks of film distribution and exhibition, especially the showing of films not only in cinemas but in public spaces and factories. The États généraux also distributed the films of Newsreel in France.[56]

Such organizations were at the forefront of politically committed filmmaking in urban environments circa 1968. Reflecting on them within the broad spectrum of filmmaking—narrative and nonnarrative, representational and antirepresentational—highlights the important distinction and overlap between cities and architecture as content in film and their deeper impact on film form and technique. The relationship between content and form was one of the most important topics for debate among filmmakers and students of film at a time when their discipline, like that of architects, saw not only fundamental theoretical reorientation but also rapid technological changes whose net effect was to make filming on location in cities more and more technically and financially viable (for example, smaller and lighter cameras, especially 16mm film cameras and early video systems, faster film stocks more suitable for filming in natural light and low light conditions, increasingly portable sound recording systems and microphones).[57]

However, because of the strong association of filmmaking, in popular opinion, with Hollywood and other commercial cinemas, many thinkers and practitioners in urbanism and architecture prior to 1968 seem to have been skeptical of its ability to achieve insight. For example, one of the most influential intellectuals of the day, and highly regarded by many students, was Henri Lefebvre, professor of sociology at Nanterre, and author of *Le droit á la ville* (1968) and *La révolution urbaine* (1970).[58] As Derek Schilling has explained, throughout much of his career, Lefebvre viewed most media as part of the problem rather than the solution of alienation in everyday life under capitalism, the press, television, advertising, and most cinema being key agents in the logic and practice of consumerism, driving excessive individualism and acquisitiveness, and mitigating against the possibility of true social conscience.[59] For example, during the political crisis of May 1958, when de Gaulle became the first president of the French Fifth Republic, Lefebvre aligned the passivity of cinema spectatorship with what he saw as the political passivity of the French citizenry: "In the film which interests you, which touches you, which concerns you, you can change nothing while it passes before you on the screen: it is a spectacle."[60] Early in the following decade, however, he signaled his appreciation of at least some of the films of Federico Fellini, Michelangelo Antonioni, and Karel Reisz, and in *Everyday Life in the Modern World* (1967) went so far as to favorably compare Jean-Luc Godard and Alain Resnais with James Joyce for their interest in "the emergence of everyday life," by which he meant its increasing (and increasingly alienating) modernity, technology, and monetization, and which he generally viewed as one of the most important themes in all artistic expression.[61] Indeed, in his recent masterful intellectual biography of Lefebvre, Lukasz Stanek points to a striking homology and contemporaneity between Lefebvre's critique of the oppressive rationalism of the brand new university campus at Nanterre and the tracking shots of that same place that played a prominent role in Godard's *La Chinoise* (1967). Indicating Lefebvre's defining belief in the (often negative) shaping influence of architecture, and its ideological basis, Stanek quotes Lefebvre's pointed answer to a question as to why the French unrest of May '68 started at Nanterre: "In order to answer the question why it started here, one should look outside the window."[62]

1968 and Architectural Institutions

Mark Rudd has explained that in the occupation of Columbia University, graduate students in architecture and urban planning played a particularly important role, taking over Avery Hall, the School of Architecture building, because they were "particularly sensitive to the needs of the community surrounding Columbia"—that is, they were especially outraged by the university's plans to build a gymnasium on the site of the nearby Morningside Park, a green space much valued by local residents, most of whom were black.[63] Opposition to those plans by students and some faculty members in the architectural school boosted the size and effectiveness of the protest overall, although most architecture students were not affiliated with either of the two main leftist student groups—Students for a Democratic Society and the Society of Afro-American Students. Architecture students' activism distinguished their politics from those of students in other professional schools such as law, business, and engineering. Engineering students, for example, were reported to be much less involved in the antiwar movement because of their relatively heavy workloads, more demanding class schedules, greater career orientation, and more conservative politics in general.[64] Blake Slonecker has explained that the School of Architecture was still paralyzed by the student strike in late May 1968, weeks after police suppression of most of the students' occupation at the end of April—indeed, "the architecture students in Avery Hall took pride in engineering the finest barricades at Columbia."[65] Moreover, architecture students were also the most heavily represented among those participating in the strike and among those arrested by police. Of a total enrollment of about 240 students in the school, about one-third were actively involved in occupying Avery Hall at any one time and about 10 percent of all those enrolled were arrested, a larger proportion than in any other Columbia department or school.[66]

At around the same time, architecture students at New York City's Pratt Institute went on strike too, demanding the resignation of the dean of architecture and a new curriculum, an action that led to two years of negotiation between the university and students and eventually produced a "restructured curriculum . . . designed to provide skills and knowledge necessary for meaningful responses to contemporary society and the profession."[67] Architecture students and faculty took leading roles in demonstrations at the Peoples' Park set up by activists on vacant land owned by the University of California at Berkeley in the summer of 1969.[68] And at Yale the following year, architecture students played a key role in that university's antiwar movement by commissioning and installing Claes Oldenburg's famous giant lipstick sculpture, *Lipstick (Ascending) on Caterpillar Tracks* (1969), in the middle of the university's main administrative plaza, Hewitt Quadrangle, where its Pop iconography and materials stood opposed to the university's neoclassical colonnade and acted as a focus for antiwar protests through the spring of 1970.[69] The *New York Times* reported of the era's activism that "if student discontent has been more virulent in any single area it has been at the schools of architecture" where young entrants to the profession, feeling especially responsible for the era's ongoing urban crisis, berated their elders who "have constituted themselves an intellectual elite."[70] Robert A. M. Stern's now-classic *New Directions in American Architecture* (1969) closed with a statement of sympathy for protesting students at Columbia and Yale.[71]

Nor was protest confined to radicalized students. The conservatism and academicism of the architecture profession and of the status quo in architecture schools was the focus of a speech given to the 1968 annual convention of the American Institute of Architects by the head of the Urban League, Whitney M. Young Jr., who focused on architecture's lack of racial integration and architects' failure to address the nation's chronic shortage of decent public housing: "You are not a profession that has distinguished itself by your social and civic contributions to the cause of civil rights, and I am sure this has not come to you as any shock. You are most distinguished by your thunderous silence and your complete irrelevance."[72] (See Figure I.2.) Jane Jacobs, author of the best-selling *Death and Life of Great American Cities* (1961), was arrested in April 1968 for

Figure I.2 Demonstrators protest charges against activist and author Jane Jacobs (not pictured), New York, May 8, 1968 (Fred W. McDarrah/Getty Images)

Figure I.3 Entrance of the École des beaux-arts, Paris, May 1, 1968 (Charles Ciccione/Gamma-Rapho/Getty Images)

demonstrating against the proposed Lower Manhattan Expressway.[73] And the architecture critic of the *New York Times*, Ada Louise Huxtable, lamented the "bulldozer approach" to urban renewal, the "asocial values of real estate," "the giant social issues of justice and opportunity for the underclass," and the need for "an environment that is civilized and humane."[74] Indeed, she complained that new architectural preservation laws enacted by the U.S. government were being weakly enforced not to disadvantage developers.[75] Nor was activism confined to the United States: the aforementioned occupation of the 1968 Milan Triennale was preceded by fire damage to the architecture school at the University of Rome as a result of fighting between police, right-wing agitators, and students;[76] and in Paris, while students forced the closure of the École des beaux-arts, citizens and urban planners worked to save the Gare d'Orsay from planned demolition, eventually achieving protection in 1973 in one of the world's most famous cases of architectural preservation.[77] (See Figure I.3.)

Effects of 1968

By that time, however, most cultural historians now agree, a new dispensation was firmly emerging—often referred to as "postmodernism"—in which political expectations were markedly lower, economic opportunity was massively reduced, and art was more and more absorbed by commodification.[78] For Stanley Corkin and Lawrence Webb, architecture and cinema were both marked by the physical crisis of the decaying postindustrial city, while city governments began to encourage film production as a route to economic growth and more effective city branding.[79] In the 1970s, this led to an austere social realism in much cinema, even in Hollywood genres, although, as Robin Wood and Douglas Kellner have explained, the latter part of the decade saw the resurgence of the blockbuster, with negative consequences for the range and quality of artistic experimentation in cinema in general, shrinking the avant-garde dramatically.[80] In architecture too, as Joan Ockman argues, while the break with modernism in 1968 was welcome, in retrospect its achievements and opportunities seem to have been undercut by a subsequent return to the old order.[81] For Tzonis and Lefaivre, the experimentation of the 1960s was displaced by a new *rappel à l'ordre* in the work of James Stirling, Renzo Piano, and Norman Foster.[82]

Reflecting on the thirtieth anniversary of May 1968, in 1998, Kristin Ross asserted that "the event has endured, resisting annihilation, insisting or asserting its eventfulness against the forms of social amnesia and instrumentalization that have sought to undo it, the sociologies that have explained it, and the ex-student leaders that have claimed a monopoly on its memory ... repentant militants intent on exorcising their militant past."[83] The year 2008 seemed notable for the range of commemorative events—for example, in mainstream media, two special documentaries hosted by Tom Brokaw for the History Channel, a *Time* magazine cover feature, and special editions of *Le Monde*, *L'Espresso*, *Der Spiegel*, and many other periodicals worldwide. Independent media in the United States such as the syndicated radio news program *Democracy Now!* hosted series of special features on the subject, and important film retrospectives took place, such as "All Power to the Imagination! 1968 and Its Legacies" at the Barbican Centre and several other venues in London, and "Sixty-eight! Europe, Cinema, Revolution?" at Yale University. Now approaching the fiftieth anniversary of 1968, it is promising that new scholarship on the subject continues to appear, although it remains to be seen what degree and kind of commemoration the protests of that year will attract.[84] Indeed, if one takes the view (which seems correct to me) that 1968 was notable for its large and numerous urban demonstrations in favor of intellectual openness, moral reflection, multiculturalism, equality, and social justice, it is arguably more important than ever that it *should be* commemorated: this book goes to press at a time when such values are under heightened threat from the rise in several supposed democracies of right-wing populist movements and politicians, and from the seemingly increasing fragility of the geopolitical situation that they thrive on and frequently encourage.

The chapters that follow are intended to make a contribution to the project of remembering and interrogating the events and legacy of 1968, its cinema and architecture, while implicitly offering a counternarrative to reactionary views in the present day. Jennifer Stob explores the artistic creativity and radically oppositional politics of the Cinétracts filmmaking group in Paris, exploring its connections to Guy Debord and the Situationist International, with reference to barricades, marches, and police charges in the Boulevard Saint Michel, the Place de la République, and the Sorbonne. Andrew Webber traces the theme of napalm and burning in films by Harun Farocki and Holger Meins in Berlin, relating them to that city's especially bitter political divisions, the rise of the Red Army Faction, and the distinctive topography and geography of the city's East and West, as well as specific sites such as the Springer building, much hated by leftist students of the day. Gaetana Marrone investigates the clash of bureaucracy, state, church, and youth revolution in Liliana Cavani's *I cannibali* (1969) and Pier Paolo Pasolini's *Teorema* (1968), exploring their critiques of the power structures of the bourgeoisie and family, and their intimate mappings of Milan, with reference to that city's factory landscapes and monumental spaces such as the Piazza della Repubblica. Jon Lewis examines the remarkable interaction of documentary filmmaking and narrative fiction in Haskell Wexler's celebrated *Medium Cool* (1969), paying attention to the detail of the film's production and of Chicago's distinctive geography and architecture—for example, Grant Park—in a film heavily indebted to the example of *nouvelle vague* directors in Paris. Stanley Corkin counterpoints Newsreel's agitprop documentary *Columbia Revolt* (1968) with narrative fiction films of New York such as Brian De Palma's *Greetings* (1968) and John Schlesinger's *Midnight Cowboy* (1969), examining their differing approaches to the rendering of Manhattan's then increasingly dilapidated physical infrastructure and pinpointing the city's condition on the eve of the Nixon era. In my own essay, I explore the exceptional tension between Los Angeles's rapid growth in the 1960s and the cinematic depiction of its deep-rooted social and political conflict in flashpoints such as the Sunset Strip and Venice, emphasizing the city's commercial strip development and its role as a magnet for European filmmakers, with a focus on Jacques Demy's *Model Shop* (1968). Jesse Lerner examines various cinematic responses to the police massacre of student protestors in Tlatelolco, Mexico City, in October 1968, against the backdrop of Mexico City's layered ancient and modern architectural history and the 1968 Olympic Games, and with an emphasis on the rise of the so-called *superochero* movement of low-budget 8mm filmmaking by leftists. Stephen Barber focuses on Toshio Matsumoto's *Funeral Parade of Roses* and Nagisa Oshima's *Diary of a Shinjuku Thief* (both 1969) in order to chart Tokyo's accelerated architectural transformation and intensifying political violence from the 1964 Olympic Games to the height of the Vietnam War, while counterpointing those with the Shinjuku district's notably sexualized counterculture.

NOTES

1. See Robert B. Ray, *A Certain Tendency of the Hollywood Cinema, 1930–1980* (Princeton, NJ: Princeton University Press, 1985); and David Rodowick, *The Crisis of Political Modernism: Criticism and Ideology in Contemporary Film Theory* (Berkeley: University of California Press, 1995).

2. Christian Metz, *Essais sur la signification au cinema* (Paris: Klincksieck, 1968), trans. as *Film Language: A Semiotics of the Cinema* (Oxford: Oxford University Press, 1974). See also Francesco Casetti, *Theories of Cinema, 1945–1995* (Austin: University of Texas Press, 1999), 75, 185.

3. Thomas Elsaesser, *The Persistence of Hollywood* (New York: Routledge, 2011), 1; Casetti, *Theories of Cinema*, 185. See also Mark Betz, *Beyond the Subtitle: Remapping European Art Cinema* (Minneapolis: University of Minnesota Press, 2009), 15.

4. George R. Collins, *Visionary Drawings of Architecture and Planning: 20th Century through the 1960s* (Cambridge, MA: MIT Press, 1979), 25–27.

5. Hence, this book aims to build on the recent growth of interest in temporally and spatially specific studies of cinematic representation such as Martin Lefebvre, ed., *Landscape and Film* (New York: Routledge, 2007); John David Rhodes and Elena Gorfinkel, eds., *Taking Place: Location and the Moving Image* (Minneapolis: University of Minnesota Press, 2011); Noa Steimatsky, *Italian Locations: Reinhabiting the Past in Postwar Cinema* (Minneapolis: University of Minnesota Press, 2008).

6. Dennis Cosgrove, *Apollo's Eye: A Cartographic Genealogy of the Earth in the Western Imagination* (Baltimore, MD: Johns Hopkins University Press, 2001), 21.

7. Ronald Fraser, *1968: A Student Generation in Revolt* (London: Chatto and Windus, 1988); Kristin Ross, *May 1968 and Its Afterlives* (Chicago: University of Chicago Press, 2002); Daniel J. Sherman, Ruud van Dijk, Jasmine Alinder, and A. Aneesh, eds., *The Long 1968: Revisions and New Perspectives* (Bloomington: Indiana University Press, 2013). See also Luisa Passerini, *Autobiography of a Generation: Italy, 1968* (Middletown, CT: Wesleyan University Press, 1996); Carole Fink, Philipp Gassert, and Detlef Junker, eds., *1968: The World Transformed* (Cambridge: Cambridge University Press, 1998); Margaret Atack, *May 68 in French Fiction and Film: Rethinking Society, Rethinking Representation* (Oxford: Oxford University Press, 2000); Mark Kurlansky, *1968: The Year That Rocked the World* (New York: Random House, 2004); Gerd-Rainer Horn, *The Spirit of '68: Rebellion in Western Europe and North America, 1956–1976* (Oxford: Oxford University Press,

2007); Julian Bourg, *From Revolution to Ethics: May 1968 and Contemporary French Thought* (Kingston: McGill-Queen's University Press, 2007).

8. Yiching Wu, *The Cultural Revolution at the Margins* (Cambridge, MA: Harvard University Press, 2014).

9. Andrew Sarris, *The American Cinema: Directors and Directions* (New York: E. P. Dutton, 1968). For histories of 1960s U.S. cinema, see, for example, Paul Monaco, *The Sixties*, History of the American Cinema, vol. 8 (Berkeley: University of California Press, 2001); Drew Casper, *Hollywood Film 1963–1976: Years of Revolution and Reaction* (Hoboken, NJ: John Wiley and Sons, 2011); Robin Wood, *Hollywood from Vietnam to Reagan . . . and Beyond: A Revised and Expanded Edition* (New York: Columbia University Press, 2012).

10. Robert Venturi, *Complexity and Contradiction in Architecture* (New York: Museum of Modern Art, 1966); Robert Venturi, Denise Scott Brown, and Steven Izenour, *Learning from Las Vegas* (Cambridge, MA: MIT Press, 1972).

11. Reyner Banham, *Los Angeles: The Architecture of the Four Ecologies* (London: Allen Lane, 1971).

12. Manfredo Tafuri, *Teorie e storia dell'architettura* (Bari: Laterza, 1968); *Contropiano*, no. 1, January–April 1969. See Harry Francis Mallgrave, *Modern Architectural Theory: A Historical Survey, 1673–1968* (Cambridge: Cambridge University Press, 2005), 406.

13. The better known version of *Powers of Ten* is the later iteration of 1977, but the film was first made by the Eameses in 1968 with the full title *A Rough Sketch for a Proposed Film Dealing with the Powers of Ten and the Relative Size of things in the Universe*. On Venturi and Scott Brown, see Martino Stierli, *Las Vegas in the Rearview Mirror: The City in Theory, Photography, and Film*, Los Angeles: Getty Research Institute, 2013, pp. 140, 155; on Koolhaas, see Fredric Jameson, "Future City," *New Left Review*, 21 (May–June 2003): 65–79.

14. David Clarke, ed., *The Cinematic City* (London: Routledge, 1997); Mark Shiel and Tony Fitzmaurice, eds., *Cinema and the City: Film and Urban Societies in a Global Context* (Oxford: Blackwell Publishing, 2001); Ewa Masierska and Laura Rascaroli, eds., *From Moscow to Madrid: European Cities, Postmodern Cinema* (London: I. B. Tauris, 2002); Mark Shiel and Tony Fitzmaurice, eds., *Screening the City* (London: Verso, 2003); Murray Pomerance, ed., *City That Never Sleeps: New York and the Filmic Imagination* (New Brunswick, NJ: Rutgers University Press, 2007); Andrew Webber and Emma Wilson, eds., *Cities in Transition: The Moving Image and the Modern Metropolis* (London: Wallflower Press, 2008); Alan Marcus and Dietrich Neumann, eds., *Visualizing the City* (London: Routledge, 2008); Yomi Braester and James Tweedie, eds., *Cinema at the City's Edge: Film and Urban Networks in East Asia* (Hong Kong: Hong Kong University Press, 2010).

15. James Donald, *Imagining the Modern City* (Minneapolis: University of Minnesota Press, 1999); Paula Massood, *Black City Cinema: African American Urban Experiences in Film* (Philadelphia: Temple University Press, 2003); Charlotte Brunsdon, *London in Cinema: The Cinematic City since 1945* (London: BFI Publishing, 2007); Lawrence Webb, *The Cinema of Urban Crisis: Seventies Film and the Reinvention of the City* (Amsterdam: Amsterdam University Press, 2015); Stephen Barber, *Projected Cities: Cinema and*

Urban Space (London: Reaktion Books, 2002); Nezar AlSayyad, *Cinematic Urbanism: A History of the Modern from Reel to Real* (New York: Routledge 2006); Barbara Mennell, *Cities and Cinema* (New York: Routledge, 2008); Yingin Zhang, *Cinema and Urban Culture in Shanghai, 1922–1943* (Stanford: Stanford University Press, 1999); Jacqueline Stewart, *Migrating to the Movies: Cinema and Black Urban Modernity* (Berkeley: University of California Press, 2005); Ranjani Mazumdar, *Bombay Cinema: An Archive of the City* (Minneapolis: University of Minnesota Press, 2007); John David Rhodes, *Stupendous, Miserable City: Pasolini's Rome* (Minneapolis: University of Minnesota Press, 2007); Mark Shiel, *Hollywood Cinema and the Real Los Angeles* (London: Reaktion Books/University of Chicago Press, 2012).

16. On comparative urbanism, see, for example, Jennifer Robinson, "Cities in a World of Cities: The Comparative Gesture," *International Journal of Urban and Regional Research* 35, no. 1 (January 2011): 1–23.

17. Not many individual scholars who might write a monograph on cinema and the city have sufficiently wide-ranging expertise to be able to deal confidently with a multiplicity of international contexts in historical depth. Webb's *The Cinema of Urban Crisis* manages this challenge in one book, dealing comparatively with a wide range of U.S. and western European cities and their various cinemas, but it is exceptional and commendable in that respect.

18. Linda Krause and Patrice Petro, eds., *Global Cities: Cinema, Architecture, and Urbanism in a Digital Age* (New Brunswick, NJ: Rutgers University Press, 2003); Pamela Robertson Wojcik's *The Apartment Plot: Urban Living in American Film and Popular Culture, 1945–1975* (Durham, NC: Duke University Press, 2010). See also Katherine Shonfeld, *Walls Have Feelings: Architecture, Film, and the City* (New York: Routledge, 2002); Richard Koeck and Les Roberts, *The City and the Moving Image: Urban Projections* (New York: Palgrave Macmillan, 2010).

19. Donald Albrecht, *Designing Dreams: Modern Architecture in the Movies* (Los Angeles: Hennessy and Ingalls, 2000); Giuliana Bruno, *Atlas of Emotion: Journeys in Art, Architecture, and Film* (New York: Verso, 2002); François Penz and Andong Lu, eds., *Urban Cinematics: Understanding Urban Phenomena through the Moving Image* (Bristol: Intellect, 2011); Richard Koeck, *Cine-scapes: Cinematic Spaces in Architecture and Cities* (London: Routledge, 2013). See also François Penz and Maureen Thomas, eds., *Cinema and Architecture: Méliès, Mallet-Stevens, Multimedia* (London: BFI Publishing, 1997); Mark Lamster, ed., *Architecture and Film* (New York: Princeton Architectural Press, 2000).

20. Merrill Schleier, *Skyscraper Cinema: Architecture and Gender in American Film* (Minneapolis: University of Minnesota Press, 2009); David B. Clarke and Marcus A. Doel, *Moving Pictures/Stopping Places: Hotels and Motels on Film* (Lanham, MD: Lexington Books, 2009).

21. Lucy Fischer, *Designing Women: Cinema, Art Deco, and the Female Form* (Berkeley: University of California Press, 2003); Tim Bergfelder, Sue Harris, and Sarah Street, *Film Architecture and the Transnational Imagination: Set Design in 1930s European Cinema* (Amsterdam: University of Amsterdam Press, 2007); Dietrich Neumann, *Film Architecture: Set Designs from Metropolis to Blade Runner* (Munich: Prestel, 1996); Anthony Vidler, *Warped Space: Art, Architecture, and Anxiety in Modern Culture* (Cambridge, MA: MIT Press, 2002).

22. Lucy Fischer, ed., *Art Direction and Production Design* (New Brunswick, NJ: Rutgers University Press, 2015). See also Charles Tashiro, *Pretty Pictures: Production Design and the History of Film* (Austin: University of Texas Press, 1998) and Juan Antonio Ramirez, *Architecture for the Screen: A Critical Study of Set Design in Hollywood's Golden Age*, trans. John F. Moffitt (Jefferson, NC: McFarland, 2004). Two other important studies of film and architecture that focus on cinema with high production values and set design are Steven Jacobs, *The Wrong House: The Architecture of Alfred Hitchcock* (Rotterdam: 010 Publishers, 2007) and David T. Fortin, *Architecture and Science-Fiction Film* (Burlington, VT: Ashgate Publishing, 2011).

23. Harry Francis Mallgrave, *Modern Architectural Theory: A Historical Survey, 1673–1968* (Cambridge: Cambridge University Press, 2005), 407, 415.

24. Mallgrave, *Modern Architectural Theory*, 408; Alexander Tzonis and Liane Lefaivre, *Architecture in Europe since 1968: Memory and Invention* (London: Thames and Hudson, 1992), 10.

25. Barry Bergdoll and Alice Thomine, "Teaching Architectural History in France: A Shifting Institutional Landscape," *Journal of the Society of Architectural Historians* 61, no. 4 (December 2002): 509–518, 510.

26. Joan Ockman, ed., *Architecture Culture, 1943–1968: A Documentary Anthology* (New York: Rizzoli, 1993), 11.

27. K. Michael Hays, *Architecture Theory since 1968* (Cambridge, MA: MIT Press, 2000), xi. Paul Virilio and Anthony Vidler have both made comparable assessments. See Vidler, *Histories of the Immediate Present: Inventing Architectural Modernism* (Cambridge, MA: MIT Press, 2008); Virilio, Sylvère Lotringer, and Michael Taormina, "After Architecture: A Conversation," *Grey Room*, no. 3 (Spring 2001): 32–53, 38.

28. "C'est Paris, le Paris de la violence et de l'enthousiasme, c'est la rue, avec ses horreurs et ses surprises, son étrangèté, sa laideur, sa poésie, son aspect immuable et que pourtant des enfants bouleversent. C'est la capitale de la consommation qui devient, en l'espace de quelques nuits, la capitale de la contestation." Philippe Labro, *Les barricades de mai* (Paris: Solar/Agences Gamma, 1968), n.p.

29. David Harvey, *The Enigma of Capital: And the Crises of Capitalism* (Oxford: Oxford University Press, 2010), 171.

30. Norman Mailer, *Miami and the Siege of Chicago* (New York: Signet Books, 1968), 85–86.

31. Ibid., 14.

32. Regis Debray, *Revolution in the Revolution?* (London: Penguin, 1967), 27, 32, and 44–50.

33. Ibid., 66–67.

34. Martin Oppenheimer, *Urban Guerilla* (New York: Crown Books, 1969), 41.

35. Ibid. 108–110, quoting from House Un-American Activities Committee, *Guerilla Warfare Advocates in the US*, U.S. Government Printing Office, Washington DC, 1968.

36. Mark Rudd, *Underground: My Life with SDS and the Weathermen* (New York: Harper Collins, 2009), 4.

37. On transnational, interurban connections of this kind, see Mark Shiel and Tony Fitzmaurice, eds., *Cinema and the City: Film and Urban Societies in a Global Context* (Oxford: Blackwell, 2001); Shiel, *Italian Neorealism: Rebuilding the Cinematic City after*

World War Two (London: Wallflower Press, 2006); "Hollywood, the New Left, and *FTA*," in Frank Krutnik, Steve Neale, Brian Neve, and Peter Stanfield, eds., *Un-American Hollywood* (New Brunswick, NJ: Rutgers University Press, 2007); and Shiel, "A Regional Geography of Film Noir: Urban Dystopias On- and Off-screen," in Gyan Prakash, ed., *Urban Dystopias* (Princeton: Princeton University Press, 2010), 75–103.

38. Daniel Cohn-Bendit, *Obsolete Communism: The Left-wing Alternative* (London: Penguin, 1969), 23.

39. Jeremi Suri, *The Global Revolutions of 1968: A Norton Casebook in History* (New York: W. W. Norton, 2007); George N. Katsiaficas, *The Imagination of the New Left: A Global Analysis of 1968* (Boston: South End Press, 1987).

40. États généraux du cinéma, no. 3, *Le cinéma au service de la revolution* (Paris: Editions Le Terrain Vague, 1968), 9–10, my translation.

41. Quoted in Philipp Gassert and Martin Klimke, *1968: Memories and Legacies of a Global Revolt* (Washington, DC: German Historical Institute, 2009), 6–7.

42. *Casabella*, November 1968, 98–99.

43. Elissa Auther and Adam Lerner, eds., *West of Center: Art and the Counterculture Experiment in America, 1965–1977* (Minneapolis: University of Minnesota Press, 2012); Timothy Scott Brown and Andrew Lison, eds., *The Global Sixties in Sound and Vision: Media, Counterculture, Revolt* (New York: Palgrave Macmillan, 2014); Aniko Bodroghkozy, *Groove Tube: Sixties Television and the Youth Rebellion* (Durham, NC: Duke University Press, 2001); Thomas Crow, *The Rise of the Sixties: American and European Art in the Era of Dissent* (New Haven, CT: Yale University Press, 2005).

44. Paul Monaco, *The Sixties, 1960–1969*, History of American Cinema series, vol. 8 (Berkeley: University of California Press, 2001); Barry Keith Grant, *American Cinema of the 1960s: Themes and Variations* (New Brunswick, NJ: Rutgers University Press, 2008).

45. Angelo Restivo, *The Cinema of Economic Miracles: Visuality and Modernization in the Italian Art Film* (Durham, NC: Duke University Press, 2002).

46. Sylvia Harvey, ed., *May '68 and Film Culture* (London: BFI Publishing, 1978); Atack, *May 68 in French Fiction*.

47. Peter Cowie, *Revolution! The Explosion of World Cinema in the Sixties* (New York: Faber and Faber, 2004), 209, 248.

48. Geoffrey Nowell-Smith, *Making Waves: New Cinemas of the 1960s* (London: Continuum, 2007), 13.

49. David James, *Allegories of Cinema: American Film in the Sixties* (Princeton: Princeton University Press, 1989), 3, 13.

50. David James, *The Most Typical Avant-Garde: History and Geography of Minor Cinemas in Los Angeles* (Berkeley: University of California Press, 2005).

51. James, *Allegories of Cinema*, 236, 267.

52. In my monographs *Italian Neorealism: Rebuilding the Cinematic City* (2005) and *Hollywood Cinema and the Real Los Angeles* (2012), I have argued that a sense of the overarching importance of urban experience, and of the built environment of cities, was a crucially important determining factor in the vast majority of, respectively, Italian and American narrative fiction films around the mid-20th century, even when the mise en scène of this or that film or group of films was primarily rural rather than urban. In the latter book, for example, this argument is supported by reference to Fred-

ric Jameson's emphasis on the increasing "disappearance of nature" in late twentieth-century literature and visual culture, which he views as a defining symptom of postmodernity—to which, in this context, I would also add a citation of Henri Lefebvre, to whom Jameson has acknowledged an intellectual debt, especially Lefebvre's analysis of the totalization of urban experience in *The Urban Revolution* (1970). See Jameson, *The Geopolitical Aesthetic: Cinema and Space in the World System* (Bloomington: Indiana University Press, 1995) and Lefebvre, *The Urban Revolution* (Minneapolis: University of Minnesota Press, 2003), originally published as *La révolution urbaine* (Paris: Gallimard, 1970).

53. *Casabella*, March 1969, 45.

54. Marc Raymond, "Politics, Authorship and History: The Production, Reception and Marginalization of *Street Scenes 1970*," *Film History: An International Journal* 22, no. 2 (2010): 133–147.

55. The original account is in États généraux du cinéma, no. 1, *Le cinéma s'insurge* (Paris: Edition Le Terrain Vague, 1968), 10–14.

56. Sebastien Layerle, *Cameras en lutte en mai 68, Par ailleurs le cinéma est une arme* (Nouveau Monde Editions, Paris, 2008), 199, 208.

57. See Barry Salt, *Film Style and Technology: History and Analysis* (London: Starword, 2009).

58. Lefebvre, *Le droit á la ville* (Paris: Anthropos, 1968) and *La révolution urbaine* (Paris: Gallimard, 1970).

59. Derek Schilling, "Everyday Life and the Challenge to History in Postwar France: Braudel, Lefebvre, Certeau," *Diacritics* (Spring 2003): 23–40, 31.

60. Henri Lefebvre, *La somme et le reste* (Paris: Méridiens-Klincksieck, 1989), 170.

61. For Lefebvre's mentions of Fellini and Antonioni, see Lefebvre, "Changements dans les attitudes morales de la bourgeoisie," *Cahiers Internationaux de Sociologie* 31 (July–December 1961): 15–40, 22; on Reisz, see *Critique of Everyday Life, volume 2, Foundations for a Sociology of the Everyday* (1962) trans. John Moore, preface Michel Trebitsch (London: Verso, 2002), 361; on Godard and Resnais, see Lefebvre, *Everyday Life in the Modern World*, trans. Sacha Rabinovitz (1967; London: Allen Lane, 1971), 11.

62. Lukasz Stanek, *Henri Lefebvre on Space: Architecture, Urban Research, and the Production of Theory* (Minneapolis: University of Minnesota Press, 2011), 186.

63. Rudd, *Underground*, 75. See also Ada Louise Huxtable, "Strike at Columbia Architecture School Traced to Anger over Exclusion from Planning," *New York Times*, May 20, 1968, 70.

64. Murray Schumach, "Art and Engineering Students in Separate Worlds: Different Motivation Found on Protests and Life Aim," *New York Times*, May 12, 1969, 50.

65. Blake Slonecker, "The Columbia Coalition: African Americans, New Leftists, and Counterculture at the Columbia University Protest of 1968," *Journal of Social History* 41, no. 4 (Summer 2008): 967–996, 980.

66. *Crisis at Columbia, Report of the Fact-Finding Commission Appointed to Investigate the Disturbances at Columbia University in April and May 1968* (New York: Random House, 1968), 142; and Ada Louise Huxtable, "Strike at Columbia Architecture School Traced to Anger over Exclusion from Planning," *New York Times*, May 20, 1968, 70.

67. National Architecture Accrediting Board, Pratt Institute School of Architecture Visiting Team Report, 2010, 24–25, https://www.pratt.edu/academics/architecture/naab/; See also *Prattfolio*, special 125th anniversary commemorative edition, 2012, 59, https://www.pratt.edu/partnerships-and-giving/publications/prattfolio/.

68. Peter Allen, "The End of Modernism?" *Journal of the Society of Architectural Historians* 70, no. 3 (September 2011): 354–374.

69. Grace Glueck, "Art Notes: At the Whitney, It's Guerrilla Warfare," *New York Times*, November 1, 1970, 124.

70. "Young Turks' Confront Architectural Eiders," *New York Times*, June 22, 1969, R1, 6.

71. Robert A. M. Stern, *New Directions in American Architecture* (New York: George Brazillier, 1969). See also Mallgrave, *Modern Architectural Theory*, 410.

72. Whitney M. Young Jr., "Unedited transcript of the speech made to the American Institute of Architects in 1968," in *20 on 20/20 Vision: Perspectives on Diversity and Design*, ed. Linda Kiisk (Boston: AIA Diversity Committee and Boston Society of Architects, 2003), 16, http://www.aia.org/aiaucmp/groups/ek_members/documents/pdf/aiap022931.pdf.

73. Jane Jacobs, *The Death and Life of Great American Cities* (New York: Random House, 1961); Richard Severo, "Mrs. Jacobs's Protest Results in Riot Charge," *New York Times*, April 18, 1968, 49.

74. Ada Louise Huxtable, "The Crisis of the Environment," *New York Times*, December 29, 1969, 28.

75. The legislation in question referred to by Huxtable was the Demonstration Cities and Metropolitan Development Act, 1966, and the National Historic Preservation Act, 1966. See Ada Louise Huxtable, "Architecture: No Time to Joke," *New York Times*, May 31, 1970, 76.

76. "200 Hurt in Rioting at Rome U. as Leftists and Rightists Battle," *New York Times*, March 17, 1968, 22.

77. John L. Hess, "Paris Urban Planners Rally to Save Gare d'Orsay," *New York Times*, January 20, 1970, 13.

78. Fredric Jameson, "Periodizing the Sixties," in *Sixties without Apology*, ed. Sohnya Sayres, Stanley Aronowitz, Fredric Jameson et al. (Minneapolis: University of Minnesota Press, 1984), 203–207.

79. See Stanley Corkin, *Starring New York: Filming the Grime and Glamour of the Long 1970s* (New York: Oxford University Press, 2010); Webb, *The Cinema of Urban Crisis*.

80. Wood, *Hollywood from Vietnam to Reagan*; Michael Ryan and Douglas Kellner, *Camera Politica: The Politics and Ideology of Contemporary Hollywood Film* (Bloomington: Indiana University Press, 1990).

81. Ockman, *Architecture Culture*, 22.

82. Tzonis and Lefaivre, *Architecture in Europe*, 11–15.

83. Ross, *May 1968*, 1, 6.

84. On 1968 and sixties politics, for example, see Martin Klimke, *The Other Alliance: Student Protest in West Germany and the United States in the Global Sixties* (Princeton: Princeton University Press, 2011); Martha Biondi, *The Black Revolution on Campus* (Berkeley: University of California Press, 2012); Robert Gildea, James Mark, and Anette Warring, *Europe's 1968: Voices of Revolt* (Oxford: Oxford University Press, 2013);

Ingrid Gilcher-Holtey, *A Revolution of Perception? Consequences and Echoes of 1968* (New York: Berghahn Books, 2014); on cinema and 1968, see Layerle, *Cameras en lutte*; Jessica Stites Mor, *Transition Cinema: Political Filmmaking and the Argentine Left since 1968* (Pittsburgh: University of Pittsburgh Press, 2012); Kathrin Fahlenbrach, Erling Sivertsen, and Rolf Werenskjold, *Media and Revolt: Strategies and Performances from the 1960s to the Present* (New York: Berghahn Books, 2014).

1

The *Cinétracts, Détournement*, and Social Space in Paris

JENNIFER STOB

"The future is imaginary, but everyone is living in it as if it had happened. It is a collective hallucination," wrote Mavis Gallant on May 26, 1968.[1] Gallant was an expat Québécoise writer living on Paris's Left Bank during the 1960s. She experienced firsthand what became known in France as *les événements de mai*, the events of May 1968. Alternately sympathetic and skeptical, her diary entries are one account of the tumultuous weeks of protest in Paris that were triggered by the actions of University of Nanterre students against the Vietnam War and their own university administration from March of that year onward. The demonstrations, barricade-building, street fighting, and institutional occupations that were undertaken primarily by university and high school students in the first two weeks of May were followed by widespread citizen engagement on May 13, when between 171,000 and 1 million Parisians flooded city streets (the former number according to conservative police estimates, the latter according to the media), in solidarity with the students and unions who had called the demonstration.[2]

Wildcat strikes in factories and public services began the day after this mass demonstration. They ended in resounding disappointment after a week of trade union negotiation with the government yielded a modest raise in salary for striking workers but not the systemic change they were hoping for. Although strikes and social revolt continued in France well beyond the summer, the month of May ended with another mass demonstration in counterpoint to the one on the thirteenth: this time, hundreds of thousands of pro-Gaullist citizens flooded the Champs Elysées to support their beleaguered president and a societal return to order.[3] In her diary entries, Gallant repeatedly stresses that all thought and action in Paris that month seemed to be a palimpsest of generational and historical conflicts: suddenly, that which had happened, could, will, and did happen, was coextensive with that which was happening inside and outside of her apartment. When the quotidian of salaried hours, public services, entertainment, and gasoline stops, she suggests, citizens are prompted by the inversion of familiar rituals to a new consciousness of their situatedness and contingency in place and time.

Gallant's description of the state of suspended futurity or potentiality that characterized this period crystallizes in her description of the May 13 demonstration that crossed through the heart of Paris. That day, she stood for hours on a pedestrian median amid the stream of bodies marching down the Boulevard St. Michel. "We, on our island," she wrote,

> are convinced we are seeing some sort of spontaneous generation, a mixture of people who have never marched together before. But the radio tells us that at Denfert-Rochereau, the destination, they are already quarrelling among themselves—the unions and the students. And while that is going on, part of the cortege is still waiting in the Place de la République to begin the march. The end of it, just before nine, is a chain of students, about forty across, holding hands. I am convinced I have seen something remarkable.[4]

Her amazement testifies to the scale and the rhythm of politicized mobilization in Paris but also to its ephemerality.

The scale, rhythm, and ephemerality of reproducible media were as essential to the remarkable quality of this event as the mixing, hand-holding, and quarreling Gallant describes. She was not the only Parisian to "live with the transistor" that month.[5] Beginning May 10, listening to the on-site breaking news broadcasts on the radio stations Europe 1 and Radio-Télé-Luxembourg (RTL) became an obsessive practice for hundreds of thousands in the French capital. Pocket radios were plentiful in the occupied Sorbonne and on the barricades themselves until May 23, when the government blocked short-wave transmission.[6] Walkie-talkies were rarer, but also playfully and strategically employed. With such technologies in the hands of those who were creating the narrative, individuals were able to assemble, disperse, and regroup with ease and exactitude. Upon hearing updates about the parts of the Latin Quarter where the street fighting was most intense, listeners could fluidly alter their individual trajectories and assist fellow protesters or avoid the conflict entirely. Simultaneous broadcast increased the potential to be at once collective and autonomous, independent and united.[7]

In the decades since 1968, a number of critical theorists have employed the term "liveness" to describe a sensory experience akin to the one that these Parisian protesters were having as they combined direct action with reproduced sound.[8] Liveness indicates a subject's sense of an event as realistic and immediate *in addition to* their distinct awareness that the virtual nature of reproducible media is converging with the event at hand. The prominence of radio broadcasts during the revolt of May 1968 was double-edged: it was enormously useful for those strategically occupying city streets, but it also de-realized their experience of occupation, distracting listeners from the present and accelerating confrontations. The advantages and disadvantages of reproducible media and the phenomenon of liveness at the heart of social revolt have only become more pronounced in contemporary culture. Despite the markedly different platforms used, media has remained a boon to and a distortion of numerous twenty-first-century global uprisings that are frequently juxtaposed with the global uprisings that took place in 1968.[9]

If Gallant's diaries characterize the "collective hallucination" of May 1968 rather ambivalently—her entry on the May 13 march suggests that perhaps the sounds and visions of unity hide others of discord—other accounts took a different tone. In an influential book of photographs, interviews, and essays published soon afterward, Philippe Labro provided an impressionistic overview of May's events that combined a factual chronology with eyewitness testimony, such as that of an anonymous student interviewed by sociologist Évelyne Sullerot who was unabashedly ecstatic in characterizing the atmosphere of the day: "I had the exultant impression that each one of us found [our]selves in a state of total consciousness: reflecting on the past, informed of the present, resolving to create the future. This provoked a deep desire in me and in all the others that I met to be informed actors, or active listeners; however you want to put it."[10] The testimonies of Gallant and this anonymous student attempt to transcribe the spontaneity, suspension, and superimposition of a revolt and its sonic reproduction into language. Where, then, are the images of this month in Paris, those that superimpose, preserve, and annotate the altered, collective uses of the city and the sociotemporal loop that encompassed it?

Televisual images of May's events were few and far between for Parisians; foreign news teams recorded the majority of those that existed. This was due primarily to the censorship that the French state imposed on its own television and radio stations and its reportorial bias in favor of the French government and police. Political scientist Boris Gobille writes that between May 2 and May 14, only two out of fifteen hours of television news treated the subject, ninety minutes of which were dedicated to official governmental or police announcements and thirty minutes to coverage of the demonstrations.[11] From May 17 until July 13, when employees of state television and radio undertook one of the longest and bitterest strikes of the summer, original televisual coverage of the events from the ORTF (Office de Radiodiffusion-Télévision Française) was reduced to nothing.

Press photography was the handiest alternative to television—only slightly more than half of the French population in 1968 watched television with the same regularity as they consumed radio and print media.[12] However, photos of major domestic events appeared in newspapers with a delay of nearly a day—in the case of photo reportages in glossy magazines, almost a week. On the Left Bank especially, newspapers and magazines were difficult to locate and sold out quickly. Any amateur or professional photographer was faced with the ethical dilemma of documenting a social movement that explicitly privileged active cooperation and partisan intervention over mass media reporting and its presumptive neutrality. Moreover, most Parisian film processing laboratories were shuttered while their technicians were on strike.

This chapter examines one instance of the quest to quickly produce, control, and circulate indexical representations of May 1968 in Paris: short 16mm films called *cinétracts* that were made anonymously as a collective project between May 1968 and March 1969. Each one under three minutes long, these films aimed to convey and prolong the extraordinary sense of time and togetherness across reclaimed city space that characterized the May unrest, while seeking to spread the ideologies that helped spark it. Forty-two *cinétracts* are known to exist, preserved in private and public collections internationally. The five or six that were filmed, developed, and projected in Paris before mid-June of 1968—for example, at 40 rue Saint Séverin, near the Place Saint Michel, in left-wing publisher François Maspéro's bookstore, La Joie de Lire—constitute some of the earliest available filmic reactions to Paris's social revolt and its repression.[13] The main period of *cinétract* production witnessed *cinétract* activity by seminal *nouvelle vague* filmmaker Jean-Luc Godard and also overlapped with his formation of the Dziga Vertov Group with Jean-Pierre Gorin (a more intimate and sustained partnership in collective filmmaking that continued into the 1970s).[14]

The *cinétracts* evolved from within a lineage of agitprop compilation film and in concert with contemporaneous experiments in the practice of revolutionarily restructuring cinema's apparatus. They represented a new formal practice and a new distribution format at the same time. Their manufacture from an archive of compiled and appropriated press photography resonated with the practice of *détournement*, advocated in the writings of the contemporary leftist collective, the Situationist International (SI). Although no Situationists are known to have participated in the creation of *cinétracts*, the SI's cofounder and most enduring member, Guy Debord, was an avid filmmaker in his own right, and the Situationists' theory of détournement can shed light on the formal strategies of the *cinétract* films. Détournement marks their difference from the vast majority of other militant films made during or in the wake of May.

In what follows, I argue that the *cinétracts* model three distinct philosophical approaches to the use of détournement to both represent resistant social space and communicate resistant ideological rhetoric. In the silent, rapid rush of photographic images that characterize the first grouping of *cinétracts* I discuss, the right to what Gallant called the "collective hallucination" of social space is commemorated impressionistically, between volleys of tear gas.[15] In a second grouping, viewers are asked to enter the state of "total consciousness" evoked by the anonymous student that Évelyne Sullerot interviewed, wherein the present and the past are radically superimposed.[16] In a third and final grouping of *cinétracts*, two registers of détournement are at work simultaneously: the juxtaposition of original and politically appropriated text takes place on and in images themselves as well as through montage. Here Gallant's account of 1968 holds another phrase (ripe for appropriation itself) that can describe the formal logic: in this grouping of *cinétracts*, language directs and controls images, exposing the "marvelous abstraction" of all visual meaning.[17]

The entire series of *cinétracts* is highly emblematic of the creative challenges that militant filmmaking can face in affirming a social ideology and affirming an urban environment's social space at the same time. To best understand these challenges, I will give a detailed overview of how this collective project functioned. The ways in which each of the three groups of films I propose represents resistant thought and resistant social space stresses again the *cinétracts*' ambition to contribute to both a revolutionary cinematic infrastructure and an activist cinematic imaginary. First, however, it is crucial to lay out a few of the *cinétracts*' most important contemporaries and historical predecessors in film and visual culture.

New (and Old) Forms of Action against Politics and Art

According to Daniel Singer, May 1968 in Paris was a demonstration to France and the world that "through direct action it was possible to force the impregnable state, and the employers, to yield."[18] He notes, however, that the French Communist Party, which had in decades past provided the "driving force" behind protest movements was this time an active impediment to the strikes and occupations.[19] Their catalyst was instead student activism, a force that was in turn significantly catalyzed by the SI. The SI group was formed in 1958, amalgamating three smaller postwar avant-gardes: the Lettrist International, the International Movement for an Imaginist Bauhaus, and the London Psychogeographical Committee. The artists and intellectuals from Denmark, France, Great Britain, Italy, and the Netherlands united by the formation of this collective found a new intellectual home in Paris's rue de la Montagne-Sainte-Geneviève, a steep and narrow street in the Latin Quarter.

A bar in that street called Le Tonneau d'Or was much beloved by Guy Debord, who was the SI's principle coordinator and theorist. Its address was used from 1958–1963 for all correspondence pertaining to the SI's eponymous journal. In it, the collective documented and lauded the ambiances found in this and many other specific patchworks of Paris's urban fabric, especially those in and around the Latin Quarter, the city's islands, the sprawling central market of Les Halles, and Saint Germain. In their articles—initially anonymous, and later signed—the Situationists decried French postwar urban planning and consumerism. They promulgated the withering away of conventional culture and politics and the rise of a revolutionary council communism founded on spontaneous creative encounters—on "situations."[20]

The Situationists' steadily widening impact on university students in France in May was evident in the pro-Situationist stances of several student agitators at the University of Nanterre in Paris's western suburbs.[21] Calling themselves the *Enragés*, their attempt to take over the university's administrative offices on March 22, 1968, kicked off the student uprising of that spring.[22] By way of the *Enragés* and other leftist student factions, Situationist-influenced thought once or twice removed had penetrated mainstream consciousness by mid-May deeply enough for a term that the Situationists had gone to great lengths to repudiate to appear in the newspaper *France-Soir*: "Situationism."[23] In a column entitled, "In order to be able to converse with your children: The Little 'Dico' of the Student Revolution," SITUATIONN-ISME was listed alongside entries such as ENRAGÉS, GROUPUSCULES, [HERBERT] MARCUSE and RECUPERATION.[24] "Its preferred mode of expression is the erotic comic strip" and its preferred technique "intellectual terrorism," journalist Alain Buhler informed the befuddled parents of young revolutionaries.[25]

Buhler's dictionary entry for "SITUATIONNISME" suggests that détournement, as a subversive mode of expression and a technique for operating on images and language alike, had begun to serve as a kind of shorthand for the group. Détournement was a practice espoused but not invented by the SI. It consisted of removing an expression from its original context and resituating it in a new context so that its theft would be evident and its message altered and subversively politicized. Perhaps the most immediately identifiable and accessible examples of the practice were those that took place in the media of protest banners, posters of the Atelier Populaire formed in the studios of the student-occupied École des beaux-arts, open letters pasted on walls, graffiti, and roneotyped flyers of the occupations movement.[26]

Yet détournement of the visual, the social, and the architectural did not exclusively take place in slogans and symbols. It was also the strategy at play when workers took over their workplaces, when thoroughfares were transformed into places for dwelling instead of driving, and when fixtures of urban scenery—tree branches, cobblestones, cars, billboards, and traffic signs—were used as barricade material. This overarching operational strategy of the student demonstrations and workers' wildcat strikes in 1968 fulfilled the Situationist decree, first declared in 1961, that "the revolution will be, among other things, the perpetual creation of signs which belong to everyone."[27]

The popularization of détournement was the topic of an article entitled "The Situationists and New Forms of Action against Politics and Art," written by René Viénet in October 1967, many months before the barricades and wildcat strikes.[28] Viénet drew attention to many promising media in which détournement could be performed, both legally (e.g., comic strips) and illegally (e.g., the takeover of radio and television channels), but the medium he dealt with at length was cinema.[29]

This was not the first time that the Situationists had devoted attention to the radical potential for filmic détournement. Indeed, Debord had thus far made three films that made use of the strategy—one before and two soon after the SI's formation: *Hurlements en faveur de Sade* (*Howls for Sade*, 1952); *Sur le passage de quelques personnes à travers une assez courte unité de temps* (*On the Passage of Several Persons through a Rather Brief Unity of Time*, 1959); and *Critique de la séparation* (*Critique of Separation*, 1961).[30] Both of the latter two films feature music and voice-overs that do not synchronize with the images shown. Modeling them on the confused ramblings of a drunken monologue, Debord stated that his objective was to make a film "as fundamentally incoherent and unsatisfying as the reality [they] dealt with."[31]

Edited together with appropriated advertising, newsreels, and comic strip imagery are a number of still photographs and original footage shot in the streets of Paris. These vignettes function as ciphers: they refuse to commemorate the site itself and point us instead to meaning elsewhere—for example, in the rapid ruination of such sites under modernist urban planning. The city's raw material that was loved and lost by Debord and the Situationists is one of several diffuse, sentimental, layered laments that sharpen the bitterness in the films' ideological rhetoric.

In contrast to Debord's cinematic destruction and incoherence through détournement, Viénet made the case for extending cinema's life and exploiting its expressive malleability: "The cinema enables one to express everything, like an article, a book, a tract or a poster. That is why we should henceforth require that each Situationist be as capable of making a film as of writing an article."[32] Viénet singled out "newsreels, previews and, above all, filmed advertisements" as inspirational formats; because these were the "most consummate and modern examples" of cinema's stagnation, they were therefore ripest for immediate appropriation.[33] His new proposal for filmmaking posited that political thought could be produced and acquired on both sides of the camera, regardless of cinematographic proficiency.

To the Situationists, the kind of film that best exemplified the study of the present "as a historical problem" was one that Soviet filmmaker Sergei Eisenstein had conceived of in 1927–1928 but never realized: a filmic interpretation of Karl Marx's *Capital*.[34] The notebook in which Eisenstein chronicled his ideas on such an adaptation reveals the three guiding theses he developed for the project: that a major text of political import could be turned into a film as "a visual instruction in the dialectic method";[35] that such a lesson could be particularly useful to nonintellectuals and could even "teach the worker to think dialectically";[36] and, finally, that the endeavor would produce a brand new kind of cinema, one that "assembles one point of view from many events" instead of "one event from many points of view."[37]

Because Viénet's theory of cinema was based on preexisting images and not new footage, a truer predecessor might be found in *The Fall of the Romanov Dynasty* (1927), one of the first feature-length compilation films by Soviet film pioneer Esfir Shub—with the caveat that the SI's antiauthoritarian communism and Viénet's emphasis on "low" materials like ads and discarded outtakes drastically differed from Shub's politics and materials. Jay Leyda has argued that Shub's masterpiece brought about "a worldwide awareness of the cultural and material value of 'archive footage,' setting in motion the principles which would lead to the establishment of the first film archives."³⁸ Certainly the *court métrages* or short films in the French documentary tradition from the 1940s onward—like those by Pierre Kast, Paul Paviot, or Alain Resnais—provide the key film historical transition from compilation film as archival, even revolutionary, truth and compilation film that used or misused both still and moving images to question the documentary impulse altogether.³⁹

Viénet's exhortation that all Situationists practice détournement in cinema constitutes a conception of radical compilation filmmaking that, in a French context, surpasses in its democratic purview the avant-gardes of the 1920s as well as those after World War II. Sebastian Layerle's historiography of French cinema in 1968 suggests that a possible exception is to be found in the Jean Vigo Group of Noisy-le-Sec, whose manifesto for a free, humanist, revolutionary cinema declared their desire to teach workers how to operate film cameras.⁴⁰ Other notable calls for the democratization and de-specialization of filmmaking include Jean Rouch's 1955 remarks advocating the widespread popularization of 16mm cameras and the advocacy for cinema's use in a psychotherapeutic context of the Atelier de recherche cinématographique in 1967. However, both Rouch and the Atelier de recherche cinématographique had in mind cinema professionals pioneering a disciplinary hybrid of film and social science rather than the actual subjects of social science learning to take up the camera themselves.⁴¹

The principle aim of the Groupe Medvedkine of Besançon was to upend just this sort of unidirectional cinematic gaze and cinematic cultural capital.⁴² It was a filmmaking collective formed under the guidance of Chris Marker only a few months after Viénet's 1967 article was published. Its declared intention to "give the working class (its representatives) new possibilities of expression" resonated at least in part with the "new forms of action" propagated by Viénet and the Situationists.⁴³ However, the Groupe Medvedkine did not emphasize self-reflexive cinematic appropriation but rather the mobility of cinema's narrative and apparatus—the kind that Soviet filmmaker Alexander Medvedkin strove to introduce into the lives of the rural Soviet working class with the innovation of an agitprop cinema train that could tour rural communities, record peasant life, and project it back to them as an audience.⁴⁴

Viénet does not explicitly situate his call for cameras and appropriated expression in relation to these antecedent Soviet and contemporary French experiments I have traced, but his article is an important milestone in the history of radical film theory and activist filmmaking on the cusp of 1968. This comparison highlights the importance that reusing found material had in contesting dominant historical narratives across dramatically different sociopolitical contexts. It also highlights the relative absence of appropriation in militant film until the widespread détournement that accompanied the May revolt. The anonymous and collectively made short films called *cinétracts* were that tendency's most important manifestation. Fragmentary and interstitial, they exemplify the Situationist belief that aesthetic détournement is linked to the promise of more expansive and extensive détournement of the material world. Furthermore, they elucidate three different conceptual approaches to the representation of resistant urban social space in a way that is emblematic of subsequent collective efforts.

Cinétract-ize!

The *cinétract* collective was one of a number of efforts launched in Paris in May 1968 that attempted to examine, dismantle, and transform the conventional apparatus of cinema, emphasizing its potential as a catalyst for social change and its power as a record and vehicle of political commitment. Examining, dismantling, and transforming the cinema as an apparatus meant understanding its operation as a system of interlocking parts (camera, projector, screen, and more), each of which involved in turn a more expansive system of social and economic institutions. For numerous French cinephiles, their first real exposure to this concept and its political implications came in February 1968, when André Malraux, Minister for Culture during the presidency of Charles de Gaulle, abruptly fired the head of the Cinémathèque française, Henri Langlois, causing a public outcry and the formation of an action committee whose press campaigns, petitions, and public demonstrations were directly responsible for Langlois's reinstatement two months later.

A number of the prominent New Wave actors, directors, and critics who had been radicalized by their protests against the firing of Langlois joined forces with the students, technicians, and other film professionals occupying Paris's major film and photography schools during May. On May 17, Les États généraux du cinéma français (The General Estates of French Cinema) was formed, one of the largest film-oriented collective experiments of the period, perhaps best known for its role in successfully calling for the closure of the Cannes Film Festival in solidarity with France's nationwide strikes.[45] Plagued by internecine conflict from the start and dormant by late June, the États généraux nevertheless garnered several influential adherents at its inception, among them Jacques Rivette, Claude Chabrol, Chris Marker, and several of the filmmakers who also participated in the *cinétract* collective.

The manifesto of the États généraux, published on May 25, perfectly echoed Viénet's statement from 1967 that cinema was a hybrid media form exquisitely suited both to "the brilliance of protest and to the restlessness of reconstruction."[46] However, the majority of the films produced in the name of the États généraux, such as *Ce n'est qu'un début* (1968), *Nantes—Sud-Aviation* (1968), and *Reprise du travail aux usines Wonder* (1968), were testimonial documentaries in the expository or direct cinema mode. The *cinétract* collective went much further in carrying forth Viénet's idea of a do-it-yourself *cinéma engagé-détourné* that could instruct and exhort without adhering to documentary film conventions. Had the SI known of these films,[47] they would have discounted the possibility that the films were truly contestational, having long criticized two of the collective's more established contributors (Alain Resnais and Jean-Luc Godard) for the way in which the associational montage of their films merely aped détournement.[48] Viénet's 1967 article even included a preemptory strike against Godard, whom he correctly suspected would adopt the cinematic techniques the article set forth.[49] Yet the events of May 1968 marked a pause in the Situationists' castigation of false friends. Debord realized that the eruption of a large-scale social revolt represented a massive political and aesthetic paradigm shift; with it, he wrote, for better and for worse, "a generation began to be situationist on an international level."[50] In their form as well as the new political consciousness they express, the *cinétracts* are an apt example of the diffusion of Situationist theory.

Like the Groupe Medvedkine, the *cinétract* project was begun through Chris Marker's initiative[51] during the third or fourth week of May 1968 and Marker linked aspects of the *cinétract* collective's sourcing of material, film development, and distribution to the organization SLON (Société pour le Lancement des Oeuvres Nouvelles), a left-wing cooperative designed in 1967 to facilitate the production, development, and distribution of just these kinds of politically conscious films.[52] As one of the ten original founders of SLON, Marker knew the influence of revolutionary cinema could be extended and strengthened by an alternative model of the vertical integration that had proven successful in commercial film industries—one aimed at developing social justice rather than lucrative markets. Key to this alternative to studio systems was Marker himself, who, more than any other French filmmaker of his generation, served as a human conduit between *cineastes*, activists, their factions, and their philosophical perspectives.

Marker and a core group of filmmakers close to him established the formal characteristics and proposed genre constraints of the *cinétract*.[53] SLON then published a roneotyped flyer, written by Jean-François Dars, entitled

"*Cinétractez!*" ("*Cinétract*-ize!"), which explained the films' purpose, production, and distribution arrangements, gave practical compositional advice, and invited anyone to participate.[54] "WHAT IS A CINÉTRACT?" the flyer began.

> It's 2 minutes, 44 seconds worth (that is, a 30m, 24 frames/second reel of 16mm) of silent film with a political, social or other theme, destined to generate discussion and action [. . .] The succession of images is a *discourse*, tied sometimes closely and sometimes loosely to the narrative discourse. The shock and the possible effectiveness of a *cinétract* is created from the variety and the play of these discourses [. . .] Normally, the *cinétract* ought to be made without montage. It must be ready FOR USE UPON ITS DEPARTURE FROM THE LABORATORY . . . The development and printing of copies are guaranteed.[55]

The *cinétract* collective was dispersed and nonhierarchical. Nineteen of its members are known by name, all of whom contributed their work anonymously. The majority were Paris-based professionals already established in the media industry, all men, and most linked by personal acquaintance with Chris Marker.[56] The first several *cinétracts* produced between mid-May and the end of June 1968 were assembled from a photographic archive in the studio of photographer and cinematographer Eric Dumage, who generously lent the filmmakers his space at 1, rue Littré near the Gare Montparnasse.[57] Marker and other founding members of the collective filmed several more *cinétracts* at the commercial studio of filmmaker Christian Quinson near the Sorbonne. There, several animation tables were at their disposal.[58] In October 1968, a group of film students and journalists in Rouen contributed eight films that furthered this particular mode of politically connecting, educating, and energizing through cinema beyond the *capitale* in a second wave of *cinétract*-izing.[59]

Much of the raw material used in the *cinétracts* consisted of photos taken by both independent photographers and professionals under contract with photo agencies. Magnum photographers Bruno Barbey, Guy Le Querrec, and Marc Riboud were among those who donated prints of their work to the collective while their agencies were busy selling the same pictures to newspapers and magazines in France and abroad. The prints were passed from friend to friend, acquaintance to acquaintance, or simply dropped off at Dumage's studio.[60] In this sense, a representational battle was staged in real time between the détournement of photos in *cinétracts* and their insertion into the mainstream media.⁶¹ The resulting pool of donated photographs, organized by the filmmakers into general thematic groupings for convenient access, resulted in several instances of the same image recurring in different films, each time in a slightly different context. Such recurrences highlighted the belief that the truth in photography was both plural and integral, manifesting itself once as the photograph was taken and many times thereafter in montage. Hence, the *cinétracts* insisted that cinema should be understood not as a mirror, a window, or an illusion, but as a surface on which we pass images to one another and around which we can commune, like a countertop or a desk.⁶²

In the purposefully rudimentary in-camera editing of the *cinétracts*, the dialectical thought of the filmmaker became synonymous with the act of pointing the camera and "seeing" a series of images. Soviet film director Dziga Vertov praised cinema for the way that its recording and editing technologies could form a miraculous new kind of "camera-eye," heightening the perception of directors and film audiences.⁶³ Like Vertov, the *cinétract* collective had revolutionary goals for cinema, but the *cinétracts*' form inverted his term and his theory. Their unremitting emphasis was on the human lens behind the mechanical one, an "eye-camera" that matched sightline to each recorded shot, which was in turn matched by the filmmaker's effort to organize his thoughts in sequence. Sebastien Layerle has characterized this project of instructing viewers in both a new experimental film mode and a set of political stances as "an education of the gaze" for filmmaker, projectionist and audience alike.⁶⁴ The pedagogical ambitions of the *cinétracts* go even further, however: the films also suggest that the act of looking through a camera, at a screen, and at other audience members, contributes to the production of alternative social space.

The idea that public space is never natural but always social, continuously produced by daily spatial practices, by schematic design, and by symbolic imaginaries was developed during the 1960s and 1970s by Marxist sociologist Henri Lefebvre.⁶⁵ Lefebvre called for "the space of a different (social) life and of a different mode of production"⁶⁶ in opposition to Paris's postwar consumer culture, theorizing cooperatively for a time with the Situationists and participating in some of the demonstrations of May 1968.⁶⁷ Despite these shared sympathies, however, he never investigated cinema's apparatus, propaganda, and fantasy as a model for social space, whereas both the SI and the *cinétract* collective sought to exploit it. With the aid of détournement, the *cinétracts* took three successive formal approaches to the representation of oppositional social spaces in the Latin Quarter and around Paris in 1968. First documenting the "collective hallucination" of these spaces, then historicizing the "total consciousness" they produced, and finally refusing to represent these spaces and creating a "marvelous abstraction" of image and rhetoric instead, these films encouraged their audiences to pass via a film's activist imaginary to activism itself.

Collective Hallucinations, Total Consciousnesses, Marvelous Abstractions

The representation of social space in the earliest group of *cinétracts*, made in the Quinson and Dumage studios, serves as ground and justification for the acts of young men and women in the city streets.[68] These films feature extensive use of rostrum camera movements such as dissolves, pans, and zooms, creating a kind of continuity editing from détourned still photographs and thereby a fleeting impression of photographic self-creation, as if the images were reenacting their subject for a few tantalizing seconds per reel. When intertitles are used in these films, they merely complement the photographic flow in a lyrical fashion rather than supplementing it with additional or contradictory information. Evoking a strange *décalage* in perceptual time that mirrors the one Gallant described in her witnessing of protesters on the Boulevard St. Michel on May 13, the term "collective hallucination" aptly characterizes this subgrouping. Far from the derogatory sense with which the word "hallucination" is sometimes imbued, its use here indicates a kind of actualized futurity—a euphoric state of subversive, shared immanence that anchors itself in a desired reality rather than the current reality.

Cinétract 004 is a prime example. The film begins with a physiology of a policeman in riot gear—a member of the CRS (Compagnies Républicaines de Sécurité)—assembled from shots that emphasize the brutal accoutrements of the riot police: goggles, nightstick, and helmet. (See Figure 1.1.) The editing accelerates as the content becomes increasingly violent, showing a surge of police chasing down and beating protesters, and culminating in a series of in-camera dissolves between multiple shots of wounded protesters lying in the street. A girl's head, faceup on a medic's stretcher, emerges out of the last dissolve, her mouth as grim as that of the CRS officer at the beginning. Hence, the film is a visual conjugation of the verb *matraquer*: to bludgeon. Like several other collective hallucinations in the series, this photo suite testifies to the government's readiness to use violence systematically and indiscriminately against its own citizens.[69]

The revolutionary advantage of this pictorial mode among the *cinétracts* corpus is its dramatic testimonial power. It presents the contested streets of

Figure 1.1 Selected frames from *Cinétract 004*, anonymous 16mm short film, Paris, 1968, showing CRS riot police in action and a wounded protestor

Paris as a kind of perpetual, subversive "urban planning" of barricade construction, cobblestone throwing, and face-to-face debate. Yet this group of films is also representative of the trickiness involved in creating a photographic flow that, while making the photographs look fresh and lifelike, can actually embalm its subject matter in remembrance. As in Marker's celebrated film, *La Jetée* (1962), composed almost entirely of still photographs, the philosophy of the photographic in this cluster of *cinétracts* is undeniably nostalgic and iconic. The fluid and impressionistic blurriness of the snapshots, many taken at night under dim street lamps, is not enough to completely dispel the sense that the scenes they portray are firmly fixed in the past. The representation of social space that they transmit centers on the Latin Quarter as a citadel for resistant students, just as it is in the narrative of May by Italian anarchist Angelo Quattrocchi and British socialist Tom Nairn.[70] In both, Paris's fifth *arrondissement* seems like a vast arena when students are victorious in barricade skirmishes, and a too-comfortable trap in the aftermath of student defeat.

These *cinétracts* of "collective hallucination" also remind us that neither still nor moving photographic representation can truly deliver upon its

Figure 1.2 Selected frames from *Cinétract 003*, anonymous 16mm short film, Paris, 1968, commemorating the death of the high school student Gilles Tautin during a police charge on strikers at the Renault factory at Flins, outside Paris

promises of mythic agency, immutability, and testimonial purity. Roland Barthes, one of the most prominent theorists of photography, consistently conveyed a simultaneous skepticism of and devotion to photography's deceptive promises in his analyses. Parsing the differences between these promises at work in photography and in film, Barthes wrote, "The cinema is not an animated photograph; in it the having-been-there vanishes, giving way to a being-there of the thing."[71] Yet these *cinétracts* blur that difference; their cinema is the very definition of animated photographs. Having détourned each photograph's subject matter to their own story line, the filmmakers were powerless to prevent this "having-been-there" from influencing each shot and consigning the social space of the Parisian uprising to the past.

Nowhere is this clearer than in *Cinétract 003*, made in mourning and in memoriam of Gilles Tautin, a high school student who had joined striking workers at the Renault factory in Flins on the northwest outskirts of Paris and had drowned while being pursued by riot police.[72] (See Figure 1.2.) In that particular *cinétract*, the youthful crowd marching with Tautin's funeral cortege through the streets of the seventeenth *arrondissement* as it heads to the Batignolles cemetery seeks to open urban space to all in a noncommodified manner—a social use of the city that geographer David Harvey has designated by the verb "commoning."[73] Unfortunately, however, the imagery of this commoning falls within the traditional symbolism of funeral rites— the film may be easily read in terms of shared, private, and individual loss rather than shared, public, and collective activity. Similarly, other *cinétracts* that attempt to represent the euphoria of collective hallucination may be misread more narrowly as mementos rather than incitements fashioned from appropriated imagery.

A second grouping of *cinétracts* attempts to avoid these elegiac tendencies of photographic flow by compelling viewers' awareness of the superimposition of history and the present during this kind of nationwide uprising. In this cluster of films, the aesthetic shift and its resulting shift in politicized meaning is evidenced in a wide range of photographic and nonphotographic source material working in juxtaposition with intertitles.[74] Many films from this second group were made in a simpler, more immediate fashion by fixing images to a wall or to the floor and filming them for several seconds in succession (as recommended in the collective's flyer). Perhaps this makeshift practice independent of animation table equipment encouraged the scripting and inclusion of written intertitles and nonphotographic images, like drawings or posters. This material was used to historicize the production of resistant social space in Paris and the factories in its near suburbs. The films' emphasis was no longer on police brutality or affirmation of the city's radical appropriation but on the role of ideological rhetoric in the practice, design, and representation of the city over time.

Cinétract 018 is exemplary of this grouping: it uses intertitles to toggle deftly between conservative euphemism and its deeply reactionary, repressive implications, doing so with a vicious sense of humor. (See Figure 1.3.) The film chronicles the demonstration of tens of thousands of French men and women who rallied in support of de Gaulle's continuing presidency at the end of May, marching up the Champs-Elysées from the Place de la Concorde to the Arc de Triomphe, the same route as (but in the opposite direction to) the French state's Bastille Day military parade. Here, the intertitles are made to speak satirically in the voice of de Gaulle's supporters, complaining that the student movement has dirtied their walls with graffiti and posters and that the marchers (workers and students alike) have polluted their city with the noise of shouted slogans. The accompanying photographs contrast the wreckage of burned-out automobiles and the chic formalwear of the de Gaulle demonstrators. They suggest that for this bourgeois population a

Figure 1.3 Selected frames from *Cinétract 018*, anonymous 16mm short film, Paris, 1968, showing images from a pro-Gaullist demonstration intercut with antiestablishment graffiti ("On salit nos murs", i.e., "We dirty our walls")

"well-behaved" citizen is not merely to behave nonconfrontationally but to completely assimilate to the culture and cadences of commodities.

Through the juxtaposition of photographs and the text that precedes and follows them, the film charges that fascist-leaning popular blocs and political figures continue to exercise undue influence in France, and that the pro-Gaullist desire for a "return to order" is inherently linked to the tyranny of colonialism at home and abroad.[75] The final seconds of this *cinétract* begin with a close-up of a former Algerian War combatant, with arms outstretched bombastically and chest studded with medals, before the camera zooms out to reveal his position at the head of a group of marchers. The dialectical contrasts in each image and intertitle suggest that there is a long history of hostility toward leftist discourse in France and that this history has serious implications for the current occupations movement. The ethical commitment to knowing the past, understanding the present, and impacting the future drives these films, just as it did the student who described the events of May, when interviewed by Evelyne Sullerot, as a "state of total consciousness." These *cinétracts* of total consciousness stress the continuity of class war instead of its repression. In 1968 is the return of the general strike of 1936, but also the French Commune of 1870, and the police massacres of Algerian protesters in 1961, they suggest. In this way, they bear an even closer resemblance to the cinema that the Situationists believed could counter the reification performed by state power and capitalism, one featuring "mediations enabling consciousness to recognize one moment in another," as Viénet had written.[76]

Only in a third distinct grouping of *cinétracts* is the détournement of an image's composition combined with the détournement of its context in a montage sequence.[77] This cluster of *cinétracts* did not use camera movement or intertitles to provide the recitative for their visual progression: they collapsed the difference between text and image. In them, photographs of the people and places of May 1968 are present, but marginal; the majority of the images used are book covers, illustrations, press clippings, advertisements, and art reproductions, virtually all of which have been altered with handwritten phrases and symbols or intertitles forming calligrams. Despite the occasional ornamental dead end, in this group of *cinétracts* there is a successful détournement of the historical reality latent inside of each instance of depiction. In other words, these films deliver radical messages directly related to Paris's social revolt, but they also critique the power of representations to perform this delivery.

The majority of the *cinétracts* that take this approach are in fact labeled "*filmtracts*," and in several instances, the film's détournement begins in the first shot, as the *filmtract*'s number has been written with marker onto the wrapper of the very 16mm film reel being exposed. Most *filmtracts* are either the work of Jean-Luc Godard or show his direct influence. The change in terminology is significant because it and Godard's inclusion of images from *La Chinoise* (1967) and *Le Gai Savoir* (1968) in some *filmtracts* could betray an obstinately authorial signature inside of a collective and anonymous project.[78] More important, however, is the fact that this new term is accompanied by the double détournement that constitutes this grouping, a second and final major shift in aesthetic strategy.

The *cinétracts* of "collective hallucination" had depended on firsthand documentation of the events of May in Paris, while those of "total consciousness" focused on historicizing instead of lyrical witnessing. Despite their differences, both groupings communicated Henri Lefebvre's concept of the "right to the city" and the responsibility to produce a more just and more pleasurable urban social space that it implied.[79] In the *cinétracts-cum-filmtracts*, however, the project of conceptualizing contestational urban social space within contestational cinema is deferred in favor of an investment in the subversive pow-

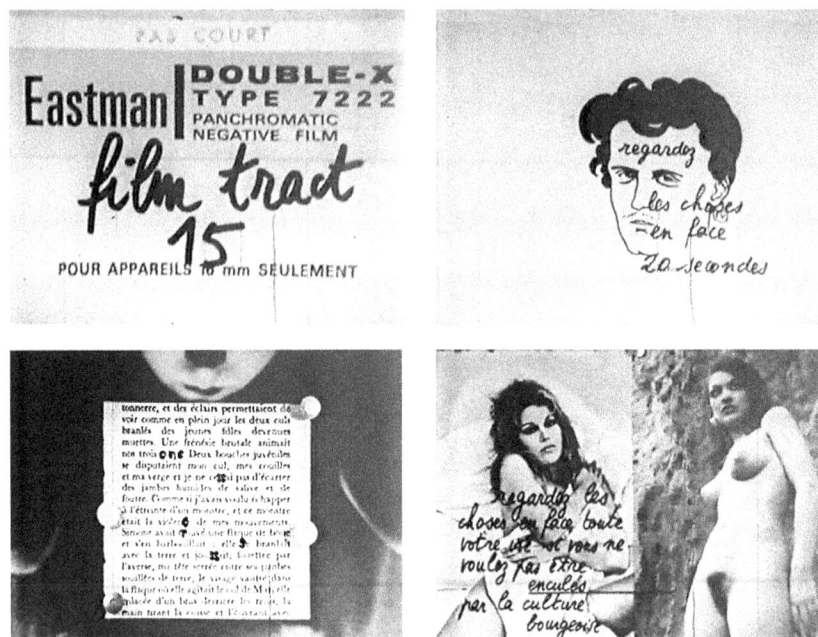

Figure 1.4 Selected frames from *Filmtract 015*, anonymous 16mm short film, Paris, 1968, calling on the viewer to "regardez les choses en face" (i.e., face the reality of bourgeois culture)

ers of détournement in language—part of a larger, well-theorized turn away from the revolutionary arena of praxis and toward philosophy after 1968.[80] Reportage on May's aftermath from the leftist newspaper *Combat* offers a phrase that can helpfully characterize this discursive turn. Gallant reports that *Combat* dubbed the month a "marvelous abstraction," tantalizing to so many activists in its utopian vagueness and promise.[81] The *cinétracts* that fundamentally question the politics of representation by embracing this vagueness as a theoretical and aesthetic platform may be thought of as "marvelous abstractions."

Filmtract 015, for example, asks the viewer repeatedly to *regardez les choses en face*, a plea that translates literally as "to look things in the face." (See Figure 1.4.) Penned across Félix Vallotton's imaginary portrait of Isidore Ducasse and on a travel advertisement depicting a snorkeler with an exotic fish, the phrase suggests that the act of "facing reality" is one of removing the mask of everyday appearances and critiquing images from their inside. Later in the film, the demand to look things in the face for five, ten, fifteen seconds or longer per détourned image seems to promise the discovery of systemic conspiracy. In two consecutive zooms, the viewer draws closer to the page of a book, as if approaching it with a magnifying glass. Lettered in bold print, the acronyms for the CRS and the Nazi SS are revealed to exist together within a page of pornographic text, linking state violence and sexual exploitation.

Earlier *filmtracts* had suggested the same link, and indeed accusations that riot police were systematically sexually assaulting young female protesters were widespread among protesters during May. The film ends by generalizing this menacing relationship, using soft pornographic pin-ups of two naked women and likening them to us, the audience, in our vulnerability to the penetration of bourgeois culture. As revolutionary as the ideas in this film might be, as much of a détournement of pin-up imagery as the last sequence might constitute, women are still posited as the mere ground for ideological figuration. The rhetoric of *Filmtract 015* is in this sense symptomatic of the dismaying gender myopia that pervaded global leftist struggle in the 1960s; clearly, more needed to be looked at straight on than this *filmtract*-er realized.[82]

All of the *cinétracts* of "marvelous abstraction" echo the thinking in Situationist Raoul Vaneigem's 1967 book, *Traité de savoir-vivre à l'usage des jeunes générations* (*The Revolution of Everyday Life*), that consumer society neutralizes critical sociopolitical inquiry and turns it into a superficial tête-à-tête with commodities.[83] Yet in the filmmaker's attempt to reveal this phenomenon, condemn it, and urge more makers and watchers of film to act against it, these *cinétracts* also resonate with the concept of facialization in the philosophy of Emmanuel Levinas and, more recently, Judith Butler. As a professor at the University of Nanterre in 1968, Levinas was certainly immersed in Paris's student unrest but interpreted it as a larger affirmation of ethical responsibility to the Other, separate from its specific sociopolitical context.[84] According to him, looking things in the face meant coming to terms with how "others make moral claims upon us, address moral demands to us, ones that we do not ask for, ones that we are not free to refuse."[85]

Unlike the *cinétracts* of "collective hallucination" and "total consciousness" that preceded them, the *cinétracts* of marvelous abstraction affirm the importance of ethical human connection that Levinas and Butler describe, and do so without recourse to the filmic process of identification. In other words, they try to build solidarity against repressive government, geopolitical injustice, consumer culture, and visual disinformation without actually depicting the faces and bodies of fellow activists in the militant film strategy that Jane Gaines calls "political mimicry."[86] Butler confirms that a face need not necessarily be shown for an image to convey the importance of intersubjectivity. Self-reflexive representation that calls its own representative powers into question can indirectly affirm the human "in that very disjunction that makes representation impossible. . . . The face is not 'effaced' in this failure of representation, but is constituted in that very possibility."[87] If films that eschew naturalistic depictions of faces and bodies still have the potential to create meaningfully subversive social imaginaries, it is clear that those that do not depict real spaces might nevertheless meaningfully imagine the alternative production of social space.

In the case of the *cinétracts*, however, their aesthetic evolution was marked by an increasing neglect of social space—the city and its inhabitants—in imagery as well as in conceptual matter. Perhaps this merely reflects the fact that the collective production of these films coincided with the gradual end of the occupations movement in Paris and its suburbs, and the return to a conventional capitalist use of the city. Yet it is crucial to note that attempts to disrupt the visual field, as in the three filmic approaches I have detailed above, may best communicate the subversive ideologies to which they adhere when they leave room within that disruption for a viable collective, contestational social space, whether that social space is or is not naturalistically pictured. The demand to *regardez les choses en face* implies a deeper, more exigent demand to *regardez les choses en l'espace*. If no individual *cinétract* manages to express both of those concepts in equal proportion, they succeed in doing so as a collective series, unitary and united.

Conclusion: Cinematic Détournement of Face and Place

From production to diffusion, from 1968 until today, the *cinétracts* were and remain an aleatory cinema of hallucination, consciousness, and abstraction. Until the 1990s, when they were compiled and leased integrally, SLON chose to distribute the *cinétracts* by splicing one or several to the beginning or end of longer political films for lease, like protest banners at the head or tail of a demonstration.[88] In this manner, the *cinétracts* enjoyed wide circulation among church groups, arts organizations, film festivals, worker's syndicates, and militant groups nationally and internationally, into the 1970s and thereafter.[89] Through their unique hybrid of objective testimony, subjective emotion, aesthetic poetry, and rhetorical vehemence, the *cinétracts* engendered Viénet's suggestion that "newsreels, previews," and "filmed advertisements" could be antimodels for a combative film form instead of simply dosing out current events and consumerism before a feature film projection.[90] As Thierry Nouel, a participant in the collective, declares, the *cinétracts* represented an entirely new cinematic genre, one "completely born from the political movement and from the reflection on images of '68."[91]

The *cinétracts* were not subversively perfect, nor could any experimental media ever hope to be.[92] They never became a full-fledged democratic media produced by amateurs as well as professionals of all social backgrounds. But through their emphasis on human engagement in a project that sought to unite artistic production and political life, the *cinétracts* were a true barometer of social activism. As the intensity of activism waned in the months after May, so did the collective's visual output. The aesthetic shifts from testimonial photomontage to dialectical image/text juxtaposition to the critique of image through text symbolizes the issues all protest movements face as they attempt to negotiate their valuation of embodied spatial resistance, of ideological history and theory, and of the subversion of conventional modes of representation.

Since 1968, of course, the media available to activists who want to convey the experiences of collective hallucination, total consciousness, and marvelous abstraction at the heart of a protest movement have become far more malleable and accessible. However, digital moving images that attempt the brief but sustained and coherent narrative arc that each *cinétract* did are notably absent.[93] The networked nature of twenty-first-century social media means that the majority of those making subversive images are doing so without the cinematic expectation of a gathered audience and a single, undivided screen as workbench. Many activists who upload and share a contestational photograph or video do so with the understanding that their contribution will be understood not as a tract or treatise—a discrete statement to be compared and contrasted in a serial or dialectical manner—but rather as a musical note in a complex symphony of other images and sounds accessible through web feeds, live streaming, instant messages, and comment sections.

Despite this conceptual death of centralized public address and reception in protest culture, détournement is alive and well aesthetically and spatially, as revolutionary praxis in both real and virtual territory.[94] Like all media that engages with the Situationist International's theories on détournement in moving images, the *cinétracts* remain a model of a communicative mode wherein gestures, words, and images can be vectors for social change. They remind us of the many advantages remaining in narrative formats of activist media—advantages such as the articulation of individual or collective radicalization, the furtherance of self-education in radical thought, and the synthesis of many facets of protest: poetic, pragmatic, and strategic. They demonstrate the value of ground *and* figure, documentation *and* self-reflexivity, consonant *and* collective modes of creation in Paris 1968, and beyond.

NOTES

1. Mavis Gallant, "The Events in May: A Paris Notebook I and II," in *Paris Notebooks: Essays and Reviews* (London: Bloomsbury, 1988), 55.

2. Daniel Singer, *Prelude to Revolution: France in May 1968* (Cambridge: South End Press, 2002), 147–148.

3. A contrasting Parisian diaristic account from a conservative point of view in stark contrast to Gallant's is Nancy Mitford, "France, May 1968: A Revolution Diary Parts I and II," in *A Talent to Annoy: Essays, Articles and Reviews 1929–1968*, ed. Charlotte Mosley (New York: Beaufort Books, 1986). Canonical English language histories include Daniel Singer, *Prelude to Revolution: France in May 1968* (Cambridge: South End Press, 2002); *Andrew Feenberg and Jim Freedman, When Poetry Ruled the Streets: The French May Events of 1968* (Albany: State University of New York Press, 2001); and Michael Seidman, *The Imaginary Revolution: Parisian Students and Workers in 1968* (New York: Berghahn Books, 2004). Noteworthy among numerous French language histories are Philippe Labro, ed. *Edition Speciale: Mai/Juin 68 "Ce n'est qu'un debut"* (Paris: Editions et publications premières, 1968); Edgar Morin, Cornelius Castoriadis, and Claude Lefort, *Mai 68 La Brèche: Suivi de Vingt ans après* (Paris: Fayard, 1988); Jean-Pierre Le Goff, *Mai 68, l'héritage impossible* (Paris: Editions La Découverte, 2006); Nicholas Daum, *Mai 68: Raconté par des anonymes* (Paris: Éditions Amsterdam, 2008); Xavier Vigna and Jean Vigreux, *Mai-juin 1968: Huit semaines qui ébranlèrent la France* (Dijon: Editions Universitaires de Dijon, 2010).

4. Mavis Gallant, "The Events in May: A Paris Notebook I," 18.

5. Ibid., 24.

6. Transmission was once again permitted on May 31, in time for de Gaulle's radio address in which he announced his refusal to step down from office. André-Jean Tudesq, "La radio, les manifestations, le pouvoir," in *Mai 68 à l'ORTF*, ed. Comité D'Histoire de la Télévision (Paris: La Documentation Française, 1987), 146.

7. Evelyne Sullerot in *Edition Speciale: Mai/Juin 68 "Ce n'est qu'un debut,"* ed. Philippe Labro (Paris: Editions et publications premières, 1968), 126.

8. See, for example, Philip Auslander, *Liveness: Performance in a Mediatized Culture* (New York: Routledge, 1999) and William Kaizen, "Live on Tape: Video, Liveness and the Immediate," *Art and the Moving Image: A Critical Reader*, ed. Tanya Leighton (London: Tate Publishing, 2008), 258–272.

9. While an analysis of this transhistorical comparison is beyond the purview of this essay, important texts that consider the centrality of social media to recent social uprisings include Manuel Castells, *Networks of Outrage and Hope: Social Movements in the Internet Age* (Malden: Polity Press, 2012); Emily Parker, *Now I Know Who My Comrades Are: Voices from the Internet Underground* (New York: Farrar, Straus and Giroux, 2014); Philip N. Howard and Muzammil M. Hussain, *Democracy's Fourth Wave? Digital Media and the Arab Spring* (New York: Oxford University Press, 2013); and Larry Dia-

mond and Marc F. Plattner, eds. *Liberation Technology: Social Media and the Struggle for Democracy* (Baltimore: Johns Hopkins University Press, 2012).

10. Sullerot in *Edition Speciale*, 126. All translations mine unless otherwise noted.

11. Boris Gobille, *Mai 68* (Paris: Editions de la Découverte, 2008), 90.

12. Cécile Meadel, "L'Information à France-Inter," *Mai 68 à l'ORTF*, Comité D'Histoire de la Télévision (Paris: La Documentation Française, 1987), 92.

13. Jean-François Dars, interview by Jennifer Stob, April 9, 2008, Paris, France; Layerle, *Caméras en lutte en mai 68*, 143; "Inventaire Ciné-mai 1968," *Cinéma 68*, no. 129 (October 1968): 27.

14. Jean-Paul Fargier and Bernard Sizaine, "Deux heures avec JLG pro. re.," interview with Jean-Luc Godard, *Tribune Socialiste* no. 23, January 1969. Republished in Jean-Luc Godard, *Jean-Luc Godard par Jean Luc Godard, tome I: 1950–1984*, ed. Alain Bergala (Paris: Cahiers du Cinéma, 1998), 332. For more on the Dziga Vertov Group, see Steve Cannon, "'When You're Not a Worker Yourself...': Godard, the Dziga Vertov Group and the Audience," *100 Years of European Cinema: Entertainment or Ideology?* ed. Diana Holmes and Alison Smith (New York: Oxford University Press, 2001), 100–119; Julia Lesage, "Godard and Gorin's Left Politics, 1967–1972," *Jump Cut*, no. 28 (April 1983): 51–58. Accessed at http://www.ejumpcut.org/archive/onlinessays/JC28folder/GodardGorinPolitics.html.

15. Gallant, "The Events in May," 55.

16. Sullerot in *Edition Speciale*, 126.

17. Gallant, "The Events in May," 83.

18. Daniel Singer, *Prelude to Revolution: France in May 1968* (Cambridge: South End Press, 2002), 9–10.

19. Ibid.

20. Guy Debord, "Rapport sur la construction des situations et sur les conditions de l'organisation et de l'action de la tendance situationniste internationale" (Paris: Internationale Situationniste, 1957). Anthologized in Guy Debord, *Œuvres*, ed. Jean-Louis Rançon, in collaboration with Alice Debord (Paris, Gallimard, 2006), 316.

21. On this subject, see René Viénet, *Enragés et Situationnistes dans le mouvement des occupations* (Paris, 1968); Jean-Pierre Duteuil, "Les groupes politiques d'extrême-gauche à Nanterre," *Mai 68: Les mouvements étudiants en France et dans le monde* (Nanterre, 1988), 110; Pascal Dumontier, *Les Situationnistes et mai 68: Théorie et pratique de la révolution 1966–1972* (Paris, 1990), 74–75; Angelo Quattrocchi and Tom Nairn, *The Beginning of the End* (New York: Verso, 1998), 4, 92.

22. Michael Seidman, *The Imaginary Revolution: Parisian Students and Workers in 1968* (New York: Berghahn Books, 2004), 27–32.

23. See "Encore un effort si vous voulez être situationnistes" *Potlatch* [June 29, 1957], reprinted in Guy Debord, *Œuvres*, 349.

24. See "Définitions," in *Internationale Situationniste. Internationale Situationniste, édition augmentée* (June 1958): 13.

25. Alain Buhler, "Pour pouvoir dialoguer avec vos enfants: Le Petit 'Dico' de la Révolution Estudiantine." *France-Soir*, May 19, 1968.

26. It is important to note that the "occupations movement" entailed not just the occupation of university buildings but also cultural institutions, factories, streets,

media headquarters, and other contested spaces, both public and private. The roneo machine was similar to the mimeograph in its production of copied text. Examples of May slogans and witticisms are abundant in Julien Besançon, ed. *Les murs ont la parole: journal mural, mai 68* (Paris: Tchou, 1968); Bruno Barbey et al. *Mai 68: l'imagination au pouvoir: trente-huit photographies de Bruno Barbey, deux-cent-soixante-dix-huit affiches* (Paris: la Différence, 1998); and Michel Wlassikoff, *Mai 68: l'affiche en héritage* (Paris: Alternatives, 2008).

27. Raoul Vaneigem, "Commentaires Contre L'Urbanisme,", *Internationale Situationniste*, no. 6, (August 1961), 35. Anthologized in *Internationale Situationniste, édition augmentée*, 233.

28. The article's title is itself a détournement of the title of an earlier Situationist text that was written by Debord in 1963 for the Situationist International exhibition, *Destruction of the RSG-6*, in the Exi Gallery in Denmark. Published simultaneously in Danish, English, and French, it was entitled, "The Situationists and the New Forms of Action in Art and Politics." Situationist chronology, http://www.cddc.vt.edu/sionline/chronology/1963.html.

29. René Viénet, "Les Situationnistes et les nouvelles forms d'action contre la politique et l'art," *Internationale Situationniste*, no. 11 (October 1967), 34–36. Anthologized in *Internationale Situationniste, édition augmentée*, 528–529.

30. See Guy Debord, *Complete Cinematic Works: Scripts, Stills, Documents*. Edited and translated by Ken Knabb. (Oakland, CA: AK Press, 2003).

31. Ibid., 35; 22.

32. Viénet, "Les Situationnistes et les nouvelles," 530. Translation accessed at http://www.cddc.vt.edu/sionline/si/against.html.

33. Ibid.

34. Ibid; as Thomas Y. Levin notes, Viénet mistakenly alludes to Eisenstein's project of filming Marx's *The Critique of Political Economy* or *The German Ideology* but was most likely thinking of Eisenstein's well-documented desire to film *Capital*. Thomas Y. Levin, "Dismantling the Spectacle: The Cinema of Guy Debord," *Guy Debord and the Situationist International: Texts and Documents*, ed. Tom McDonough (Cambridge: MIT Press, 2002), n. 93, 444.

35. Sergei Eisenstein, "Notes for a Film of *Capital*," in *October: The First Decade, 1976–1986*, trans. Maciej Sliwowski, Jay Leyda, and Annette Michelson, and ed. Annette Michelson, Rosalind Krauss, Douglas Crimp, and Joan Copjec (Cambridge: MIT Press, 1987), 128.

36. Ibid., 122.

37. Ibid., 130.

38. Jay Leyda, "Esther Shub and the Art of Compilation," in *Imagining Reality: The Faber Book of Documentary*, ed. Mark Cousins and Kevin MacDonald (London: Faber and Faber, 1996), 56.

39. For more on French postwar *court métrage* history, see Dominique Bluher and Philippe Pilard, eds. *Le court métrage documentaire français de 1945 à 1968: Créations et créateurs* (Rennes: Presses Universitaires de Rennes, 2009).

40. Sebastien Layerle, *Caméras en lutte en mai 68: "Par ailleurs le cinema est une arme . . ."* (Paris: Nouveau Monde, 2008), 106. Layerle's text is an excellent compilation of the various groups active in the militant cinema sphere before, during, and after this period.

41. Layerle, *Caméras en lutte en mai 68*, 119; Jean Rouch, "À propos des films ethnographiques," *Positif*, no. 14–15 (November 1955): 145–149.

42. A collective formed from Chris Marker's contact with the workers of the Rhodiacéta textile factory as well as other cinema and worker's syndicate professionals associated with the Popular Cultural Center of Palente-les-Orchamps (CCPPOO). For more on the Groupe Medvedkine, see Trevor Stark, "'Cinema in the Hands of the People': Chris Marker, the Medvedkin Group, and the Potential of Militant Film" *October*, 139 (Winter 2012): 117–150.

43. Groupe Medvedkine, "Texte Manifeste du Groupe Medvedkine de Besançon," unpublished document, three copies circulated, 1968. In Layerle, *Caméras en lutte en mai 68,* 285; Viénet, "Les Situationnistes et les nouvelles," 530.

44. See Chris Marker's *Le Train en marche* (1971). Similar ambitions for militant cinema are also expressed in the writings of Cesare Zavattini throughout the 1960s; see Giorgio Bertellini and Courtney Ritter, "Zavattini, Above and Beyond Neorealism," *Cinema Journal* 54, no. 3 (2015): 1–5; Cesare Zavattini, "Proposals for a Television Open to Reality and Democracy," trans. Giorgio Bertellini and Courtney Ritter, *Cinema Journal* 54, no. 3 (2015): 7–9; and Cesare Zavattini, "Free Newsreels," trans. Giorgio Bertellini and Courtney Ritter, *Cinema Journal* 54, no. 3 (2015): 9–11.

45. "Etats Généraux du Cinéma: Historique," *Cahiers du Cinéma*, no. 203 (August 1968): 25.

46. Ibid.

47. No evidence exists that members of the Situationist International knew of the *cinétracts*. Instead of making films themselves during May 1968, a number of Situationists militated with student protesters as part of the Occupation Committee of the People's Free Sorbonne University and then, after mid-May, as part of the Council for the Maintenance of Occupations. Fearing government reprisals after the June 12 laws banning numerous radical leftist organizations, Debord and several other Situationists left Paris in June, taking refuge against government reprisal first in Brussels, then in the Vosges. See Jean-Louis Rançon, "Chronologie 1957–1972," in Guy Debord, *Oeuvres*, 306. Godard makes his familiarity with the Situationists (in particular, their comics) clear in a 1969 interview. Godard, *Jean-Luc Godard*, 334.

48. See, for example, "Le rôle de Godard," in *Internationale Situationniste, édition augmentée,* 470–471 and "Sunset Boulevard," ibid., 282–286.

49. Viénet, "Les Situationnistes et les nouvelles," 531.

50. Guy Debord, "La Véritable Scission dans l'Internationale" [1972] reprinted in *Œuvres*, 1092, 1105. Translation accessed at http://www.cddc.vt.edu/sionline/si/sistime.html.

51. Godard, *Jean-Luc Godard*, 332. Yvette Romi gives a different account of how the project developed, writing that Jean-Luc Godard approached the March 22 movement and offered them his assistance. In collaboration with them, he made about thirty *cinétracts*—he behind the camera and they gathering the visual material for the montage. Yvette Romi, "Godard contre la culture," *Le Nouvel Observateur*, July 15–21, 1968, 36.

52. Hélène Raymond, "La scansion du montage dans les Cinétracts de 1968," in *Une Histoire du Spectacle Militant: Théâtre et cinema militants 1966–1981,* ed. Christian Biet and Oliver Neveux (Vic la Gardiole: l'Entretemps editions, 2007), 274.

53. According to Sebastien Layerle, direct formal inspiration for the *cinétract* format may have been the very first film containing images of May's street battles to be distributed and projected, made collectively by students of the SNE-Sup (the National Union of Higher Education) under the direction of Guy Chalon. Ten minutes long, composed of photographs snapped by Elie Kagan, intertitles, and an accompanying soundtrack, it was entitled *C.C.P.*, a winking reference to the French acronym for compte chèque postale. "By freezing the brutality of the gestures and underscoring them with a counterpoint of well-chosen sounds, the fixity of the documents adds to their disquieting character," wrote Louis Séguin, reviewing *C.C.P.* in *Positif's* summer '68 issue. Undoubtedly, the use of appropriated material in militant film by Cuban documentary filmmaker Santiago Álvarez also informed the style of the *cinétracts*; Marker was intimately familiar with Cuban film culture and had himself made a film on the country in cooperation with the Cuban Institute of Cinematographic Art and Industry (*Cuba Si*, 1961).

54. Inger Servolin on behalf of ISKRA, interview by Jennifer Stob, June 19, 2008, Paris, France.

55. CINETRACTEZ! flyer, collection of ISKRA, undated.

56. Lists with the names of *cinétract* filmmakers can be found in the following publications: Nicole Brenez and Joëlle Lê, "Quelques Titres des Ciné-tracts," in *Jeune, dur et pur! Une histoire de cinema d'avant-garde et expérimental en France*, ed. Nicole Brenez and Christian Lebrat (Cinémathèque Française: Paris, 2001), 333; Layerle, *Caméras en lutte en mai* 68, 144: Raymond, "La scansion du montage," 276; Christian Lebrat, "Il faut créer un Vietnam dans chaque musée du monde," interview with Gérard Fromanger, in *Cinéma Radical*, ed. Christian Lebrat (Paris: Editions Paris Experimental, 2008), 142: Layerle, *Caméras en lutte en mai* 68, 146.

57. Jean-François Dars, interview by Jennifer Stob, April 9, 2008, Paris, France.

58. Ibid.

59. The *filmtracts* of Jean-Luc Godard inspired a group of five people in Rouen, France (three film students, including Thierry Nouel and Alain Laguarda and two journalists) to make their own *filmtracts*, which were later screened with postfilm debates at high schools in Rouen and in a community center for disadvantaged youths in the town's suburbs. Thierry Nouel, interview by Jennifer Stob, February 19, 2008, Paris, France.

60. The Cinétract Collective were hardly the only group during and directly after Paris's May 1968 to assemble an impromptu archive of photographs; other examples include the photo contest of CRS police organized by the Committee for the Defense of the Revolution in late May (gold, silver, and bronze paving stones for first, second, and third place, respectively) and the exposition of 270 photographs taken by professionals and amateurs alike at a youth center in the rue Mouffetard in June. Comité de défense de la révolution "Safari-Photos" flyer, collection of the Bibliothèque Nationale de France, undated; André Fermingier, "Expositions: C'est déjà une légende," *Le Nouvel Observateur* July 3–9, 1968, 41.

61. Ironically, this once generous gesture has now made the films a victim of French copyright law: ISKRA cannot digitize and sell copies of them because of the daunting

task of divvying up royalties. A few examples of publications that ran some of the same photographs used to make *cinétracts* include: *L'Express*, May 13–19, 1968; *France Soir* May 22 and 25, 1968; and *Le Nouvel Observateur*, May 8–14, 1968, and June 7, 1968.

62. The realignment of art's address from contemplative vertical plane to horizontal work surface in this postwar period is also discussed in Leo Steinberg's seminal essay, "The Flatbed Picture Plane," *Other Criteria* (Chicago: University of Chicago Press, 1972) 61–98. Tom Holert suggests the term's relevance to militant cinema in "Harun Farocki, Tabular images: on *The Division of All Days (1970)* and *Something Self Explanatory (15x)* (1971)," in *Harun Farocki, Against What? Against Whom?* ed. Antje Ehmann and Kodwo Eshun (London: Koenig Books, 2009), 75–92.

63. See Dziga Vertov, "WE: Variant of a Manifesto," in *Kino-Eye: The Writings of Dziga Vertov*, ed. and intro. Annette Michelson, and trans. Kevin O'Brien (Berkeley: University of California Press, 1984), 5–9.

64. Layerle, *Caméras en lutte en mai 68*, 251.

65. Henri Lefebvre, *The Production of Space*, trans. Donald Nicholson-Smith (Cambridge: Blackwell, 1991), 33.

66. Ibid., 60.

67. See Kristin Ross, "Lefebvre on the Situationists: An Interview," *October* 79 (Winter 1997): 69–83.

68. The *cinétracts* in this grouping are numbered 001, 003–005, 011 and 017.

69. "Matraque" is the French word for the nightstick or billy club carried by the CRS. For a compelling history of the French police matraque from its colonialist origins to its omnipresence and figurative importance in '68 and after, see Kristin Ross, "The Police Conception of History," *May '68 and Its Afterlives* (Chicago: University of Chicago Press, 2002), 19–64.

70. Angelo Quattrocchi and Tom Nairn, *The Beginning of the End* (New York: Verso, 1998), 65.

71. Roland Barthes, "Rhetoric of the Image" (1964). *The Responsibility of Forms: Critical Essays on Music, Art and Representation*, trans. Richard Howard (Oxford: Farrar Straus and Giroux, 1985), 45.

72. Michael M. Seidman, *The Imaginary Revolution: Parisian Students and Workers in 1968.* (New York: Berghahn Books, 2004), 239. The circumstances of Tautin's death are unclear, with some eyewitness accounts claiming that police pushed Tautin to his death in the waters of the Seine.

73. David Harvey, *Rebel Cities: From the Right to the City to the Urban Revolution* (New York: Verso, 2012), 73.

74. The *cinétracts* in this grouping are numbered 002, 018, 021, 026–030 and R-106.

75. This represents the logical conclusion of France's state project to simultaneously de-colonize, neo-colonize and self-colonize as a consumer society in the two decades following World War II, analyzed in Kristin Ross, *Fast Cars, Clean Bodies: Decolonization and the Reordering of French Culture* (Cambridge: MIT Press, 1995).

76. *Internationale Situationniste, édition augmentée*, 531. Translation at http://www.cddc.vt.edu/sionline/si/against.html. See also *Internationale Situationniste, édition augmentée*, 35.

77. The *cinétracts* in this grouping are *filmtracts* 007–016, 023, 040 and R-107.

78. Raymond, "La scansion du montage," 277.

79. See Henri Lefebvre, *Le Droit à la ville* (Paris, Editions du Seuil, 1968).

80. See, for example, the history of this uncoupling of critical theory and praxis as recounted in Frankfurt School Marxism by Martin Jay, *The Dialectical Imagination: A History of the Frankfurt School and the Institute of Social Research, 1923–1950* (Boston: Little, Brown, 1973).

81. Quoted in Gallant, "The Events in May," 83.

82. The dearth of women *cinétract*-ers is all too representative of France's film and photographic culture in the 1960s. A concise overview of French feminism in and after May 1968 can be found in Claire Duchen, "May '68," *Women's Rights and Women's Lives in France, 1944–1968* (New York: Routledge, 1944), 190–211.

83. "The good sense of consumer society has carried the old expression 'to look things in the face' to its logical conclusion: to merely stand face to face with things." Raoul Vaneigem, *Traité de savoir-vivre à l'usage des jeunes générations* (Paris: Gallimard, 1974), 28.

84. Emmanuel Levinas, *Collected Philosophical Papers*, trans. Alphonso Lingis (The Hague: Martinus Nijhoff, 1987), 150.

85. Judith Butler, *Precarious Life: The Powers of Mourning and Violence* (New York: Verso, 2004), 131.

86. Jane Gaines, "Political Mimesis." *Collecting Visible Evidence*, ed. Jane M. Gaines and Michael Renov (Minneapolis: University of Minnesota Press, 1999), 84–102.

87. Ibid., 144.

88. Inger Servolin on behalf of ISKRA, interview by Jennifer Stob, June 19, 2008, Paris, France.

89. Ibid.; Gary Elshaw, "Cinétracts," chapter in "The Depiction of late 1960's Counter Culture in the 1968 films of Jean-Luc Godard" (master's thesis, Victoria University, Wellington NZ, 2000), http://www.garyelshaw.com/jlg/index.html. In a report issued in 1982, ISKRA (the nonprofit distribution collective into which SLON transformed after 1971) calculated that with one hundred fifty films in distribution and twenty films expedited per week for screenings of roughly one hundred people, more than one hundred thousand people were exposed to titles from their catalogue every year, among them the *cinétracts*. Claude Veuille et Claire Kirby, "Iskra Gazette," CinémAction, suppl., nos. 1–20 (August 1982): 6.

90. René Viénet, "Les situationnistes et les nouvelles formes d'action contre la politique et l'art," *Internationale Situationniste* no. 11 (October 1967), 34. Translation: http://www.cddc.vt.edu/sionline/si/against.html

91. Thierry Nouel, interview by Jennifer Stob, February 19, 2008, Paris, France.

92. Some of their failures of mission as well as depiction are recounted in Sonia Bruneau, "Le symbole de l'alliance étudiants-ouvriers: une représentation de l'Autre dans les films de Mai 68," in *L'Autre en images: idées reçues et stéréotypes*, ed. Elodie Dulac and Delphine Robic-Diaz (Paris: L'Harmattan, 2005), 155–171.

93. The revolutions of the Arab Spring, the consciousness-raising of North America's Occupy movement in 2011 and the Black Lives Matter movement begun in 2013 can all serve as examples here.

94. Given this dual occupation of social space, W.J.T. Mitchell argues that the representative images of contemporary global protest culture are spaces: "not figures, but the negative space or ground against which a figure appears . . . The scores of plazas, squares and open urban spaces." W.J.T. Mitchell, "Image, Space, Revolution: The Arts of Occupation," in *Occupy: Three Inquiries in Disobedience*, ed. W.J.T. Mitchell, Bernard Harcourt, and Michael Taussig, (Chicago: University of Chicago Press, 2013) 101, 109.

2

Milan, the Cine City of 1968: Metamorphosis and Identity

GAETANA MARRONE

Cinematic Paradigms: An Introduction

In the documentary film *1960* (2010), director Gabriele Salvatores tells the story of a young boy's relationship to his older brother Rosario who left his village in southern Italy in order to find work and adventure in the industrial North. *1960* maps a portrait of Italy at the height of the "economic miracle" (1958–1963), a period in which the class composition of Italian society underwent radical changes. Salvatores had access to the rich national television archives of Rai Cinema, which produced the film, and he intercuts the personal storyline (told in voice-over) with newsreel footage of the historical events that defined an extraordinary year that saw the Olympic Games in Rome, the release of Fellini's *La dolce vita*, and the election of John F. Kennedy as U.S. president.

In Salvatores's film, the story of a family searching for a son who has emigrated to the North defines the changing cultural contexts and shifting power relations of the economic miracle—also known as the "boom"—at a time when the Italian family, which had always played a vital role in forging the country's political and civic development, became an issue of ideological contention. Historically, the family has played a prominent role in Italian political campaigns, often used as a means of expressing the competing parties' cultural agendas and value systems.[1]

Given that Italian cinematic tradition had always favored Rome as the cine city *par excellence*, the ideal backdrop when recounting the postwar tales of the *poveri ma belli* (poor but beautiful), in the 1960s the world of the factory worker remained an unknown territory to be discovered. At the same time, as the capital of the economic miracle, Milan consolidated its role as *the* industrial and financial city in Italy, besides retaining its leadership as the center of publishing and advertising. The home of Alfa Romeo, Innocenti, and Pirelli, which founded its famous Calendar in 1963, Milan came to represent Italy's revolutionary creativity, as it witnessed the rise of architects of fashion such as Armani, Ferré, Versace, Krizia, and Prada. No city symbolized better the wealth and power of Italian neocapitalism.[2] Then in the late 1970s, another center of immense power emerged in Milan when a private entrepreneur, Silvio Berlusconi, created a vast media empire with television, dubbing, and mixing studios that gave work to a good number of people. His Mediaset Group would eventually become the largest commercial broadcaster in the country, making Milan an alternative center to Rome for film production and changing forever the way cinematic works were approached by producers. Films were no longer intended for theatrical release but would be directed to the small screen. As Gian Piero Brunetta points out, at this time we came to speak of made-for-TV products, with a gradual dilution of creativity and standards of quality.[3]

The Milan of the economic miracle inspired films that provided a window onto the profound historical contradictions of these prosperous times. If the Italian cinema of the 1950s was a reflection of the mystifying optimism of the middle class, a departure from the neorealist years when filmmakers dramatized social conditions in a national populist vein, the 1960s offered a fertile ground for young directors who made a commitment to works of opposition and intervention. But the crisis of spring 1968, when students and workers occupied the streets of Milan, signaled that the "boom" had come to an end. Widespread instability and uncertainty ensued. The bomb that exploded at the Banca Nazionale dell'Agricoltura in Piazza Fontana on December 12, 1969, killed sixteen people and wounded eighty-eight. The hasty police account of responsibility led to a massive public scandal—two anarchists, Giuseppe Pinelli and Pietro Valpreda, were wrongly accused, the former dying in mysterious circumstances in police custody a few days after the bombing, the latter unjustly imprisoned for years.[4] This radicalized the younger generation, leading to the *anni di piombo* (years of lead), when the protests of revolutionary groups turned violent throughout the 1970s. Milan-based journalist Giorgio Bocca has described the reaction to this heady atmosphere: "Youth culture which has all the natural gifts that come with being twenty, such as being happy to be alive and being optimistic, but which has fabricated enemies and sufferings, baffles the provincial man who has experienced the poverty of Italy. He has the impression that the world is turning upside down."[5] After Piazza Fontana many Italians felt that they had been betrayed by their State. Bocca was among those who signed a document published by *L'Espresso* against police commissioner Luigi Calabresi following Pinelli's death. The far-left Lotta Continua would later execute Calabresi outside his apartment in Via Francesco Cherubini on May 17, 1972.[6] Capping what Mario Capanna calls the "formidable years," the student upheavals of 1968 were followed by a bloody armed struggle.[7] The "strategy of tension" pursued by the government to manipulate and control public opinion began in Milan's Piazza Fontana and its dire consequences would be assessed in Gianni Amelio's *Colpire al cuore* (*Blow to the Heart*, 1982), one of the first films to tackle the issue of terrorism.

In Salvatores's *1960*, when Rosario's family arrives in Milan with great expectations, they are met by "darkness." The city once imagined by Rosario as "a kind of wonderland" wears "the same suit that is worn by the dead on their last journey," its magic appeal forever lost.[8] So we ask: in 1968, were they all ideologically inebriated in the factories and universities? Were they all proclaiming the impossible? Something did not work out with the youth revolt, but the emerging social future was even harder to imagine. Were those who wanted to change the world reviving a defunct one?[9]

Mapping Film Itineraries in a Problematic Urban Space

Culturally, Milan remained the stronghold of the intellectual left and also came to signify crucial moments in the nation's history. Italian directors continued to show not only that cinema coexisted with an ethical commitment and social awareness but also how valuable it might be as an ideologically expressive medium. The political films produced in the early 1960s are notable for their renewal of traditional cinematic forms but also for retaining the cultural and social ideals that once inspired the richness of national cinema. Filmmakers felt the need to expand the ways of telling stories of the present.

The early 1960s were dominated by Luchino Visconti, Michelangelo Antonioni, Federico Fellini, and, among the new directors, Ermanno Olmi and Pier Paolo Pasolini. Except for Fellini, these artists chose Milan for some of their most compelling works. Eduardo De Filippo's *Napoletani a Milano* (*Neapolitans in Milan*, 1953) and Camillo Mastrocinque's *Totò, Peppino e la . . . malafemmina* (*Totò, Peppino and the . . . Bad Woman*, 1954) represent Neapolitan migrants as *homo oeconomicus* fighting for survival in Milan during the preboom years. In both films, within the city's industrialized universe, only laughter seems to offer a modicum of redemption. De Filippo's film ends with a high angle shot of a tram at the mouth of the Arengario underpass, interpreting the main character's dream of uniting his beloved Naples with Milan. But there are still overwhelming fractures separating one culture from another, North and South. The industrial growth and labor migrations of the late 1950s are captured in Visconti's *Rocco e i suoi fratelli* (*Rocco and His Brothers*, 1960), with its tragic account of an immigrant family from the South disintegrating after moving to Milan. One of the most memorable scenes in cinema history is the arrival of the Parondi family at the main train station, where the mist and the smoke increase their sense of displacement, and they are overwhelmed by the city's brightly lit store fronts as they look out of a moving tram during a nighttime journey. In reaching their final destination at the outskirts of the city, in Via Dalmazio Birago, they encounter a tenement block, a row of bleak public houses lacking the characteristic courtyard of the old Lombard architectural style.

Visconti had chosen to recount a social phenomenon that had yet to be studied in depth. It is worth noting that the film was made in 1958 and that Visconti spent a lot of time in Milan among people who had emigrated from the South. At this time, Milan's periphery began to dominate the city, as new neighborhoods sprang up to accommodate new immigrants. This periphery was made up of a mosaic of shapes; it was flat, gray, and foggy.[10] Visconti's longtime screenwriter Suso Cecchi d'Amico remembers that she "wanted to put the accent on how people from a city ruined and corrupted people who were more tribal, more pure."[11] In the film, the model for survival in a desperate age becomes Ciro, the brother who manages to remain honest, works hard at the Alfa Romeo auto plant, attends evening classes, and is engaged to a Milanese girl. By the end of the film, Visconti explains

> [Ciro] not only has demonstrated a non-romantic, steady ability to integrate and become part of a new lifestyle, but he has also acquired the understanding that many duties come with many rights. After all, the ending of *Rocco* turned out more symbolic than I even thought, I'd say emblematic of my convictions on the Southern question: the working brother tells the younger one what he envisions for the future of the country, which represents the ideal unitary model found in Antonio Gramsci's writings.[12]

The last scene is of Ciro joining his fellow workers as they go toward the factory, while the little brother, who is always dreaming of returning to the South, follows his own path toward a brightly lit open road. Ciro inspires a new immigrant approach in dealing with a different kind of reality. Despite the anguish and difficulties of being uprooted, he embodies improved prospects in life.

Antonioni's *La notte* (1961) shows a different plight at the other end of the social spectrum, that of an upper-class couple, a successful Milanese writer and his wife Lidia, at odds with their unstable feelings. Urban architecture provides an implicit comment on these characters' running away from rather than facing their problems. Their restlessness is externalized in the couple's hectic drive through the city's traffic in Corso Europa or in Corso di Porta Vittoria. In the Milan suburbs, Lidia is lured into watching some toughs engaged in a violent fight, but she also witnesses some young people launching toy rockets in a field. As Seymour Chatman has aptly noted, her very act of looking at Milan communicates not only her estrangement from her husband but also from the Milanese high bourgeoisie, tracked solely "by what is shown of the stark and unrelieved concrete buildings and streets of Milan and its *periferia*."[13]

After making a series of documentaries for the Milan company Edisonvolta, Ermanno Olmi came to national attention with *Il posto* (*The Sound of Trumpets* or *The Job*, 1961). In it, he examines with a dispassionate eye the impact of the city's rapid economic transformation in the world of labor. Olmi's proletarian characters, played by nonprofessional actors, suffer at having to adjust to an alien industrial and bureaucratic environment. The film focuses on a young man from Milan's hinterland whose mother sends him off to the city to apply for a job. Olmi is sensitive in portraying this simple boy's loss of identity as he is engulfed in a mechanical routine that anticipates his anonymous life to come as a white-collar worker. At the time, little was known by the Italian public of the frustrating conditions of this lower stratum of the urban working class. By 1968, Milan, a powerful economic center and a laboratory for change, had become a cinematic site that reflected the difficulties and expectations inherent in the macroeconomic changes of Italy's economic miracle. One of the most significant consequences of urbanization and rural exodus was the disconnection of migrants from their native environments and, ultimately, from themselves. Furthermore, the new consumer society preached new values that would generate subversive responses. Indeed, the boom produced a greater individualism in the Italian working and lower middle classes. Filmmakers such as Pier Paolo Pasolini would champion a revolutionary dream of change, while raising questions that challenged Italy's Left, both Old and New.

Industrial Desert and Class Crisis in Pasolini's *Teorema* (1968)

The economic miracle offered a unique opportunity for a progressive political class to address the imbalances in Italy's capitalist development. A group of industrialists emerged (in Milan, employers such as Pirelli) who were aware that their survival would rely on a program of workforce reforms. Radical changes took place in the employment sector until demand for labor began to exceed supply, while increased costs and other labor difficulties also proved to be a significant problem, even for those industrialists who cautiously supported a center-left coalition.[14] But if the Italian business class underwent considerable transformation, this was also a time of missed political opportunity. An unorthodox Marxist, Pasolini became increasingly concerned with the profound transformations affecting collective and individual life. In earlier films—*Accattone* (1961), *Mamma Roma* (1962), and *Uccellacci e uccellini* (1966)—he had depicted the poverty of the Roman periphery, but he turned to the Milan of spring 1968 in *Teorema* to warn of the damaging effects of the new worker who aspires to become a *padrone*.[15] Of all of his films, *Teorema* most clearly shows his imaginative courage in representing the turbulence of a neocapitalist society, where the world of the working class appears atypical and even ideologically damaged by capitalism. In this intensely personal film, Pasolini adopts a "primitive" style dominated by the rich figurative culture of the Lombard landscape. The camera canvasses the cityscape with its factories and villas, the rows of poplars, the square fields, the yellow reeds along the river Po, against which characters are captured as examples of estrangement. The pace is slow with many austere but beautifully composed static images.

The film's dramatis personae is made up of a variety of characters whose interaction points to the most problematic cultural and social processes of the era. These are dramatically introduced with an outrageous new model for guaranteeing social harmony: at the outset of the film, a wealthy industrialist donates his factory to his workers, a privileged figure usually dialectically opposed to workers introducing a redistribution of wealth that makes a mockery of revolutionary class struggle. The subsequent story, Pasolini explained in the eponymous novel (which he published in March 1968, before the film's premiere in September), "concerns a petty bourgeois family— petty bourgeois in the ideological, not the economic sense. In fact, the case of many rich people who live in Milan."[16] The wealthy industrialist and his family are visited by The Guest, an extraordinarily handsome young man (Terence Stamp) who spends a few days in their home. (See Figure 2.1.) His sexual magnetism has a profound effect on each member of the household, each of whom is inevitably seduced by him with devastating results. Self-awareness occurs at several levels. The maid, Emilia (Laura Betti), tries to gas herself but is saved; the teenage son and daughter, Pietro and Odetta, are transfixed by his presence; the mother, Lucia (Silvana Mangano), is sexually reawakened and realizes the barrenness of her social status; the father, Paolo

Figure 2.1 The Guest (Terence Stamp) and the mother, Lucia (Silvana Mangano), in the garden of the Milanese villa in *Teorema* (Pasolini, 1968)

(Massimo Girotti), confronts his homosexuality and loses all sense of his class role.

Midway through the film, as unexpectedly as he appeared, the mysterious visitor is summoned away, leaving behind five people alienated from the codes of behavior they once knew and observed. They are unable to cope with the intense yearnings that have been unleashed and each of them seeks an answer or escape. Emilia undergoes a kind of mad religious experience, returning to her roots in the countryside, to the sacred solitude of the peasant life, where she achieves a kind of sainthood, performing miracles for the local people. Then she travels back to the outskirts of Milan, to a construction site for public housing, in which she ends the film being buried alive, symbolically, at the bottom of a muddy pit. Her physical journey from the Milanese villa to her village and back to Milan's industrial periphery is the opposite of the one undertaken by the new proletarians, who aspire to the economic status of the bourgeoisie. For Pasolini, religion thus survives as an authentic belief only in the peasant world. Preindustrial civilizations have not disappeared, but they remain buried.

"This is not a realistic story, it is a parable," proclaimed Pasolini in the enunciative section of the novel.[17] Rather than being a story, it is a *referto* (report), providing purely indicative data about the identity of the characters. Each encounter between the young man and the members of the family takes on an emblematic, poetic quality. The contents of the characters' minds are not verbalized and do not rely on the tradition of the "language of narrative film prose."[18] They must be inferred from stares, looks, and glances. From a philosophical point of view, these gestures and gazes are the result of certain ideological necessities; from the formal point of view, the principle of repetition conceptualizes the ahistoric past of mankind. Northrop Frye noted that in a tragic story repetition leads logically to catastrophe.[19] For example, recurring images of a desert landscape, which Pasolini called "the landscape of what is contrary to life," evoke the unconscious memory of our existence, worn away by time.[20] Volcanic clouds cast deep shadows over the desert (actually Mount Etna), the dry sands blown by the wind conveying a sense of the beginning of creation that confirms the poetic character of the film, as Alberto Moravia pointed out in his review.[21] This is an abyss into which Pasolini casts all hope, that attests to the negation of historical redemption for the capitalist class. In fact, film critic Serafino Murri sees *Teorema* as the beginning of Pasolini's progressive, intellectual isolation, an artist who would soon be publicly attacked by the militant Left as well as by the conservative Catholic press, as a sort of "monster of dissent."[22] But, one might add, he would also become the crusader of the political, ideological, and moral dissent of an entire nation.

Pasolini's method of repetitive frames disrupts the iconography of a contemporary "normal" life. In particular, each character's frozen stare is an image (not supported by any natural sound) that anticipates a kind of strategic withdrawal from action. It reveals how Pasolini moves beyond statement into the very heart of events. *Teorema* impresses by its skillful handling of the visual image as it does by its narrative paucity. In interior scenes, the lens is situated frontally, an approach supported with flat shadowless lighting that creates a certain distance from the characters. The effect is as if the viewer is looking at a two-dimensional icon with a lack of perspective. But at the same time, many of the shots have a kind of phallic violence. The contorted gestures, the bodies in *silhouette*, are reminiscent of the artist Francis Bacon (whose work is cited in the film); they convey the impression of looking into a distorted mirror. Close-ups frame the characters, who are made to seem like primitive sculptures. By returning to a primitive style (frontal, inner, erotic), Pasolini shows how the perspective of the image becomes timeless. Compositions are geometric and alienating.[23] Static lines, such as those of converging tram tracks or rows of poplar trees, recede into the background and imply a sense of transience. *Teorema* was initially conceived as a verse tragedy, then as a literary inquiry, and finally as a cinematographic scientific report that rests on the very poetic composition of the image.

Pasolini's experimental approach is introduced *tout court* by the film's prologue, which shows a frenzied reporter (played by journalist/writer Cesare

Garboli) interviewing some workers on the day their employer has given them his factory, and questioning them about what they think. This opening sequence is entirely shot in a *cinéma vérité* style, as if a television news report, with a handheld camera and available light with background sound. From this point onward the narrative will be a polemical demonstration of this breaking news event. In fact, as a public act, the donation of the factory is nothing more than a function of "the degeneration of the life of the world" that Pasolini associated with the bourgeoisie.[24] The impulse of the *padrone* can only be triggered by guilt, not by love; it participates in the transformation of the working class, indeed of all men, into petty bourgeois. Thus, it is "a historical assassination."[25] In an interview with the BBC, Pasolini explained:

> This is the first film I have shot in the bourgeois milieu with bourgeois characters. Up till now I have never done this because I could not bear to have to live with people I could not stand for months on end, fixing the script and shooting the film. But my hatred for the bourgeoisie is really a kind of physical repugnance toward petit bourgeois vulgarity, the vulgarity of hypocritical "good manners," and so on. And perhaps it is above all because I find their cultural manners insufferable. . . . But I chose people who were not particularly odious, people who elicited a certain human sympathy—they are typical of the bourgeoisie, but not of the worst bourgeoisie.[26]

The tragic ambiguity of the film's prologue is confirmed by the enunciations of the theorem, the data recording how the bourgeois behaves in his or her particular space: Paolo at the factory, Pietro at the Liceo Parini (historically a site of the students' revolt), Odetta at the Catholic Istituto delle Marcelline, and Lucia in her bedroom. The introduction of each character is monochromatic, as are the recurring static shots of the factory throughout the film—in a film set, after all, in Milan, whose factories symbolized, more than anything else, the nation's economic miracle.[27] Modern architecture appears and is judged as a sort of urban totalitarianism, a statement of economic power, without beauty or soul—as in the opening scene, filmed in front of the old Innocenti Factory in the Lambrate district, and when Paolo is seen leaving the factory for home in his car, driving through Via Riccardo Pitteri.[28]

The almost colorless, sepia-toned world of the characters is further defined through their mechanical movements punctuated by the eerie music of Ennio Morricone: they not only occupy an architectural space; they "possess" it socially. Then, color is introduced by cutting to the exterior of their magnificent neoclassical villa in Via Palatino in the elegant San Siro quarter.

The controlled, artificial life of this typical well-to-do Milanese family is turned upside down by the arrival of the Guest, who is "socially mysterious"—that is, unfamiliar with the values of an industrial civilization.[29] The revealing power of his body evokes emotions through which each member of the family has to face his or her existence from a new perspective devoid of mediocrity and vulgarity. Sex in the film has the effect of breaking down habitual responses, thus flaunting the heterosexual and social norms that regulate bourgeois behavior. Silence accompanies the Guest's gestures as he molds creative experiences that are authentic and unstoppable. The way each member of the family obsessively stares at his body suggests that the physical encounters are symbols in something akin to a strange liturgy that cannot be limited, as Marc Gervais suggests, to an exclusively sexual interpretation.[30] At the beginning, it is an ostentatious contemplation of the young man's scandalous beauty, which is followed by an imaginative interiorization of what is seen, and eventually a surrender to an overwhelming desire. Thus, the "so divinely degrading" glances of the Guest are met with the "desperately begging" look of those who are used to possessing and now crave to be possessed.[31] Lucia's waiting for him naked on the terrace of the chalet, as if possessed by a dream, and the bewitched Odetta staring into the camera lens make the audience aware of the act of looking.

In *Teorema*, the Guest's body tells the whole story with a mixture of directness and ambiguity. The dialectic between the young man and the family reflects their inner psychological development and historical transformation. His powerful glances haunt the characters once he abandons them, taking away with him the mystery of his apparition. What follows is a series of setbacks. They begin to sense the vulgarity of their daily routine, filled with empty, fake, logically controlled gestures, from which the dominant class cannot escape. Pietro's compulsive drawing of the Guest's portrait and Odetta's catatonic stupor are the direct expressions of their emotion. Bourgeois rationality now yields before the need to re-create the lost experience. On the central figure of *Teorema*, Pasolini declared: "I adapted my character to the physical and psychological person of the actor. Originally, I intended this visitor to be a fertility god, the typical god of pre-industrial religion, the sun-god, the Biblical god, God the Father. Naturally, when confronted with things as they were, I had to abandon my original idea and so I made Terence Stamp into a generically ultra-terrestrial and metaphysical apparition: he could be the Devil, or a mixture of God and the Devil."[32] Ultimately, the film suggests that a sense of desolation and emotional disorientation pervades the everyday life of the historically dominant class. Thus, it is the death drive, Thanatos, that connects each corollary of the theorem.

Pasolini's grounding of sex in class identity is an invitation to turn our attention toward a much deeper unease in late-1960s Italy, a time when industrial management and political power became even more closely intertwined, with ruinous consequences. He points to the false values of a civilization that is "Other" compared to preindustrial and peasant cultures. As he wrote just months before his death, in an article entitled "Il vuoto del potere in Italia" ("The Power Void in Italy"), the degenerative process of industrialization has led to "the disappearance of the fireflies"—a process he explicitly identified with the Milanese-born chemical giant Montedison: "I would give up the entire Montedison for just one firefly."[33]

Behind this is a further assumption that the light of nature cannot be blended with the artificial light of history. In Paolo's last scene at the factory, as he is driving his car, he asks himself what it would be like to divest himself of his property, and donate the factory to his workers. But "the bourgeoisie loves nothing," Pasolini warns; at best their love is decorative, "certainly not historical, that is to say real and capable of advocating a new history."[34] The sacred sex of the Guest demands the total abdication of the institutional mechanisms commanded by the ruling class. Each member of the bourgeois family is reduced to impotence, as in Lucia's purposeless driving through the anonymous back streets of Milan or Paolo's wandering at the Stazione Centrale, located in Piazza Duca d'Aosta in the center of the city.

In the film, the sense of dawning is heightened by Mozart's *Requiem*, which is associated with Paolo when he is bedridden and dazed by physical pain, or the Guest's reading of Tolstoy's *The Death of Ivan Ilyich*.[35] The compound rhythm of Mozart's music also accompanies Odetta's psychological awakening, as it does her mother's desperate search for something lost when she explores the great industrial metropolis and picks up a young boy, who has come from the provinces to study at the university. At the end of the film, the chorus of "Kyrie" is heard as Paolo, the father and industrialist, walks through the desert, naked and tragically aware of his defeat. (See Figure 2.2.) His terrible scream, his lineaments disfigured by a beastly despair, his body engulfed in the abyss as the camera moves behind him, all express the rejection of the vitality exemplified by the sacred Guest. In the fleeting present, "just as in [his] life, as in Milan," the father cannot confront history: his scream is "fated to last beyond any possible end."[36] In the last poem of Pasolini's novel, "Oh, my naked feet, . . ." the Lombard city appears as the symbol of social reality as well as of Paolo's existential displacement. The question remains: "Is he who was searching in the streets of Milan the same as the one who now searches on the roads of the desert?"[37]

Teorema heralds a cinematic technique that Pasolini defines as "sacred," in the way he approaches the camera movements and careful photographic

Figure 2.2 The father and industrialist, Paolo (Massimo Girotti), walks through the desert (actually, Mount Etna), naked and tragically aware of his defeat in *Teorema* (Pasolini, 1968)

compositions.[38] Some critics have spoken of a "miracle play."[39] More than Pasolini's other protagonists, Paolo is an individual who exemplifies the historical challenges of 1968. In industrial cities such as Milan, the factory became a hub of social interaction, around which workers' lives revolved, as captains of industry like Pirelli tried to look after the welfare of their employees. For Pasolini, within this progressive environment, the individual has no hope of redemption. He foresees an eventual depoliticization of Italy, in which Italians will adapt to their own "degradation" and "suicidal disillusionment and amorphous ennui."[40] This resonates even more forcefully today.

The Architecture of Public Drama: Liliana Cavani's *I cannibali* (1969)

Milan also figures prominently in Liliana Cavani's *I cannibali* (*The Cannibals*), freely adapted from Sophocles's *Antigone*. Cavani targets living history and the way in which the formula of revolution is applied to young rebels, anticipating the collapse of all traditional assumptions about the stability of political authority at a time when the militant body of the 1968 generation was still getting organized. Her cinematic style, which is haunting and mobilizing, imaginatively translates a classical myth into a ground for contemporary cultural debates.[41] In the film, Milan becomes a paramount example of the clash between the highest totalitarian forces and revolutionary youths, bearing witness to a natural rebellion conducted in the name of Nature. "Today," said Cavani in the film's press book, "our cities are like many Corinths, where the tyrant gives orders against nature. That is an obscene authority, the real scandal nature resists. . . . We have seen symptoms of rebellion. My film wants to bear witness to this type of natural rebellion."[42]

It is from this perspective that Cavani attempts her fictional account of the experiences that came to define and shape the sociopolitical landscape of an industrial city-state during the late 1960s. She also warned: "Today's young rebels have alarmed not only the bourgeoisie but also the repressive bureaucracy. They risk becoming a toy in the hands of politicians and the upper level of the hierarchy."[43] In the film, the city appears increasingly disciplinary (in Michel Foucault's sense), confined by a repressive state apparatus that polices urban space.[44] With few exceptions, characters are named by appellations that translate hierarchical forms of control and surveillance, such as Father (the Prime Minister), Guard, Sergeant, Officer, Policeman, and so on. Meanwhile, Milan represents and expresses the larger national reality in all its complexity. On her choice of the Lombard city, Cavani declared: "I wanted to capture a modern city. In Rome, you are never sure where to place the camera, because you always seem to get a cupola of Borromini or the Temple of Augustus in the background. On the other hand, Milan, and its historical downtown, is very contemporary, so the audience can identify with a city of today. The film was entirely shot in Milan, for eight weeks, during the spring of 1969."[45] In this modern setting, under a totalitarian regime, the dead bodies of insurgents who have conspired against the state are left on display in the streets and in public places to discourage further conspiracies. Multilingual announcements affixed to walls warn the citizens against any removal of the dead. This order is defied only by the daring of Antigone (Britt Ekland), who comes from an upper-class family and is engaged to the son of the prime minister. Only a mysterious stranger (Pierre Clementi), a modern Tiresias, who speaks an unknown language and communicates by allusive gestures, will assist in performing the funeral rites for her dead brother Polynices. They are both denounced by the citizens and eventually arrested and interrogated. Tiresias is subjected to psychiatric observation and paraded by the media like a freakish spectacle. Antigone is tortured, and both are publicly executed, but the film's ending suggests their deaths will inspire new rebels to follow their example.

In *I cannibali*, the language of gesture is the affective means that provides communication. It is formally established in the prologue. The film opens by the sea, where children find the body of a young man (Tiresias) who appears to have been swept ashore. When they try to awaken him, and the man gets up and begins to follow them, hunters arrive at the scene and shoot all the children dead. The handheld camera gazes upon the action as if it is in danger of being discovered. "When Tiresias awakens," wrote the director in the working script, "he begins to utter a terrible prophecy already in progress."[46] He will carry these violent images with him while he roams through the city streets.

I cannibali then continues with an extensive crosscutting sequence in Milan, which juxtaposes corpses and skyscrapers. Tension abounds in the static, symmetrical shots of claustrophobic buildings. We see the Piazza della Repubblica, one of the city's largest piazzas, built in 1865 on the site of the old Stazione Centrale, with its International Style towers and residential high-rises designed by some of the nation's leading architects (including Giovanni Muzio and Luigi Mattioni). The cold gray dawn casts upon the cityscape a metallic sheen of light. The images of bodies on the pavement scream their horror. We read in the published treatment: "What could have possibly happened in this city that is so astounding? Bodies everywhere: laying along the sidewalks, in the middle of streets, isolated, piled up, men and women, some dressed in work clothes, others in suits. What is astonishing is that no one stops to look. The passers-by walk with their heads up high avoiding reality down below. Pedestrians, cars, trams, buses all go about their business as if nothing is happening."[47] Supporting these surreal images is the title song, "The Cannibals" (composed by Audrey Nohra and Ennio Morricone), which calls out to mankind to become conscious:

Call me cannibal, I won't die.
Savage cannibal, I won't die.
Crazy cannibal, I won't die.
Pagan cannibal, I won't die.
I'm happy and wild and free.
Kill me if you can, I will never lie down dead.
I'll just fly away on my sky-blue horse.
I'll just fly away, happy that my mind is free.[48]

Cavani emphasized the absolute importance of featuring Milanese piazzas, streets, and public places as protagonists, filled with the dead bodies of the rebels. (See Figure 2.3.) She recounted a funny episode that occurred while filming:

> I had imagined the city as a theatrical stage. Revolts do not happen in interiors. They belong in the streets. I was with a group of students who were instructed to sit on cars, to lay on the ground and play dead.

Figure 2.3 Tiresias (Pierre Clementi, center left) and Antigone (Britt Ekland, center right) walk past dead bodies in the streets of Milan in *I cannibali* (Cavani, 1969)

We had pasted revolutionary posters on walls against dictatorship. The brother of a friend of mine happened to pass by. He was a university student struck by the scene, and said: "My God, Milan is in uprising and I nearly missed it all!" Then he realized that he had stepped into a film set. We had recreated the spirit of what was happening in the city.[49]

In evoking in many ways the violent turmoil of its time, *I cannibali* is a powerful critique of bourgeois rationality. The opening sequences establish Cavani's approach with the camera, at once mobile and invisible, present and hidden. The 2.35:1 wide-screen anamorphic format helps define the physical relationship of the characters to the environment. What is typical of *I cannibali* is the use of relatively brief shots to build up a scene, punctuated by the rhythmic assonance of sounds.

The film portrays human life in terms of unrelieved bondage, a nightmare of political tyranny. The central images are images of torture, dismemberment, and mutilation. The city takes the form of a labyrinth, where emotion and anxiety communicate a lack of social interaction. Cavani wrote the screenplay at the end of 1968, and her approach involved gathering together real events taken from newspapers and magazines, especially photojournalism, as well as her own observations of life. As she explained in an interview with Claire Clouzot in 1974, Cavani soon realized that any cinematic account of violence and revolution would carry emotional impact for the viewer for just a short time: "Information cannot engage us politically. It has the numbing effect of a horror film . . . I wanted to place this man in a situation where he could no longer avoid the corpses in front of his home, in a city full of bodies. He could no longer turn the page without stepping on them."[50]

The film's title sequence, which follows the prologue by the sea, is a photographic collage of ultimate horror: the published treatment of the film refers to human bodies piled "like garbage that gets in the way."[51] We are reminded that, in an advanced industrial society, the camera defines reality essentially as a spectacle for the masses and as an object of surveillance for their rulers. Images are enlisted in the service of important institutions of control (the police, the family), as symbolic icons and pieces of information.[52] In an interview with Ornella Ripa, Cavani maintained that she simply filmed whatever people could see every day and that her film materialized "the monsters of the spirit."[53] She relies on the kind of pathos that we associate with the iconography of industrialized photography, as, for example, in the bold interplay of concrete and emotion in the architectural setting of the mental institution where Tiresias is detained. In such disturbing images, it is dominant neocapitalist ideology that codifies what constitutes an event. *I cannibali* is the director's way of responding to contemporary ideological contestations.[54]

Images shock us only if they represent something novel: the horrible appearing ordinary. The title sequence sums up a terrifying vision of a death-haunted world, establishing the act of violence as a primary gesture. In the film, the decomposing corpses amassed upon the streets of downtown Milan appear as flattened shapes against the outline of imposing buildings, such as the Breda Tower overlooking Piazza della Repubblica.[55] These images are as realistic as the mysterious images of an apocalyptic world. The photography presents a range of flat grays, lacking shadows, and with a hallucinatory effect that has an essential thematic significance: under Creon, man has defied ancient laws and has entered into a nightmare world. These haunting images will be retelevised throughout the film to remind citizens of the terrible events inscribed by the power that has besieged the city.

Antigone's refusal to obey the laws of the city-state is a gesture that transcends the performance of Polynices's symbolic burial. Throughout the film, her corporeal vibrancy and silence contrast with the stagnation and wordiness of the figures of power. Cavani uses the language of myth and universal symbols to avoid the revolutionary speeches that had become a cliché by 1969:

> As everyone knows, two months following the events of May 1968, all slogans, posters and catchy phrases were sold out and over-used by the establishment . . . *I cannibali* is not the chronicle of a revolution (I would have needed an entirely different language) but the spectral analysis of reality beyond the various episodes which characterized the demonstrations. I believe it is a comprehensive analysis, and primarily a discourse of generations.[56]

Dialogue is kept to a minimum. Antigone and Tiresias *must* not speak, because in a revolution a word is already the beginning of a compromise toward defeat. During the months of the great unrest, language becomes meaningless. Cavani wanted to make a film against all kinds of speeches and restore the value of silence and pure gesture. Antigone and Tiresias's revolt has no slogans; they work alone, not as a group: "I was startled to see that books were being sold with revolutionary catchphrases and so were buttons and paving stones. In Italy, there was even a Boutique of Contestation."[57] The language of gesture is an effective one, providing a powerful form of communication in *I cannibali*. Tiresias's prophetic function is highly developed in this direction; he is specifically required to communicate through signs: drawing (the fish), sound (utterances of words from an African dialect), and exemplary gesture (the burial of the dead).

From the beginning of the shooting script, entitled *Il tamburo di carne* (Drum of Flesh), the character of Antigone is outlined in terms of both her mental and physical state: the expression of her face suggests anxiety as she looks down at bodies upon bodies lying on the ground. Under a flat overcast sky, she is caught fleeing through a maze of streets, hollow corridors, stairways, and claustrophobic buildings. The film opposes the vectorial idea of hegemonic forces to the idea of movement inherent in Antigone's corporeal visuality. She is the charismatic witness of the metropolitan scene, her figure's movement consistently underlined by a series of close-ups of her feet.

Cavani effectively balances the recording and creative powers of the film medium. To this end, she utilizes a long telephoto lens with a shallow depth of field that achieves an optical effect of diffusing the background, a type of graininess, evocative of a nightmare state. The streets appear ominous, reinforcing the image of the metropolis having supreme claim on the citizens. Cavani has explained that "various scenes had to be shot at dawn, also because the light has a beautiful quality; this is the only film in which I used a 750mm lens in order to create the look of news films shot during the war."[58] The soundtrack also functions as commentary, its eeriness resulting from extended moments of silence. Among the natural sounds we do hear, the most audible are echoing footsteps. Cinematographer Giulio Albonico had the challenging job of shooting in an improvised documentary style due to the actual difficulty of filming in the streets of a metropolis, pressed for time, blocking nonprofessional extras, coping with traffic, and dodging police surveillance.

Cavani denounces rituals of political execution and the lust of the ruling class for sadistic power by isolating the implacable eye of the photographic lens that underlies the humiliation of being constantly watched. The exercise of discipline exhibited in the opening sequences is intended to suggest a normalizing effect on the citizenry. Its success depends on a mechanism that coerces by means of observation: the telephoto lens gives a sense of simultaneous distance from and closeness to the multitude of bodies. The camera becomes the eye that must see without being seen, an art of the visible, which secretly constructs a new knowledge of man. The techniques of subjection exploited by the apparatus of the state are projected onto the film's settings, which feature military and police headquarters, prisons, madhouses, government buildings, and places of execution: the spatial nesting of hierarchized surveillance—what Foucault called the means of correct training.[59]

Cavani's narrative shapes the topography of a carceral city: a network of gazes that supervise one another. The architectural mapping of the city allows for an articulated control of the individual in both external and internal space. From Antigone's first appearance in the metro, she is constantly being pursued and watched by observers. Once she runs into Tiresias at a snack bar, and decides to follow him on foot through the streets; later, both she and Tiresias are pursued by soldiers in numerous chase scenes, which are filmed in transitional spaces (streets, paths, alleys, corridors). Milan becomes a theater of shock and horror, in which every movement Antigone makes is observed in detail, each gaze being part of the functioning of power.

For example, the sequence of Antigone and Tiresias running naked through the streets of Milan has a nightmarish quality and was described by Cavani as "a grotesque crossing through the places and the institutions that represent power."[60] The chase maps out a maze of winding streets, hidden depths, and downward paths. The camera follows Antigone and Tiresias inside an Officers' Club, rushing down some stairs, against a background of white walls. A place fit for concealment, this building is marked by tunnel-like corridors leading to hollow, narrow rooms. The fugitives hide in the sauna, where they strip off their clothes and witness an unusual act of subjugation: a procession of naked high-ranking officers, crouched on all fours, crawling between the legs of an adolescent boy in an oversized military uniform. The boy delights in physically abusing the officers, but they offer no resistance to his cruelty. At dawn, pursued again, hunted by police dogs, Antigone and Tiresias resume their flight in the streets: as they run, the silence of their bare feet contrasts with the pounding of military boots.

Later, Antigone is questioned in an aseptic, white room at the military police headquarters, forced to sit on an office chair with wheels and spun around from one interrogator to another in a disorienting motion. (See Figure 2.4.) This is intensified by rapid camera movements and blurred shots, which lend aggression to the examination process and its intersecting observations. The camera tracks back and forth, positioned at the same level as the

Figure 2.4 Antigone is questioned by military police in *I cannibali* (Cavani, 1969)

key interrogator, thus enforcing his subjective point of view. The police officers who surround Antigone in this torture scene alternately slap, strike, and insult her, the optical montage effectively expressing the extraction of the truth by relentless interrogation and pain. Here we also witness a process of discursive divestment: Antigone utters cryptic sentences but then speaks no more. Throughout this penal liturgy, she resists the gaze of control. Beaten until she collapses, she who has been given motion is finally constrained to stillness and silence.

A similar authoritarian control is exhibited in the scene of Tiresias at the television station, where he is being telecast by the news media who have tracked him down before the police can get to him. Tied up and kept under surveillance, he is a figure of misery and ridicule, looking around in bewilderment, his countenance antithetical to the self-assured posture of the anchorman. The "criminal" is then displayed through multiple television monitors, which also bring images of Antigone into every household in the city. Psychologists have been invited to take part in a panel discussion to evaluate his case, but the puzzled Tiresias breaks free, turning the news program into a comedic chase scene amid studio equipment and cables. Obviously excited by this unexpected turn of events, the anchorman urges his viewers "to enjoy the show," reassuring them that the captive cannot run very far. Hence, the anchorman is a voice of bourgeois hegemony, controlling an instrument of observation and capitalist reification.[61]

Cavani further depicts the geopolitics of the carceral city and its cynical enclosure of citizens in the scenes at the neuropsychiatric hospital, where Tiresias is secluded after his capture. The architectural orchestration of mental institutions as agents for training docile bodies is shown in perpendicular high angle shots that establish the courtyard from the point of view of a watchtower. Other shots compose the detailed geometry of a panoptic fortress: several black apertures are arranged octagonally in a fixed space of internal control in which the slightest movement is supervised and recorded by the guards. A juxtaposition of bird's eye views of the octagonal dungeon reinforces the feeling of looking down a tunnel, as if humans have fallen into an abyss.

The final sequence questions the civic function of the urban piazza in Italian architecture, which historically represented a distinctive form of public life, a space to satisfy the desires of crowds.[62] Cavani cinematically stages the execution of Antigone and Tiresias, conducted by the military police, at the very center of a piazza, in downtown Milan. As the citizens gather around to gaze on them from multiple angles, the camera remains fixed on this central space. Close-ups of machine guns firing indicate the event of their deaths. The technopolitics of punishment is based on the idea of preventing future disorders, but, all of a sudden, undifferentiated figures appear in the background and begin to remove the rebels' bodies. Antigone and Tiresias's deaths transform the ending into another beginning of the same ineluctable process: they will be imitated by others. This ending suggests that the coming of Tiresias, a seer and a prophet, has exorcized the spell of the present and rescued man from the city of dreadful night.

Uncharted Territories

For Pasolini, tragedy and myth become the vehicles that interpret the present, that depict its deep-reaching transformations as well as forms of degradation in the industrialized Milanese world. These are evident throughout his focus on the urban fabric in *Teorema*, but one of the most striking scenes takes place near the end of the film, at the Stazione Centrale, the monumental railway building designed by Ulisse Stacconi and realized during the fascist period.[63]

The station, which Anna Maria Ortese has called "a port of work, a bridge of necessity, and estuary of simple blood," was the main gateway to Milan for immigrants, like Visconti's Parondis.[64] It is here that Pasolini chooses to dramatize a final physical ritual of divestment: as Paolo slowly undresses, completely ignored by the crowd, a cold light falls from the dome above, emphasizing the majestic architectural structure. The whole episode is filmed in a documentary style, the camera following Paolo in a long dolly shot, which establishes the cathedral-like glass and steel arches of the station (designed by Alberto Fava) that appear behind him. He stops and looks up in awe, as if overpowered by a religious awakening, reminiscent of St. Francis. Then he slowly begins to take off his business suit. The camera cuts to his bare feet and, as he walks, there is an abrupt cut to the same feet stepping into the desert sands. The Stazione Centrale sequence locates Paolo's symbolic and real divestment as a revolutionary act, and his nakedness projects a visual image of an impossible dream of emancipation from economic bondage. Paolo must accept his fate; his attempt to master historical change is in vain. For Pasolini, the volcanic desert is the visual form of time outside history.

Certain dates stand out in the contemporary history of Italy and Milan. In mid-November 1967, the city's Catholic University of the Sacred Heart was the first private institution to be occupied by protesters. It marked one beginning of a more general cultural revolution, commonly interpreted as being a spontaneous and antiauthoritarian mass protest movement. It spread from the "Cattolica" into the factories, and then into society as a whole. Milan, more than any other Italian city, became a microcosm as well as the epicenter of revolutionary action. Cinematic representations of Milan such as *Teorema* and *I cannibali* portray a city divided culturally, socially, and spatially. Pasolini and Cavani are certainly *the* auteurs who did the most to interpret the political and institutional history of the revolutionary movement in that city. After 1968, during the "years of lead," Milan remained a protagonist on the national scene, but the violent political events that followed the Piazza Fontana bombing were an unmistakable sign that Pasolini's "fireflies" were disappearing. Milan, a city whose cinema gave the public access to the world of workers, industrialists, and student revolutionaries, increasingly reflected a disturbed present in which the lights of the big city no longer excited young men with ambition. Gabriele Salvatores's recent documentary *1960*, which I mentioned at the outset of this chapter, represents a new response to this national crisis, in which Milan is a city of departure rather than hopeful arrival. The cinematic depiction of Milanese urban space from the height of Italy's boom to the upheavals of 1968 shows that the architectural character and social hierarchies of the Lombard city are invaluable indicators of dramatic change in Italy's economic and institutional culture.

NOTES

1. On the family in postwar Italy and its historical, sociopolitical, and economic variables, see Nicholas J. Esposito, *Italian Family Structure* (New York: Peter Lang, 1989); Lesley Caldwell, *Italian Family Matters: Women, Politics and Legal Reform* (London: MacMillan, 1991); Pierpaolo Donati and Riccardo Prandini, eds., *La cura della famiglia e il mondo del lavoro: Un piano di politiche familiari* (Milan: Franco Angeli, 2008).

2. On the social dimension of neocapitalism, see Ernest Mandel's article "The Economics of Neo-capitalism," from the 1964 *Socialist Register* https://www.marxists.org/archive/mandel/1964/xx/neocap.html; also Lelio Basso, *Neocapitalismo e la sinistra europea* (Bari: Laterza, 1969).

3. Gian Piero Brunetta, *Il cinema italiano contemporaneo: Da "La dolce vita" a "Centochiodi"* (Rome-Bari: Editori Laterza, 2007), 492–493.

4. Giuseppe (Pino) Pinelli, a Milanese railroad worker, who was arrested on the night of the bomb attack, presumably fell from a window of the central police station on December 15, 1969. Pinelli spent forty-eight hours under interrogation in the office of the police commissioner, Luigi Calabresi. His name was cleared six years later and the far-right Ordine Nuovo was accused of the Piazza Fontana bombing. Pietro Valpreda, a ballet dancer associated with the "Bakunin Circle" in Rome, was accused on the evidence of a taxi driver, whose testimony eventually proved false. Valpreda was kept in prison for years and cleared of the crime in 1985.

5. Giorgio Bocca, *Il provinciale: Settant'anni di vita italiana* (Milan: Arnoldo Mondadori, 1991), 217–218.

6. Calabresi's assassination inaugurated an era of fierce political violence. In March 1972, Milanese publisher Giangiacomo Feltrinelli was found dead at the foot of a high-voltage power pylon, killed by his own explosives during a sabotage attempt at Segrate. Feltrinelli operated an armed clandestine left-wing group called GAP, supposedly to fight a right-wing coup in Italy.

7. Capanna, a philosophy student at the Catholic University of Milan, led the students' collective action during the late 1960s and early 1970s. He later published the autobiographical *Formidabili quegli anni* (Milan: Rizzoli, 1988), a recollection of the events that had dominated the public debate in the city.

8. Cited from the film dialogue. Unless otherwise noted, all translations are mine.

9. See Bocca, *Il provinciale*, 224.

10. See John Foot, *Milan since the Miracle: City, Culture and Identity* (Oxford: Berg, 2001), 5–6. See also Raffaele De Berti, "Milano nel cinema: L'immagine della città sullo schermo," in *Un secolo di cinema a Milano*, ed. R. De Berti (Milan: Editrice Il Castoro, 1996), 431–447.

11. John Boorman and Walter Donahue, eds., *Projections 6: Film-makers on Film-Making* (London: Faber and Faber, 1996), 167.

12. Cited in Gianni, Rondolino, *Luchino Visconti* (Turin: UTET, 1981), 403–404.

13. Seymour Chatman, *Antonioni or, the Surface of the World* (Berkeley: University of California Press, 1985), 96.

14. See Paul Ginsborg, *A History of Contemporary Italy: Society and Politics 1943–1988* (London: Penguin, 1990), 73–74, 270–271.

15. As Enzo Siciliano reports, *Teorema* was initially set in New York, a city Pasolini first visited in October 1966 in order to attend the New York Film Festival, which was showing *Uccellacci e uccellini* (*Hawks and Sparrows*), and best represented the bourgeois conservatism of the Western world. See Enzo Siciliano, *Vita di Pasolini* (Florence: Giunti, 1995), 408.

16. Pier Paolo Pasolini, *Theorem*, translated with an Introduction by Stuart Hood (London: Quartet Books, 1992), 3. The book was first published by the publisher Garzanti in March 1968, over five months before the film premiered at the Venice Film Festival on September 4.

17. Ibid., 11.

18. Pier Paolo Pasolini, in *Heretical Empiricism*, ed. Louise K. Bernett, trans. Ben Lawton and Louise K. Barnett (Bloomington: Indiana University Press, 1988), 174.

19. Northrop Frye, *Anatomy of Criticism: Four Essays* (Princeton, NJ: Princeton University Press, 1957), 168.

20. Pasolini, *Theorem*, 71. On the image of the desert as a reflection of the characters' inner reality, see Gian Piero Brunetta, *Forma e parola nel cinema*, Introduction by Gianfranco Folena (Padua: Liviana, 1970), 112.

21. Alberto Moravia, *Al cinema: Centoquarantotto film d'autore* (Milan: Bompiani, 1975), 108. The opening sequence ends with a quotation: "God led the people about, through the way of the wilderness" (*Exodus*, XIII, 18).

22. Serafino Murri, *Pier Paolo Pasolini* (Milan: Editrice Il Castoro, 1994), 97. Although the film was awarded the OCIC prize by the left Catholics, it was accused of obscenity by the conservative wing of the Church who attacked Pasolini for his ideological and theological positions.

23. Cf. Noel Purdon, "Pasolini: The Film of Alienation," in *Pier Paolo Pasolini*, ed. Paul Willemen (London: British Film Institute, 1977), 47.

24. From an interview published in *La Stampa*, July 12, 1968, cited in Murri, *Pier Paolo Pasolini*, 7.

25. Pasolini, *Theorem*, 171.

26. Oswald Stack, *Pasolini on Pasolini* (London: Thames and Hudson/BFI, 1969), 155.

27. In *Rocco e i suoi fratelli*, Visconti closes with the Alfa Romeo factory gates overlooking Via Gattamelata, during the time when the Giulietta automobile was the Italians' dream car. Also the Innocenti Lambretta became the dream scooter of 1960s youth. This same Innocenti site was also used by Mario Monicelli in *Romanzo popolare* (*Come Home and Meet My Wife*, 1974), a film focusing on the world of the factory workers, who appeared no longer controlled by organized labor.

28. The historical Lambretta factory was founded in 1922 in Rome by Ferdinando Innocenti. In the early 1930s, Innocenti moved his business producing seamless steel tubing to Milan. After World War II, he decided to launch a motor scooter competing in cost with the bigger motorcycle companies. The factory closed in 1993. Initially the remaining old buildings were used for automobile production (including the Maserati) and were later demolished to construct apartment blocks. At the time Pasolini filmed *Teorema*, the Innocenti buildings were the farthest from the center of Milan. It is worth mentioning that during the so-called Forty-Five Days following the fall of Mussolini (from July 25 to September 8, 1943), the workers at the Innocenti factory marched through the streets of Milan carrying placards demanding an immediate end to the war (see Ginsborg, *A History of Italy*, 12).

29. Pasolini, *Theorem*, 24. Ernesto G. Laura suggests that the Guest evokes God's entry into human history. "Teorema," *Rivista del Cinematografo*, no. 41, September–October 1968, 546.

30. Marc Gervais, "Pier Paolo Pasolini: Contestatore," *Sight and Sound* 38 (Winter 1968–1969): 5.

31. Pasolini, *Theorem*, 34.

32. Stack, *Pasolini on Pasolini*, 156–157.

33. Pier Paolo Pasolini, "Il vuoto del potere in Italia," *Corriere della Sera*, February 1, 1975, reprinted in *Scritti corsari* (Milan: Garzanti, 1975), 160–168.

34. From an interview published in *Vie Nuove*, October 18, 1962, cited in Murri, *Pier Paolo Pasolini*, 9.

35. On the role of the *Requiem* in the film, see Jean-Louis Bory, "Le Grand Scandaleux," in *Ombre Vive: Cinéma III* (Paris: Union Générale d'Èditions, 1973), 21. It is reported that Mozart believed that the *Requiem* was meant to be played for his own funeral.

36. Pasolini, *Theorem*, 176–177.

37. Ibid., 175.

38. Pier Paolo Pasolini, "Una discussione del '64," in AA. VV., *Pier Paolo Pasolini nel dibattito culturale contemporaneo* (Alessandria: Amministrazione Provinciale di Pavia, 1977), 95.

39. Cesare Garboli, *La stanza separata* (Milan: Mondadori, 1969), 266.

40. Pier Paolo Pasolini, *Trilogia della vita*, ed. Giorgio Gattei (Bologna: Cappelli, 1975), 11.

41. Sophocles's tragedy recounts the ordeals of Antigone, the daughter of Oedipus and Jocasta, who defies a fateful edict decreed by her uncle Creon, the new King of Thebes, which forbids the honorable burial of her brother's body. Creon has ordered that the corpse of Polynices be left lying in the plain, as an example to those who are the enemies of the country. Anyone who disobeys the royal order will be sentenced to death. Cavani's film focuses on the transgressive context of the play as defined by Creon's threat to his citizens.

42. Liliana Cavani, "*I Cannibali*: Un Cri d'alarme," French press book (1972), Liliana Cavani personal archive.

43. Interview with Liliana Cavani by Gaetana Marrone, Rome, May 10, 1990.

44. See Michel Foucault, *Surveiller et punir: Naissance de la prison* (Paris: Gallimard, 1975).

45. Interview with Liliana Cavani by Gaetana Marrone, Rome, May 26, 2009. Published as "L'impegno di Liliana Cavani: Il '68 e *I Cannibali*," in *Zoom d'oltreoceano: Istantanee sui registi italiani e sull'Italia*, ed. Daniela De Pau and Simone Dubrovic (Manziana-Rome: Vecchiarelli Editrice, 2010), 45–58.

46. "*I cannibali*," Liliana Cavani personal archive.

47. Liliana Cavani and Italo Moscati, "I cannibali," *Sipario* 25, no. 286 (February 1970): 41.

48. The lyrics of "The Cannibals" are in English.

49. Interview with Liliana Cavani by Gaetana Marrone, Rome, May 26, 2009.

50. Claire Clouzot, "Liliana Cavani: Le Mythe, le sexe et la révolte," *Ècran*, no. 26 (June 1974): 38.

51. Cavani and Moscati, "I cannibali," 41.

52. See Susan Sontag, *On Photography* (New York: Delta Books, 1977), 21, 178.

53. Ornella Ripa, "Solo i cannibali salveranno la città," *Gente*, May 11, 1970, 108.

54. Cavani was brought up in two separate economic and political worlds: her mother's working-class militant anti-fascism and her father's conservative, high-bourgeois values. Throughout her career, she has maintained secular, apolitical ideals.

55. The Breda Tower, built in 1954 on a design by Luigi Mattioni, was Italy's tallest skyscraper until the Pirelli Tower was completed by Giò Ponti in 1960. For the film

sets, see *Milano, si gira! Gli scorci ritrovati del cinema di ieri*, ed. Mauro D'Avino and Lorenzo Rumori, preface by Carlo Lizzani (Rome: Gremese, 2012), 43, 76, 99.

56. Clouzot, "Liliana Cavani," 37. On Cavani's film and the Italian political climate of 1968, see in particular Callisto Cosulich, "Cadaveri a Milano," *A.B.C.*, March 27, 1970, 25–28; Marco Sorteni, "Una cinepresa sull'anima dei giovani," *Domenica del Corriere*, May 26, 1970, 36.

57. Interview with Mary Blume, "Liliana Cavani and the Young," *International Herald Tribune*, April 15–16, 1972, 14.

58. Interview with Liliana Cavani by Gaetana Marrone, Rome, May 26, 2009.

59. Foucault, *Surveiller et punir*, 173–174.

60. Cited from the film treatment (Cavani's Personal Collection).

61. On television as a system of capitalist social subjection, see Gilles Deleuze and Félix Guattari, *A Thousand Plateaus: Capitalism and Schizophrenia*, trans. and foreword by Brian Massumi (Minneapolis: University of Minnesota Press, 1987), 458–459.

62. As an architectural object, the piazza is a place of encounters and social interaction. For Milanese-born architect and designer Aldo Rossi, the piazza was a classical, urban artifact that withstands the passage of time and gives structure to the city as a great theatrical encampment of civic living. See his *L'architettura della città* (Venice: Marsilio, 1966). One of the last scenes, in which Tiresias searches for Antigone through a pile of bodies, was filmed in old Milanese quarter of Largo Marinai d'Italia, with its Liberty building, which, in 1974, would house Dario Fo's "Collettivo teatrale la Comune."

63. The first Milano Centrale station opened in 1864 and was designed by French architect Louis-Jules Bouchot, its architectural style reminiscent of the Parisian buildings of that time. It was in operation until 1931 when the current station was inaugurated by Foreign Minister Galeazzo Ciano. Architect Stacchini modeled his original design after Union Station in Washington, DC.

64. Anna Maria Ortese, *Silenzio a Milano* (Turin: La Tartaruga, 1998), 44.

3

Inextinguishable Fire—or How to Make a Film in Berlin in 1968

ANDREW J. WEBBER

In this chapter, I consider how filmmaking responded to, and helped shape, the particular conditions of political upheaval in Berlin around 1968. The chapter adopts its title from two of the most incendiary films of the time, the agitprop shorts *NICHT löschbares Feuer* (*Inextinguishable Fire*, 1969),[1] by Harun Farocki, and *Herstellung eines Molotow-Cocktails* (*Making of a Molotov Cocktail*, 1968), by Holger Meins, which is often known by the alternative title *Wie stellt man einen Molotow-Cocktail her?* (*How Do You Make a Molotov Cocktail?*)[2] Both films embody forms of actionism, the programmatic staging of art as intervention in sociopolitical realities, that characterized the Berlin radical cultural scene in 1968. Such actionism would be incorporated in more direct style in the subsequent development of militancy around the RAF (Rote Armee Fraktion, or Red Army Faction), of which Holger Meins would be a high-profile member. Although the flames of the Molotov cocktail represented a direct reaction to the "inextinguishable fire" of the napalm used by U.S. forces in Vietnam, they also inevitably responded in Germany, and in Berlin in particular, to the burnings of books and of people by Nazism. These were fires that were not yet extinguished in the revolutionary Left's view of the restoration politics of the Federal Republic, and were still in need of counteraction.

In what follows, I will consider the production and deployment of these and other films, their position in the general cinematic landscape of this post-Oberhausen period in Germany, and their relationship to international developments in alternative cinema.[3] A key focus for militant interventions in the international system of film production and distribution were film festivals, increasingly seen by film activists as celebrations of free market capitalism and cultural elitism. The Berlin International Film Festival, or Berlinale, had a particular status in this regard, serving as it inevitably did as a screen-cum-storefront for vaunting and flaunting the freedoms of Western capitalist culture. Although the center of the spectacle in the late 1960s was located in a film palace—the Royal Palast, strategically placed in the main shopping strip of West Berlin—its publicity also faced toward potential consumers living under communism just across the border, with large-scale posters set up to be seen from the Eastern side. The 1968 Berlinale thus seemed particularly ripe for disruption by student militants, with commentators predicting revolutionary explosions, which, in fact, did not really materialize.[4] Godard's *Weekend* (1967) was the most high-profile international feature film, its excoriation of consumer culture as explosive traffic pileup standing in for the storming of the festival, which had been anticipated in response to the militancy of Godard and others shortly before at Cannes.[5]

Although the Cannes Film Festival had been discontinued half-way through, after Godard and other directors withdrew their films, the Berlinale went ahead with little serious disturbance. The potential debacle was displaced instead to the Technical University where a group of younger German filmmakers (including the signatories to the Oberhausen manifesto, Alexander Kluge and Edgar Reitz) were given a podium to debate with the students but were shouted down and pelted with eggs for their perceived compromises with the interests of the establishment. Although Godard, Truffaut, and other protagonists of the *nouvelle vague* sought positions at the vanguard of the 1968 events in Paris, with Godard's famous battle cry of revolutionary takeover, "A la grande salle!" ("To the main auditorium!"), their counterparts in Germany were for the most part outflanked by the more radical positions in the students' movement. In Berlin, too, the auditorium, both in the universities and the cinemas, was the principal arena for activist debate; although, in Berlin, whether in the lecture theater or the film theater, it seemed that concerted action between angry younger film directors and outraged student revolutionaries in changing the conditions of film production and consumption was impossible. An opportunity was thus created for a new generation of student filmmakers, who saw film as a ready medium for the sort of "happening"—the performative interventions—that characterized much of the student activism of the time. They took their cue in part from Godard and other more antiestablishment directors (such as Jean-Marie Straub and Danièle Huillet,[6] Michael Snow,[7] and Peter Nestler[8]), but they also sought to introduce a new and more radical cinematic praxis in direct response to the political exigencies of the time.

My argument here focuses on the ambiguous relationship between aesthetics, politics, and mediality that surrounded the agitprop agenda of Berlin's answers to Godard. Alongside discussion of short films and film projects by Farocki and Meins, I consider Helke Sander's film essay, *Brecht die Macht der Manipulateure* (*Break the Power of the Manipulators*, 1968), which polemically attacked the ideological manipulation of the political situation in Berlin, Germany, and the wider world by the powerful Springer media group.[9] Sander, Farocki, and Meins were all active in the newly founded Deutsche Film- und Fernsehakademie Berlin (DFFB, the German Film and Television Academy),[10] whose activities form part of the fraught history of academic institutions as laboratories for political dissent and activism around 1968. I also want to evaluate the particular status of Berlin as a city divided between Western and Eastern blocs and the implications of this division for the politics and the political "film theatre" of 1968. The topographical conditions of the divided city had a particular role to play in this inflammatory episode of film history. Thus, the ostentatious high-rise building of the passionately pro-West Springer media concern, erected between 1959 and 1965, was sited provocatively in the immediate vicinity of the border between East and West. With the construction of the Berlin Wall in 1961, the strategic symbolism was intensified, as the glittering, gold-clad bastion of the capitalist order and its most partisan media served to look over in to, and be demonstratively visible from, the East.[11] In 1969, a massive architectural response came from the other side of the Wall, with the construction of the Leipziger Straße complex of high-rise blocks, commonly known as the "Springerdecker" or "Springer coverers." On the Western side, the corporate architecture of the Springer tower was a prime object for assault from the streets, a target at once for incendiary films and other devices.[12] (See Figure 3.1.) The titles of Springer newspapers, "Bild" and "Welt" (literally, "Picture" and "World"), emblazoned allegorically at the top of the building, made a claim to picturing the world that the leftist radicals were determined to attack.

Berlin, Hanoi, Tehran

West Berlin in the late 1960s was predisposed in particular ways to be a site for left-wing activism. Berlin was a city with a strong radical Left tradition, embodied by such iconic figures as Rosa Luxemburg and Karl Liebknecht, the revolutionary socialist leaders who had been executed in 1919 by proto-Fascist freikorps paramilitaries. But it was a city that had subsequently been

Figure 3.1 Barbed wire protects the modernist office building of Axel Springer publishers, Sunday, April 14, 1968 (Keystone Pictures/ZUMA Press/Alamy Live News)

overwhelmed by the brutal rise to power of National Socialism, which co-opted the city as the command center for its "topography of terror," with countless victims.[13] The dire historical legacy of Nazi terror, and what was perceived by young people on the Left as the gross failure of their parents' generation to come to terms with that fascist legacy and the share they had in it, added an acute burden to the German version of the political battles of the 1960s. And the particular situation of Berlin in the postwar period, the city divided between East and West and a prime stage for their geopolitical standoff, made it all the more ready to act as a battleground and show ground for insurgence in 1968. On the one hand, Berlin was a highly militarized city, occupied by opposing forces; on the other, the particular constitutional or-dinance of West Berlin, where the requirement for military service operating in the Federal Republic did not apply, meant that many young people with pacifist or antiestablishment views were drawn to the city. Cold War Berlin, combining opposed military zones, was a kind of impossible proxy conurba-tion of Washington on one side of the Berlin Wall and Moscow on the other. It was a place for posturing across the divide between the blocs and always a potential flashpoint for global conflagration. And as such it had a special resonance with the brutal version of the Cold War confrontation being fought out in Vietnam. But both West and East Berlin were also the places in the respective halves of the divided Germany that were inhabited by the highest numbers of those who resisted the official line and were accordingly designated in official discourse as actually or potentially in league with the other side. Although in the East the possibilities for active resistance— including in the form of dissident filmmaking—were distinctly limited,[14] on the Western side there were many who would be willing, in dissident films and other forms, to smash the shop windows of high capitalism, and run amok in, and set fire to, its displays.[15] The windows of the Springer offices had a particular symbolic status in this, repeatedly featuring in agitprop films as implicit or explicit targets, in particular for stones wrapped in Springer newspapers.[16]

As in Paris and elsewhere, the revolt of 1968 in West Berlin was largely orchestrated and enacted by students, with sit-in, teach-in, and go-in events in the auditoriums of both the Technical University and the Free University and student demonstrations on the streets. And, also as in Paris, the medium and institution of film represented a prime arena for political action. Accordingly, the DFFB, founded in 1966 to be an institution of renewal for the German film industry, was destined to become a key production site for the ideological battles of Berlin's version of 1968. From its first term, relations between the institution and a significant number of its students were fraught, with struggles for control of the educational agenda and for rights of ownership of the Academy and the works produced within it.[17] Political consciousness was raised by "film-ins," and in May 1968 students occupied the Academy and renamed it for the early Soviet political filmmaker, Dziga Vertov, in protest against what they called "Nazi laws" at federal level and their ramifications at the level of institutions like the film school.[18] In Germany, as elsewhere, orthodoxies both of education and of film production had come under critical scrutiny as part of the general upheaval in attitudes to power and control during the early 1960s. Hierarchical systems of university education were challenged, not least by an increasingly radicalized student movement around the "Sozialistischer Deutscher Studentenbund" (SDS, the League of German Socialist Students). This had five hundred members in Berlin in 1968 and counted the most prominent German student leader, the charismatic Rudi Dutschke, among its ranks.[19] The SDS and its pursuit of a new model of "Critical University" provided much of the core ideological thinking and activist momentum for the so-called Außerparlamentarische Opposition (Extraparliamentary Opposition or APO).

At the same time, an emerging generation of student filmmakers had to find its place in relation to the ossified conventions of postwar German cinema but also the established Oedipal revolt of the Oberhausen Manifesto group, many of whom were old enough to be their fathers and were often accused of connivance with the establishment (hence, the theatrical humiliation inflicted upon Kluge, Reitz, and others in the podium discussion at the Technical University). A film school founded in 1966 was inevitably going to produce a volatile cocktail of critical film and educational politics, and so it was with the DFFB. When the Shah of Iran visited Berlin on June 2, 1967, crowds of protestors—among them students of the DFFB—gathered in front of the Deutsche Oper, the West Berlin opera house. The Shah's henchmen beat protestors—and bystanders—with planks, with no intervention from the Berlin police, and two DFFB students made a record of the event with a film entitled, *2. Juni 1967*.[20] This became a model for the use of film as documentary resource, providing evidence of activism and the response to it. The violent treatment of the protestors—in particular when one of them, Benno Ohnesorg, was shot in the back of the head by a policeman—was a defining moment for the formation of a more radical response to what was regarded as a return of police-state terror to the streets of Berlin.[21] Increasingly, leftist students insisted upon the coextensiveness of Berlin with Hanoi and Tehran, binding the particular national conditions of the city (also as a site of superpower occupation) to the internationalist cause.[22] And taking the camera onto the streets to shoot film would be a key mode of their response, with cinematic guerrilla action, as we will see, always standing in an ambiguous relationship to more physically immediate forms of intervention in the events of the day.[23]

Incendiary Devices: Holger Meins

Holger Meins was something of a martyr figure for the radical left in Germany following his death after a hunger strike in November 1974: an artist-turned-terrorist who was also at the center of some of the most powerful and disturbing scenes of the RAF drama, and as such was framed as a kind of performance artist. Meins epitomized the character of much of the prototerrorist and terrorist activities of the time as also a kind of production, aware of its status as an object of media attention and manipulation and seeking to maintain control of its impact. The television images of his arrest in Frankfurt in June 1972 and the photograph of his emaciated corpse after his fatal hunger strike in prison two years later became defining elements in the iconography of the radical Left. In these pictures, the would-be autonomous producer of images was subjected at once to the disciplinary control of the state and to the gaze of the media, in powerful and vengeful collusion. In the television footage of his arrest, he was seen as a howling animal, dragged more or less naked from his hideout: dehumanized and humiliated for the viewing public and painful to behold for sympathizers. Years later, the scene was recalled as such by Tilman Baumgärtel in an interview with Harun Farocki, who assumed that the police stripped Meins in an act of abject exposure of a criminal for the cameras.[24] Farocki described the images of Meins's emaciated corpse as a continuation of this act, suggesting a disinterred skeleton or an "image of terror from the Thirty Years' War."[25]

In this evocation, Meins appeared as a kind of hunger artist, radically rejecting consumption controlled by the state, but also an image maker who had lost control of his performance and of the kind of graphic associations that it might evoke. In another account of Meins's death, Farocki suggested that the skeletal image might also—perhaps necessarily in the German context—be seen as an imitation of the dead or barely living bodies from the death camps, and expressed the hope that it was not Meins's intention to produce such an effect for the cameras.[26] That extreme form of comparison was ever present in the conflict between the state and the dissidents of 1968 and after but also ambivalent in its agency, projected back and forth.[27] The scenes of Meins's arrest and mortification might therefore be understood as the enactments of a *lex talionis* on the part of the state, performing retribution at once for the part he played in acts of terror and for his role as a producer of *acts* of terror. As an image-artist, Meins, in his notorious short film *Making of a Molotov Cocktail*, had played with fire on-screen in the lecture theaters of Berlin, projecting *acts* of arson onto the city streets. While the extent of his direct involvement in actual acts of political violence remains uncertain, his status as enemy of the state and its institutions rested as much as anything upon the production of incitements to violence, in films, posters, and flyers. The firebrand outlaw was to be subject to ritual exposure through the apparatus of the media that had been the object of his militant practice in film and other media, and not least, as we shall see, of the acts of arson that he demonstratively played out on-screen.

Meins's working notes in the DFFB archive show that while he was a student filmmaker in Berlin in 1967–1968, he saw film as a matter of intense collaboration between aesthetics and politics and between the imperatives of theory and praxis. Meins came to the DFFB with experience of working in film (assisting the Hamburg-based underground director, Hellmuth Costard) and he stood out as a "real cineaste" with an advanced education in film, according to Farocki.[28] The sophistication of his thinking about film is clear from his essayistic work and sketches for projects, which are especially concerned with structural questions of argumentation, with form serving the interests of political content. In the Brechtian tradition, this means the need for alertness to the contradictions of sociopolitical conditions and a dialectical resistance to unifying structures, especially as these might conform with the subjective needs of the filmmaker.[29] The auteurist model of the director using the film to fulfill a personal idea—with a palliative, therapeutic effect for both producer and consumer—is challenged by the collective imperative of critical intervention. In this form, film is proposed as an integral force in the work of oppositional groups in Berlin, providing the basis for an activist film commune. And this involves a particular engagement with the city and its prevailing conditions, with a commitment to a new form of the old genre of the *Straßenfilm* or street film,[30] understood here as filmmaking that participates in the life of the streets in a practice of agitation. As Ulrike Meinhof put it in a famous TV interview, for the activists of 1968 the "street" was the focal arena to be occupied.[31] And film was a key apparatus in opening it up.

Meins's projects demonstrated this communard participation in various forms. He proposed a film about gang life in the Märkisches Viertel housing estate, in the northern Berlin district of Reinickendorf, whereby the gangs would be not just the objects but the coproducers of the film. Other projects involved filming from within institutions of state control—courthouses and prisons, locations with considerable poignancy for the making of film on the boundaries of legality and for a filmmaker who would end his days in prison. A more substantial project that he completed was the episodic film, *Oskar Langenfeld: 12 Mal* (*Oskar Langenfeld: 12 Times*, 1966), which followed the everyday experience of a homeless Berliner. The essay film works in the style of direct cinema, with the director as participating observer, engaging the film's protagonist in dialogue about the conditions of his life, and concluding, as if to pronounce judgment on it, with a repeated call to make him say "Mist" ("crap"). As Farocki recognizes, this is an accomplished work of engaged documentary, indicating something of the potential that Meins would have had in that genre.[32]

It is, however, for the short agitprop film, *Making of a Molotov Cocktail*, produced during his time at the DFFB, that Meins is best known, ironically enough given that the film's authorship has been subject to question, if not mystification, during the decades since its production and subsequent disappearance. It is a film that has been marked by uncertainty both as to those involved in its making (and hence, as accessories, in the demonstrative making of the Molotov cocktail) and in its title, the mutations of which indicated something of the stake that different actors and institutions have in the film as a cause célèbre of Berlin 1968. The attested title of the film—*Herstellung eines Molotow-Cocktails*—alludes, ironically, to systems of production, suggesting a counterproduct to the mass-market capitalism that it is intended to disrupt and to the production systems of the military-industrial complex. This will be a production by hand, with the implication that it will obviate the alienation of conventional processes of making, engaging the producer as user in full knowledge and control of the conditions of production.[33] In another version of the title, the film becomes *Über die Herstellung eines Molotow-Cocktails* (*On the Production of a Molotov Cocktail*), as if to suggest that this is a neutral documentary study, intended for disinterested educational enlightenment. But the film cannot, of course, be understood so innocently: its act of showing the making of the incendiary device is in itself an incendiary act, intended to light fires. That is, it is best understood after Meins's Brechtian model as a "Lehrfilm," by analogy with the *Lehrstück*—teaching or learning play—and expressly intended to act as an education in activist behavior.[34] In as far as the film is demonstrative, rather than just documentary, it presents the gestic act (by several hands) as an exemplar for a counterform of mass production. This is the logic that the Springer Group drew out in its manipulation of the title for ideological purposes, so that it became—for the purposes of its lawsuit against Horst Mahler—*Wie stellt man einen Molotow-Cocktail her?* (*How Do You Produce a Molotov Cocktail?*).[35] This version of the title emphasized the intention of the production to be copied and implied a desire on the part of the viewer to be shown how to do it.

Berlin Is Burning: Harun Farocki

Meins's Molotov cocktail film was evidently ignited by the Vietnam War and what the extraparliamentary opposition saw as the collusion of the German authorities and conservative media in it. He planned a set of screenings that would include the film, or its replacement by a "practical demonstration," proposing to provide the answer to two questions: "What has Berlin got to do with Vietnam?" and "What have both got to do with our films?"[36] In Harun Farocki's *NICHT löschbares Feuer* (*NOT Extinguishable Fire*, 1969), these questions are more explicitly addressed. The burning scandal of Vietnam is transported to Berlin while also shown to be located in the factories and offices of global capital, by means of a Brechtian mock-up of the Dow Chemical plant in Michigan which produced napalm.[37] If the production of napalm is traced to the U.S. factory, however, the factory is in its turn reproduced in West Berlin, which for Farocki and other activists was under occupation by the United States. They saw the city as deeply implicated in both the military-industrial and ideological fabrications of the Cold War West, and they wished to convert it into a site of resistance on both levels. Berlin was also the historical site of the

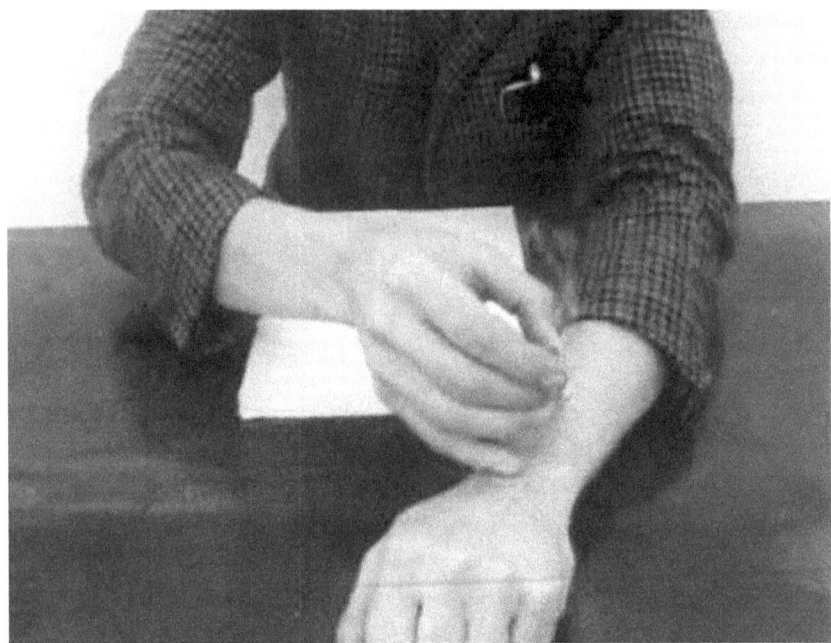

Figure 3.2 The burning of skin in *NOT Extinguishable Fire* (Farocki, 1969)

development of Brechtian techniques of revolutionary political performance, and in works like *NOT Extinguishable Fire* the young radical filmmakers working in the city extended that tradition of political agitation in new forms. As with Meins, Farocki's logic is also one of pronounced demonstration. Meins shows how to make counteractive incendiary devices; Farocki shows the workings and outcomes of the military-industrial complex to which those devices respond.

The twenty-five-minute film takes the form of a sequence of scenes aiming to perform both the system of production of napalm and its terrible effects. It begins with an act of demonstration, imitating in estranged form the setup of educational screenings in the mainstream media. Farocki appears in the guise of a television announcer. He first reads out the testimony of a Vietnamese witness to, and victim of, the effects of napalm from the Vietnam Tribunal in Stockholm (May 1967), reciting this in a studied form of underperformance, his eyes fixed upon the papers before him. At the end of the recitation, he looks up, as he breaks out of the role and engages the audience in direct apostrophe, asking how it might be possible to demonstrate the appalling effects of napalm. This he then proceeds to show in a radical act of performance, as he stubs out a cigarette on the back of his lower forearm. (See Figure 3.2.) The act is designed to give some sense, at least, of how napalm burns on the skin of its victims.

As Thomas Elsaesser has noted, this scene might be aligned with the notorious opening of Buñuel and Dalí's *Un Chien andalou* (1929),[38] and this was indeed one of the films that students of the DFFB viewed as part of their training.[39] For Elsaesser, *NOT Extinguishable Fire* follows *Un Chien andalou* in raising radical questions about the indexical character of the film medium, its immediate reference to the reality of things. It is a matter of film's ontological status as a kind of second skin, relating to—in some sense grafted from—the embodied experience that it records. In these terms, we can understand the demonstrative extinguishing of the cigarette on the skin of the presenter as an act of cinematic hapsis, a visual effect that also forcefully engages the sense of touch. As in *Un Chien andalou*, the optical field is co-opted by a powerful effect of tangible violence. As *Un Chien andalou* has been read as an intensely self-reflexive film, and its eye-slitting prologue as a strategic assault on the established conditions of the medium,[40] so *NOT Extinguishable Fire* can be seen as an extreme, experimental test of the ability of the conventional film medium to record such violence as the burning of napalm upon the skin. If the self-reflexive logic of *Un Chien andalou* is to threaten a cutting of the film, that of Farocki's film is to threaten a burning out of the pellicle of the film by a representation that exceeds its mediation, a threat contained by the recourse to the cigarette as prop. Neither the film nor the skin of the presenter is extinguished by fire, as demonstration and viewing are sustained. Although the presenter expresses concern that viewers may shut their eyes to an actual demonstration of napalm, to avoid having their "feelings hurt," the strategic, haptic effect of the scene is indeed to inflict a form of affective injury, albeit one that is only to a limited degree comparable with the injurious force of the real thing, napalm.

In Farocki's film, the act of violence is moved from a framework of surrealism to one of stylized realism, and from the eye (also readable as camera-eye) to the skin above the hand (also readable as the manual instrument of film production and montage). Although in *Un Chien andalou* Buñuel used a close-up to foreground the eye (the director himself wielding the razor that cuts it), followed by another close-up of ants emerging from a wound in the palm of a hand, in Farocki's film the eye is initially averted. However, the director-protagonist has his hands filmed prone before him, so that they are foregrounded, as if reaching out of the image in an excessive showing of skin. In both cases, the logic of the scene is fundamentally performative: the films show a revolutionary act, but as *act*, contained by an apparatus of performance. It is what Farocki calls in his film essay *Der Ausdruck der Hände*

(*The Expression of Hands*, 1997) "Handlung"—the performative "action" of hands. He takes the scene of intense observation of the hand from *Un Chien andalou* as an example to show that the action performed here is optical as much as manual.

Un Chien andalou is set up as a kind of dressing room scene before the theater proper of the film, while the prelude to *NOT Extinguishable Fire* establishes an austere mise en scène—the figure seated at a table—which is a signature feature of Farocki's filmmaking. The table serves as a site of filmic demonstration, of reportage, and—implicitly—of production: a cutting-table.[41] In particular, it references the setup of television and the news report, subtly subject to effects of estrangement in its performance—with Farocki himself acting as presenter. Although the setup is emphatically flat and frontal, by analogy with a television screen, the hands of the presenter embody a reaching beyond the comfortable conventions of distance between viewer and performance, even as his gaze remains fixed on the paper before him. The pronounced neutrality of the presentation is interrupted at one point in the course of the recitation, as the presenter looks up and at the viewer. This occurs as he pronounces the word "anzeigen," translated by the subtitles as "to report," but this is not in the uninvolved style of a television presenter, rather as a witness reporting a crime so that its perpetrators can be held to account. Its root is "zeigen"—"to show"—and its performative emphasis here carries the effect of the Brechtian axiom that the actor's job is to "show that showing is taking place." The gestural force of this moment as deixis, as deliberate pointing out, marks a breaking out of the role of presenter and into that of accuser, asserting the performative authority to pronounce judgment, to level accusation. And the eye-to-eye encounter with the viewer is a necessary corollary of that pronouncement, requiring registration and recognition.

The dark glasses that we see in the top pocket of the presenter also serve to unsettle the performance of television presenting. Such glasses were standard wear for Farocki and other young radicals of the time, a matter of styling but also representing the shielding or disguise of identity.[42] Here, the glasses indicate that this is a theatrical performance of impersonation. They are a subtler index of the pantomimic element that runs through the films under review here, and the broader activism of which they are part. The paper bag masks of the Shah and his wife in Farocki's playful 1967 short *Worte des Vorsitzenden* (*Words of the Chairman*), a film conceived in response to the couple's visit to Berlin, are the most stylized example. In the case of the glasses in the top pocket, the implication is that—even as this is a self-conscious performance—the gaze must be exposed without protection. *Un Chien andalou* cuts the eye—and by implication the camera-eye—

in order to open up a new mode of vision; Farocki's film does violence to the vulnerable skin—and by implication the skin of the film, in an act of stigmatization. It is a performative branding of the film activist and of the activist's film with something that can only begin to approach the effect of napalm.[43] And—by haptic effect, metonymically transferred between skin and eye—it enacts a mimetic branding of the unprotected gaze and hand of the viewer as potential activist, inflicting a strategic form of the injury—the hurt feelings—to which the presenter refers. The question remains whether the injury is enabling, or rather a mark of the failure to find adequate means of representation and intervention. Is this self-mortification as a response to the irresistible enormity of systems of violence, a self-reflexive alternative to acts of counterviolence aimed at the other which is identified as producing terror? What the final sequence of the film—"How can this be turned round?"—suggests, with the engineer carrying a vacuum cleaner in one hand and a machine gun in the other, is that the only way of countering the system of production of exploitation and violence is for those engaged in it to determine what they produce. This means production and consumption on the domestic level (the vacuum cleaner) must be seen as bound up with those of geopolitical violence (the machine gun).

The filmic act of demonstration announces its inadequacy, only able to give a limited sense of what it would show: irremediably scorched skin and scorched earth. Accordingly, the burning inflicted with the proxy prop is achieved by its stubbing out: the cigarette is extinguished, even as it gives some sense of the *not* extinguishable fire of napalm. At the same time, the manipulation of the cigarette and the self-inflicted burn wound are part of an incendiary network that structures the film after its prologue. The stylized mise en scène, as the film enacts the workings of the Dow Chemical concern, involves self-consciously iterative returns to tables (writing desks, coffee tables, laboratory tables), frequently in conjunction with cigarettes and other agents and objects of burning.[44] And at the same time, the self-conscious TV setup of the prologue is relayed through repeated acts of viewing footage from Vietnam, mediated by multiple television screens. The television footage ends each time with the view of a burn wound that also appears in the sequence directly following the prologue, with fingers and a surgical instrument investigating the wound, picking at its skin. In each case, the opening of the wound, with its function as leitmotif, introduces—opens up—the following section of the film. The serial structural effects of *mise en abyme* are designed to project the traumatic impact of the prologue into the representation of an apparatus of production that works by excluding the effects of the violence that it produces. By branding the episodes that follow with the mark of the prologue, the film insists in its formal disposition upon showing how the parts of a structure of assembly are implicated in each other, an exposure of a systematic chain of production and usage that the division of labor in the Dow plant is designed to obscure from those who do its work.

As the repeated scenes of television viewing indicate, those who are implicated in the production of the weapons of mass destruction are rendered as "Zuschauer" or "viewers" of their effects, and this exposure of spectatorship also serves to question the position of those watching the film in which those scenes are embedded. The self-consciously ready-made character of the film set, with posters serving to simulate landscape locations, is designed to show that Berlin as the site of the film's production lies behind the mock-up of the Dow factory as the site of napalm production. If Berlin is connected with Vietnam here in this pirate mock-up of a television show broadcast from the outpost of the "free West,"[45] it is no less exposed as associated with the Michigan of Dow Chemicals. The bombs that are shown falling on television screens in Farocki's film are put into a medial relation with Berlin, much as the translation of Vietnam into Berlin in his 1968 short *Ihre Zeitungen* (*Their Newspapers*) is managed by a montage of bombs dropped over Vietnam and bundles of Springer newspapers falling over the streets of Berlin.

Breaking Fire: Helke Sander

The two films discussed so far co-opt the logic of (television) documentary for their essayistic acts of exposure of the way things are and how they might be changed. Helke Sander's *Break the Power of the Manipulators* is also conceived as much as a record of the activism and actionism of the revolutionary student filmmakers as the imperative call to direct action announced by its title.[46] It is as much a countermanipulative *handling* and *showing* of evidence— resisting acts of "Verschleierung" (veiling or covering up)—as a performative instruction to engage in breaking the power of those who control the status quo, and not least the key ideological territory of the city of Berlin. Here, as in her other DFFB films, Sander exemplifies the desire of the student filmmakers to stake a claim to the streets and the buildings of Berlin, co-opting them as locations for political film work, with or without permission.[47]

The film begins with the Berlin street as a didactic instrument, with flow diagrams chalked on pavement, illustrating the connections that the activists perceive between institutions of state, mainstream media, and prevailing sociopolitical conditions. This establishing setup, projecting the subversive thinking of students from the academy onto the streets, in order to take possession of them, will recur to frame the various scenes of the film. That this is not mere blackboard abstraction is indicated when the chalk is repurposed later in the film as an evidential instrument in a reconstruction of the scene of the shooting of student leader Rudi Dutschke. The opening scene following the frame is a comic mock-up of an interview with the president of the Federal Republic on why he reads the Springer broadsheet, *Die Welt*. This leads into a montage sequence of industrialists heading for the "island" of Berlin, their conversations about the need to quell dissent to build capital in the city, cued by *Die Welt*. The first word to be chalked on the street at the start of the film is "Brecht," and the pun announces that here too activist film theater will be guided by Brechtian methods. The performers are self-evidently impersonators of their characters; the conversations are stylized (also in their derivation from print journalism); the camera is resolutely static, creating fixed tableaux; and the mise en scène is demonstratively mocked up. Thus, in a discussion between the industrialists in the car heading for Berlin, the rear screen is clearly missing so that the camera can record from behind their heads. The counterpart to these scenes of ideological connivance between those in control of capital and the Springer broadsheet are those that follow showing working-class characters manipulated in their thinking by the discourse of the tabloids. In this, the film references acts of newspaper reading in the classic Berlin-based activist work of 1932, *Kuhle Wampe*, for which Brecht wrote the screenplay.[48] The global title of Springer's broadsheet might be seen as asserting possession of the world in answer to the question raised by the full title of the earlier film: *Kuhle Wampe oder Wem gehört die Welt?* (*Kuhle Wampe or Who Owns the World?*).

The remainder of the film is then devoted to the activism of the students, working in the tradition of the young socialists in *Kuhle Wampe*. It shows scenes of discussion around the SDS's Springer Tribunal, with such protagonists as Dutschke and Peter Schneider, intercut with speeches from the Berlin city parliament denouncing the student activists. The logic of the Tribunal is to insist upon the coextensiveness of Berlin with the battleground of Vietnam. Schneider makes the case for a cultural politics of student revolt in the spirit of Brecht, whose anticonformist political theater, if it should not qualify as "Theater," would simply be given another name: "Thaeter." This is followed by an example of what might be called a "thaetrical" intervention by filmmakers, when Sander, Farocki, and cameraman Skip Norman disrupted the Berlin Press Ball, unfurling agitprop banners at the table of Axel Springer. The adoption of costumes and habitus of establishment figures is not just the technique of filmic demonstration that runs through the works considered here, but it affords direct intervention, which is then also recorded on film.[49] The footage of the intervention is framed by two discursive scenes.

Figure 3.3 Burning vans outside the Springer building in *Break the Power of the Manipulators* (Sander, 1968)

The first shows Sander, Farocki, and a third filmmaker, sitting around a table in their dark glasses, in a stylized discussion of the countervailing demands of aesthetics and politics and the need to achieve the right sort of accommodation between them. The camera is embraced here as a weapon to be taken up before the gun to show the actions that "prepare for the collapse of this society," while—in the Brechtian style—poetry is asserted as integral to the message that the ballistics of the antiauthoritarian revolt have to deliver (a wrapping for stones that will break plate glass). In the second scene, after the Press Ball footage, the three protagonists of the intervention appear in a "making-of" scene, taking turns to appear in their evening dress costumes and give a record to the camera of their activist performance.

The film ends with a taking stock of the position of political filmmaking in Berlin in 1968. Sander is shown addressing a student rally with a manifesto for the work of the filmmaker, making documents of the events of the time, but also asserting a function of activism and agitation. As if in response to the nefarious activities of the Dow Chemical concern in Farocki's film, the subversive work of the filmmakers is represented here as a form of "technical-chemical" production. The speech is shot from behind, so that the filmmaker, with cigarette in hand, takes the place of the capitalists in the car, plotting the takeover of Berlin at the start. Although the film ends with a rousing street rally and the singing of the "Internationale," led by a group of activists with allegorical identity signs around their necks—"Student," "Presenter," etc.—it also registers the stalling of the attempt to overcome the activities of the Springer concern through a radical "Gegenöffentlichkeit" or counterpublic sphere. The shots of burning Springer vans have more the character of historical document than inflammatory incitement. (See Figure 3.3.) As Sander later recounted, the film found little resonance with the oppositional forces of 1968.[50] As such, it looks toward a set of different post-1968 trajectories. Sander would engage increasingly with filmmaking around feminist concerns, and Farocki around broader Marxist ones, both of them adopting the position of El Lissitzky, as voiced by Farocki in Sander's film: "I don't however wish to exchange politics for art, but to mediate between the two." Meins, on the other hand, would abandon the camera for the gun after his student filmmaking career. The rest is history, and the stuff of history films.[51]

NOTES

1. The emphatic form of the title (*NOT Extinguishable Fire*) is often elided in references and is lost in the standard English translation.

2. Although the attribution of the film to Meins has often been framed as less than certain, his personal notes in the archive of the Deutsche Film und Fernsehakademie Berlin (DFFB) make it clear that he was indeed the director. The DFFB papers are now held in the archive of the Deutsche Kinemathek in Berlin, and I am grateful for the opportunity to access the papers and discuss them here.

3. The promulgation of the Oberhausen Manifesto by a set of younger filmmakers at the Eighth West German Short Film Festival in 1962 is generally seen as the birth of German cinema's new wave, disrupting the conservative disposition of the postwar cinema of the fathers. The press conference that launched the movement carried the title "Papas Kino ist tot" ("Daddy's cinema is dead").

4. The discourse of the time was saturated with (more or less) figurative references to explosions. Recording the failure of the revolt at the Berlinale, the film critic, Enno Patalas, wrote in the leading liberal weekly, *Die Zeit*, that "there's a desire to blow the establishment to high heaven. Quite right. But where should the powder be put and how should the fuse be laid?" ("Das Elend mit der Taktik" [The Misery of Tactics], *Die Zeit*, July 5, 1968). And an article in August 1968 in the progressive journal *Filmkritik* saw the violent refusal of the students to have their films screened at the festival (as a concession from the organizers in response to their protests) as amounting after all to a "fatal explosion"; quoted in *Zehn Jahre Deutsche Film- und Fernsehakademie Berlin 1976*, ed. Hans Helmut Prinzler (Berlin: DFFB, 1976), 85.

5. Two years later, the 1970 Berlinale was indeed terminated by protests, following the scandal of the selection for screening of Michael Verhoeven's *O.K.*, which

transposed a Vietnam War crime—a gang rape and killing of the rape victim by U.S. soldiers—to the Bavarian woods. The breakdown of the festival, after the threatened walkout of the President of the Jury, American director George Stevens, led to a substantial revision of the festival's structure.

6. *The Chronicle of Anna Magdalena Bach* by Straub and Huillet was also shown at the Berlinale in 1968, but although conceived as a work of protest against the political and economic status quo, not least in the film industry, its studied aesthetic means, with elaborate attention to compositional detail in *longue durée* and the historic removal of its narrative, are very different to the formal and thematic preoccupations of the films to be discussed here. The film appears to chart an alternative path to the programmatic logic of the subtitle of their 1965 film, *Nicht Versöhnt* (*Not Reconciled*): *Only Violence Helps Where Violence Reigns*.

7. Harun Farocki notes how he and Meins had been deeply impressed by Michael Snow's *Wavelength*, one of the few films they chose not to disrupt when they attended the Knokke Experimental Film Festival in December 1967/January 1968. See Tilman Baumgärtel's conversation about Meins with Farocki, "Holger dachte Ästhetik und Politik zusammen" ("Holger Thought Aesthetics and Politics Together"), http://busyreadywhat.org/Authors/Farocki,%20Harun/farocki%20ueber%20meins.html (accessed April 28, 2016).

8. Straub and Nestler are mentioned as potential models in notes by Holger Meins, held in the DFFB archive. Nestler, an early exponent of the radical film essay (such as *Aufsätze* [*Essays* 1963]) or *Ein Sheffielder Arbeiterclub* (*A Working Men's Club in Sheffield* [1965]) was frozen out of documentary film production for German television in the mid-1960s and emigrated to Sweden.

9. In 1968, the Springer Group controlled 70 percent of the newspaper market in Berlin. See Gerd Conradt, *Starbuck Holger Meins: Ein Porträt als Zeitbild* (Berlin: Espresso, 2001), 72.

10. When it opened in 1966, the Academy was heavily oversubscribed, and Rainer Werner Fassbinder was one of those who failed to be selected. This suggests an interesting counterfactual narrative for Fassbinder but also for film in Berlin in 1968.

11. The Springer building, standing in the area known during the Weimar Republic as "Die Zeitungen" ("The Newspapers") after the press concerns located there, occupies a site with a particularly fraught history, from the revolutionary street battles of 1919 onward. See Andrew J. Webber, *Berlin in the Twentieth Century: A Cultural Topography* (Cambridge: Cambridge University Press, 2008), 123, 173.

12. A number of the agitprop films produced at this time used the Springer highrise as a demonstrative target for attack from the streets.

13. The "Topography of Terror" is the commemorative name that has been given to the central area of Berlin where the headquarters of the Gestapo and other organs of the National Socialist state were located. It can be extended to the terrorizing control that was exerted over the space of the capital, and from there over the wider domains of the Third Reich. See: http://www.topographie.de/en/ (accessed August 21, 2014).

14. In the German Democratic Republic, dissidence generally took the form of attention to formal experiment and complex subjectivity, in defiance of the party line—an example would be Konrad Wolf's *Der geteilte Himmel* (*Divided Heaven*, 1964), based on Christa Wolf's narrative of the same name.

15. In the most high-profile case, Gudrun Ensslin and Andreas Baader were among those who used incendiary devices to set fire to two department stores in Frankfurt (April 2, 1968).

16. A particularly explicit example was Ulrich Knaudt's *Unsere Steine* (*Our Stones*, 1968).

17. The DFFB archive holds many documents that testify to the character of these institutional struggles over rights and contractual duties. In particular, a group of students were charged with having broken into the projection room of the Academy and stolen copies of their films in order to show them without permission at the Pesaro Festival of New Film.

18. See the flyer written by Thomas Giefer, cited in: Tilman Baumgärtel, *Vom Guerillakino zum Essayfilm: Harun Farocki, Werkmonografie eines Autorenfilmers* (Berlin: b_books, 2002), 73.

19. Dutschke narrowly survived when he was shot on a Berlin street by a right-wing extremist in April 1968, and many on the left held the conservative press—the Springer concern in particular—responsible for inciting the assassination attempt.

20. This was shot by Thomas Giefer, who also filmed other demonstrations around that time.

21. It emerged in 2009 that the police officer who killed Ohnesorg—Karl-Heinz Kurras—was secretly working for the Stasi, the East German State Security Force.

22. The programmatic identification of Berlin with Hanoi or Tehran arose recurrently in the discourse of radical groups. When the Brussels department store, A l'innovation, was burned down, the Kommune 1 published a flyer under the title "When will Berlin Department Stores Burn?" claiming that Brussels had become Hanoi, with Berlin next in line.

23. There is, of course, a well-established tradition of understanding the shooting of films as a form of virtual force, and the radical filmmakers at work in Berlin around 1968 repeatedly deployed the rhetoric of film as instrument of counterviolence. See also the poster by students of the DFFB, which trains a camera and gun barrels in the same direction, in Baumgärtel, *Vom Guerillakino*, 35.

24. See Farocki, "Holger dachte Ästhetik und Politik zusammen." The two media scenes are also the repeated focus of the memory work in Gerd Conradt's book and film, *Starbuck Holger Meins* (2002).

25. Ibid.

26. Harun Farocki, "Staging One's Life: Images of Holger Meins," in *Harun Farocki: Working on the Sight-Lines*, ed. Thomas Elsaesser (Amsterdam: Amsterdam University Press, 2004), 83–91, 83.

27. Thus, the Springer Press gratuitously compared the breaking of their windows to the *Reichskristallnacht*.

28. See Farocki, "Holger dachte Ästhetik und Politik zusammen."

29. Meins's notes in the DFFB archive embrace some of the key tenets of Brecht's epic theater, such as the principle of proceeding through breaks rather than organic continuity and the focus on humans as changeable and as agents of change.

30. The *Straßenfilm* was a key genre, cast between urban realism and melodrama, in the cinema of the Weimar Republic, and its co-option for more radical purposes here involves a strategic understanding of the city street as the proper scene of film activism.

31. The interview is included in Conradt's film, *Starbuck Holger Meins*.

32. For Farocki's account of the film, see his "Staging One's Life," 87–90.

33. The focus on work by hand and passing between hands is clear in the reconstruction included in the film *Starbuck Holger Meins*. The manual emphasis clearly goes beyond a wish to protect the identities of the participants.

34. Interviewed in *Starbuck Holger Meins*, Farocki sees such actions as the disruption of the Knokke Film Festival as concerned with learning for the performers, on the *Lehrstück* model.

35. The lawyer and activist Horst Mahler was accused by the Springer Group of being responsible for the damage sustained by their headquarters in the protests of 1968. See Tilman Baumgärtel, "Die Rolle der DFFB-Studenten bei der Revolte von 1967/68," http://www.infopartisan.net/archive/1967/266705.html (accessed September 1, 2012). In its report of the event with the screenings, the Springer paper *Berliner Morgenpost* (February 3, 1968) described these as introduced by the slogan, "Wie stelle ich einen Molotow-Cocktail her?" (How Do I Produce a Molotov Cocktail?), and co-opted this for the title of the article.

36. See Holger Meins file, DFFB archive.

37. For an account of the history of napalm production, use, and representation and the role played by Dow Chemical, see: Robert M. Neer, *Napalm: An American Biography* (Cambridge, MA: Harvard University Press, 2013).

38. Elsaesser, ed., *Harun Farocki*, 18.

39. See Helke Sander-Lathela file, DFFB archive.

40. See, for instance, the reading of the film in my *The European Avant-Garde, 1900–1940* (Cambridge: Polity Press, 2004), 156–165.

41. See also Elsaesser, ed., *Harun Farocki*, 26.

42. Farocki notes this in an interview in *Starbuck Holger Meins*.

43. For Baumgärtel, the scene marks Farocki's subscription to artistically mediated rather than direct action. Tilman Baumgärtel, "Bildnis des Künstlers als junger Mann: Kulturrevolution, Situationismus und Focus-Theorie in den Studentenfilmen von Harun Farocki," in *Der Ärger mit den Bildern: Die Filme von Harun Farocki,* ed. Rolf Aurich and Ulrich Kriest, (Konstanz: UVK Medien, 1998), 155–171.

44. The laboratory tables are used to demonstrate the effects of napalm but also to stage the stylized exploratory conversations between researchers, who speak through elaborate screens of laboratory apparatus. The figure of Mr. Dow is shown lighting a cigarette while justifying the use of napalm to his secretary.

45. The DFFB students played with the idea of establishing a pirate television channel broadcasting from next to the Berlin Wall.

46. The film is not Sander's in any straightforward authorial sense, any more than those ascribed here to Meins or Farocki are theirs. As the chalked credits at the start indicate, this is understood as an ensemble production, with both named collaborators, such as Farocki, and "others from the anti-authoritarian camp."

47. The DFFB archive includes, for instance, official requests by Sander to film in Tempelhof Airport and the city abattoir, as well as for access to the Moabit prison and courtroom by Meins and the Möckernbrücke subway station by Farocki.

48. The later scene in a subway train, with a chorus of approval for the Springer tabloid, *Bild*, alludes to a similar scene at the end of *Kuhle Wampe*. The chalking of circles around Dutschke's shoes also echoes the chalk outline of the corpse of the young jobless Bönike in the earlier film.

49. Another example of such masquerade technique was the infiltration by student filmmakers of a Hoechst factory to expose exploitative workplace practices.

50. See http://www.helke-sander.de/filme/brecht-die-macht-der-manipulateure/ (accessed September 1, 2014).

51. The afterlife of Berlin 1968 is featured, for instance, in Edel's *The Baader Meinhof Complex* (2008).

4

Slouching toward Chicago in Search of Peace and Love: *Medium Cool* and Chicago 1968

JON LEWIS

In Chicago in August 1967, a full year before the Democratic National Convention of 1968, three thousand delegates from over two hundred progressive organizations descended on the city to attend the National Conference for a New Politics.[1] Prominent on the agenda was the "Dump (President Lyndon) Johnson" campaign introduced by the future congressman Allard Lowenstein and the activist Curtis Gans at a convention of the National Student Association a few months earlier. One group at the convention floated a provocative and unrealistic third-party slate with the Reverend Martin Luther King Jr. at the top of the ticket and the pacifist children's health care author Dr. Benjamin Spock as his vice president. Others promoted more mainstream and more practical alternatives from within the Democratic Party: the antiwar senators Eugene McCarthy from Minnesota, Frank Church from Idaho, and George McGovern from South Dakota. Though none of these senators had publicly announced an intention to enter the race so long as Johnson planned to run, many in the New Left were already looking forward to mounting a challenge to the incumbent at the convention the following August.

Two months later, in October 1967, the Mobe, the National Mobilization Committee to End the War in Vietnam, organized a demonstration outside the Pentagon. The event drew an astonishing one hundred thousand antiwar protestors. To discuss plans for building on the momentum achieved by the protest, the Administrative Committee of the Mobe convened again in December in New York. In attendance: Rennie Davis, a Chicagoan and prominent SDS (Students for a Democratic Society) organizer; the Mobe chairman David Dellinger; and Tom Hayden, SDS founding member and author of that organization's formative document, all of whom in a year's time would become famous defendants among the so-called Chicago Seven.[2] It was at this meeting that the leadership of the antiwar movement stopped talking about backing peace candidates and started talking about organizing something big and dramatic on the streets of Chicago during the convention.[3]

Planning for convention week protests was foremost on the agenda two months later at a meeting in Lake Villa, Illinois, about fifty miles from Chicago. Among the estimated two hundred participants, in attendance were Davis and Hayden as well as Abbie Hoffman and Jerry Rubin, the cofounders of the Yippie faction. A consensus emerged that success in Chicago hinged upon the number of protestors willing to make the trip and make the scene.[4] Exactly what those protestors might do once they got to Chicago remained very much a topic to finesse over the coming months.

"My Kind of Town (Chicago Is) . . ."[5]

> In any other city, they would have technologies to silence the beasts with needles, quarter them with machines, lull them with Muzak, and have stainless steel for doors and aluminum beds to take over the old overhead trolley—animals would be given a shot of vitamin-enrichment before they took the last ride. But in Chicago they did it straight, they cut the animals right out of their hearts—which is why it was the last of the great American cities . . . greedy, direct, too impatient for hypocrisy, in love with honest plunder . . . Yes, Chicago was a town where nobody could ever forget how the money was made. It was picked up from floors still slippery with blood.
>
> —NORMAN MAILER, *Miami and the Siege of Chicago* (1968)[6]

In the late summer of 1968 when the Oscar-winning cinematographer Haskell Wexler arrived in Chicago with a skeleton cast and crew to shoot a feature film eventually titled *Medium Cool* (released a full year later in August 1969), he did so because something cinematic and dramatic, something historically significant seemed certain to happen there. The newspapers had serially reported on the various plans and provocations of the New Left. And Chicago mayor Richard J. Daley had responded with the promise of a city inhospitable to out-of-town protestors. The antiwar and civil rights movements were banking on a huge turnout that, like the Pentagon protest, would by its sheer scale and scope provide a public forum for their policies and goals. Daley, who rather embraced his role as a standard bearer for the law-and-order crowd, was gearing up for a showdown.

In his discussion of the weeks leading up to the convention, Todd Gitlin, the noted historian of the sixties, contends that the forces converging upon Chicago had one thing in common; they were all really angry: "Rage was becoming the common coin of American culture," Gitlin writes, and, in August 1968, this rage "dovetailed with strategy," as the leaders of the antiwar movement were driven "to test themselves ... finding out how far [they] were willing to go for [their] beliefs, and finding out how far the American government was willing to go in suspending the better part of its tradition to stop [them]."[7] Wexler, who had been following the news as he developed his film project, planned to be there to get it all on film.

Haskell Wexler was born in Chicago in 1922 and his first credits as a cameraman were in industrial and short documentary films produced there. In an interview with the *Chicago Sun-Times* film reviewer Roger Ebert published a month before the film opened, Wexler put his successful decade-long run as a Hollywood cinematographer in context to his Chicago roots: "I am a Chicagoan . . . Chicago is a real place and LA is a motel." Wexler's keen understanding of Chicago landscape and architecture imbue *Medium Cool* with a sense of what "Chicago is" . . . especially, what Chicago was like in the summer of 1968. But that understanding and appreciation fueled a profoundly negative piece of public relations for the city. In the interview, Wexler expressed his regrets: "I hope people won't think *Medium Cool* is against Chicago, I feel romantic about the place. And I wanted to make the movie in Chicago, I guess, mostly because I know the place and I know the feel of it. I didn't have to ask anyone where Fullerton was, or Diversey."[8]

Wexler shot virtually all of *Medium Cool* on location in Chicago. And his commitment to location sets and setting made for an unusual feature film shoot. With most commercial American films there is a fundamental gap and a fundamental production-stage division of labor between setting and narrative. The establishing shots of buildings, streets, landmarks, and remarkable geographic spaces and places are meant primarily to locate the story and situate the viewer. This footage suggests in the grammar of moviemaking that the fictive drama is taking shape in some real, recognizable place. In most commercial films, the narrative is shot separately and out of sequence, following a production plan and daily call sheet depending on access to soundstages, various constructed sets, production equipment, cast, and crew. The primary and second units' productions are then assembled in the editing room to create continuity and verisimilitude between the narrative sequences and the nonfiction geographic and architectural footage. What happens with these two types of footage in *Medium Cool* is at once more interesting and less calculated; the convention riots captured by

Wexler on the streets of Chicago became the primary narrative; the scripted scenes, adapted rather freely from an original story idea preliminarily titled *The Concrete Wilderness*, became what scriptwriters call "the satellite story." The fictive characters from the satellite story (the TV cameraman John Cassellis, the former West Virginia schoolteacher Eileen, and her precocious son Harold) literally wander into the kernel or A-story on the city streets. As a result, the film transgresses the boundaries of documentary and fiction, roughly following the urban historian Lewis Mumford's elegant cinematic metaphor for the contemporary metropolis as "a stage upon which the drama of social life may be enacted . . . with the actors taking their turns as spectators and the spectators as actors."[9] Taking the metaphor to its logical next step, the scripted actors in *Medium Cool* take their place as spectators in a drama that is bigger and more interesting than the one in which they had been hired to perform.

Wexler's merging of narrative and location work in *Medium Cool* is exemplary because his location choices were not a matter of luck or of happenstance; if we track the well-publicized advance planning for the demonstrations we can see how he managed to so often be in the right place at the right time. For example, in July 1968, Rubin and Hoffman applied for a permit for demonstrators to camp in Lincoln Park about two miles north of the Chicago Loop and a second permit to rally adjacent to Soldier Field and the Field Museum of Natural History on the lakefront south of the Loop—an area now known as the Museum Campus. The Mobe applied for permits to rally at the International Amphitheater, where the convention was to be held, and in Grant Park. All these sites figure prominently in the scripted narrative. For example, Wexler set Eileen's search for her son Harold along the demonstration route, lingering significantly in Lincoln Park. And he shot a lovely scene of Harold on stage under the bandshell in Grant Park delivering his innocent but nonetheless telling parody of the convention speeches. (See Figure 4.1.)

In the interview with Ebert, Wexler acknowledged that his anticipation of real events made for a powerful setting for his film.

> EBERT: "You knew you'd be making the film during the Democratic convention . . . [and] when things broke loose, did you decide on the spot to include that in your film?"
>
> WEXLER: "The script didn't specify long shots in Grant Park, or anything like that . . . But there were riots in the script. We anticipated them. We knew something would happen somewhere, and we knew that our TV reporter would naturally be involved in them."[10]

Figure 4.1 Harold on stage under the bandshell in Chicago's Grant Park in *Medium Cool* (Wexler, 1969)

The challenge for Wexler was not a matter of finding the demonstrations but instead a matter of using the demonstrations dramatically. Much of the demonstration footage is composed of groups of people walking from one place to another; the action itself is for the most part visually uninteresting. But in *Medium Cool*, this aimless locomotion functioned beautifully for Wexler as a means of building suspense in the fictional narrative and in his retelling of the riots. The footage of the ambling throng suspends an action that was all but inevitable in 1968 (as he shot the footage) and for filmgoers in 1969 already part of a historical record. The footage carries a narrative function: the deflection of violent conflict to the end of the second act of the film's story. Although Wexler deftly regards a stylistic intersection between documentary and fiction film footage, his point is not to confuse or efface the distinctions between appearance and reality, fiction and nonfiction. Instead, he uses the handheld *cinéma vérité* style and elsewhere long lenses to simulate the "fly on the wall" technique popular at the time to diminish narrative at the expense of setting, to situate his story in a certain city at a certain specific and significant moment in time. The style allows him to tell a fictional story realistically and to give that story a historical setting and significance.[11]

In his conversation with Ebert, Wexler discussed the relationship between the documentary and narrative footage in the film: "Nothing is 'real.' When you take a camera down to Michigan Ave. and point it at what's happening, you're still not showing 'reality.' You're showing that highly seductive area that's in front of your camera."[12] But Wexler is really talking about another duality here: between subjectivity and objectivity. In an effort to evocatively capture a big American city at a big moment of history, in an effort to create a politically powerful and provocative work of art, he effaces distinctions between the real and the staged and in the process diminishes, as he suggests above, the significance of the distinctions between subjectivity and objectivity. As the influential film reviewer Vincent Canby of the *New York Times* wrote at the film's initial release:

> [*Medium Cool*] is an angry, technically brilliant movie that uses some of the real events of last year the way other movies use real places—as backgrounds that are extensions of the fictional characters. In addition to directing and photographing *Medium Cool*, Wexler also wrote it, designing a screenplay to utilize the anticipated demonstrations at the Democratic Convention as the climax of the movie itself. The result is a film of tremendous visual impact, a kind of cinematic "Guernica," a picture of America in the process of exploding into fragmented bits of hostility, suspicion, fear, and violence.[13]

Writing for the *Sun-Times*, Ebert focused on the emblematic function of Wexler's documentary and location footage: "Wexler doesn't see the hippie kids in Grant Park as hippie kids. He doesn't see the clothes or the life style, and he doesn't hear the words. He sees their function; they are there, entirely because the National Guard is there, and vice versa. Both sides have a function only when they confront each other. Without the confrontation, all you'd have would be the kids, scattered all over the country, and the guardsmen, dressed in civilian clothes and spending the week at their regular jobs.

So it's not what they are that's important—it's what they're doing there."[14] And the there there was Chicago, August 26–29, 1968.

"Jesus, I Love to Shoot Film"

> I have to tell you that the line 'Look out Haskell, it's real!' was done afterwards. I put it in because we were not shooting sounds [at the time]. But it was my intention and it was on my mind. If someone read my mind at the moment I was shooting and the fucking tear gas was coming at me in slow motion . . . something in me said those very words. When you're looking through the camera, in a sense you're not there: you are looking at the movie you're trying to make. When the tear gas came at me, it was a strong enough jab from the so-called real world to remind me that that ground glass with the etched 1.85 is no barrier to your lungs, to your eyes, to your face.
>
> —Haskell Wexler (2001)[15]

For one of the film's early documentary sequences, Wexler shot the city's elaborate preparation for the demonstrations. During these mock "riot games" we see in rehearsal National Guardsmen, police officers from the Chicago Police Department (CPD), and U.S. Army soldiers, all of whom were dispatched to Chicago to patrol the streets between August 26 and August 29. What we see in this scene is at once disturbing (army jeeps outfitted with concertina wire, combat-ready, meant for use in suppressing civil unrest) and comical (the police and guardsmen playacting as hippie protestors, donning dirty shorts and T-shirts, wearing wigs and makeup, looking much as they suspect the enemy might look in the coming days, but alas looking less like hippies than rowdy frat boys in drag on Halloween).

The scene includes an official filmed statement from the Brigadier General Richard T. Dunne, the commander of the Emergency Operations Headquarters of the Illinois Army National Guard. We see Dunne first in some found footage shot by the military, filmed in a static medium shot in what looks like an empty banquet hall. Wexler then cuts on image, so we hear Dunne's disembodied voice (a sound bridge, in editing parlance) while the action on screen chronicles the beginning of the riot simulation exercise. This separation of live image and recorded voice track—a technique employed a number of times in the film—is used here to juxtapose Dunne's placid, droning delivery of lines like "The Emergency Operations Headquarters was established last winter [1967–1968] for the purpose of planning and controlling operations in the event of civil disturbances," to disconcerting images of the jeeps and uniformed soldiers outfitted for war, destined to face off against demonstrators on the city's streets.

Doubling Wexler and fellow cameraman Michael D. Margulies's work as filmmakers of the riot simulation is the actor Robert Forster as Cassellis, (inoperable) TV camera on his shoulder, capturing the dry run in character. The scene ends with a disturbing and complex mix of humor and horror, of playacting and foreshadowing, as one of the soldiers shouts: "Let's get the guys with the cameras." The Guardsmen run at and then past Forster/ Cassellis and continue to advance toward Wexler. A Guardsman's hand covers the lens, a gesture Wexler uses in his editing of the sequence as a wipe to cue the end of the scene. What is on the one hand another self-conscious reference to the presence of the camera in direct cinema (what Wexler intended when he shot this footage in the days before the convention)[16] would prove to be disconcertingly prescient as television journalists would be rather frequent victims of the Emergency Operations force.

In the months after the convention, when Wexler edited this footage in post-production, he realized that he had something more profound than the Pirandellian "play within a play" or "film within a film" conceit. So in continuity editing, he cannily juxtaposed this sequence to events that roughly matched those predicted in the exercise, events that, when they played out on the streets of Chicago, could hardly be viewed as a joke. The nuanced docudrama, then, in *Medium Cool* offers a sixties' American neorealism: real locations, a mix of professional and nonprofessional actors, a focus on poverty and the real lives of real Chicagoans. Here and elsewhere in the film, there is the risk of exploitation; when Wexler shot the training exercise, for example, he knew that a realization of the rehearsal was bound to occur. And, assuming that one goal, if not the primary goal, was the acquisition of great footage and not the prevention of or aversion to violence, Wexler and his cast and crew indisputably got what they came for.[17]

The degree of success Wexler enjoyed in acquiring powerful footage prompted the director on more than one occasion to indulge some on-screen self-examination and self-incrimination, observing and analyzing through his fictive counterpart, John Cassellis, the peculiar ethical dilemma posed by his endeavor. John is introduced in a shocking early sequence as an "ambulance chaser," obtaining car accident footage for the local news before calling the cops or an ambulance. The point even this early on is not that the cameraman is crass or insensitive. Instead, we are meant to view him as naive, because like many other Americans who witness the events in Chicago, he is, whether he likes it or not, about to be radicalized. In such a narrative arc, John becomes smarter about his line of work, which we see as he storms into the station manager's office to object to the FBI screening of the footage he's shot. But indicatively, political awareness doesn't do him much good professionally—he gets fired—or personally, as he fails to survive the convention. When John listens to King's "I Have a Dream" speech in Eileen's apartment on TV, we discover that his naiveté is rooted in a single-minded devotion to the image above and beyond the spoken word: "Jesus, I love to shoot film." In the mounting spectacle on the streets of Chicago, John's myopic remark seems for Wexler a trenchant bit of self-reflection as well as a setup for the character's radicalization as the week drags on.

In an earlier scene, during a postcoital conversation with his girlfriend, Ruth, John renders explicit his devotion to doing his job as an objective cameraman. His single-mindedness, his apolitical attitude at this point in the film, comes under fire when Ruth ponders, as a parallel to John's occupation as a news gatherer, the ethics of the documentarians who shot the recently released *Mondo Cane* (Paolo Cavara, Gualtiero Jacopetti, and Franco E. Prosperi, 1962).

> RUTH: You remember that scene on an island where they tested an atom bomb.
> JOHN: Ya.
> RUTH: Well, there were these big turtles. You know tortoises—who at a certain time in their lives would walk to the sea to lay their eggs. They found that the radiation thing threw the turtles' sense of direction, so instead of heading to the sea, they went inland and they died.
> JOHN: (sarcastic) Oh, I'm crying.
> RUTH: Dammit! Look-it. Somebody took those movies, right? I mean, do you think... did they, after they took those movies... did they reach down and turn those turtles around? Or did they put them in a jeep and drive them back?
> JOHN: How the hell do I know what they did? Those were Italian cameramen.

John's inability or reluctance to appreciate Ruth's argument would have further resonance for Wexler in his dealings with some of his real-life human subjects, most importantly Harold, Eileen's son, who is played in the film by Harold Blankenship, a local boy Wexler found on the streets of Uptown Chicago's Little Appalachia. Paramount paid Harold $300 a week—a lot of money for the boy and his family. But while the exchange of cash for this brief period of acting work required for the film might have been standard operating procedure for the employment of local nonunion talent, what Wexler did and what he did not do for Harold raises certain fundamental questions regarding the filmmaker's responsibility to not just the film he or

Figure 4.2 The squalor of Little Appalachia in Chicago in *Medium Cool* (Wexler, 1969)

she is making but to the larger community into which the film intrudes. Using Wexler's analogy (as expressed by Ruth and misunderstood by John), did Wexler have the responsibility to turn Harold around? Or was his responsibility to gather news and assemble footage (like John in the film; like Cavara, Jacopetti, and Prosperi, the directors of *Mondo Cane*) and to leave the larger questions inherent in the footage for another day, another agency more attuned to the social issues in play?

Blankenship's performance, if that's what we should call it, is fully improvised. It had to be; he couldn't read. When John tries to forge a relationship with Harold (the character), he takes him to the boxing gym and then back to his apartment for a shower—the real Harold Blankenship's first ever. Much as Harold and many other denizens of Uptown's "hillbilly heaven" felt like outsiders in the big city in 1968, Harold must have found the lives and lifestyles of the L.A.-based cast and crew alien as well. The shoot was probably a lot of fun for Harold, but it is fair to wonder what the filmmakers' responsibility to him should have been while the film was being shot and, perhaps more importantly, afterward. Should someone have taught him to read and helped him to escape the squalor of Little Appalachia? (See Figure 4.2.) Or is the role of the documentarian, which is what Wexler is most of the time during the production and postproduction of *Medium Cool*, simply to chronicle and report, an endeavor John in the film discovers to be empty, complicit (with the authorities who seize his film, for example), and impotent ("the whole world is watching," but nothing gets changed).

Whatever happened to Harold Blankenship after *Medium Cool* is a question answered by the documentary filmmaker Paul Cronin in his 2006 film *Sooner or Later*.[18] Intercut with images from *Medium Cool*, we find Harold thirty-eight years later back in West Virginia and rather down on his luck. He is living with his sister and her husband and reflects back on a feckless existence characterized by serial disappointment, unemployment, and past problems with alcohol and drugs. Conspicuously absent is a discussion of his experiences with Wexler and others from the cast and crew of *Medium Cool*. His entire Chicago experience is dismissed in a sentence or two; the place wasn't for him, and while things haven't gone all that well back home either, the film does well to show a man comfortable in his surroundings if at the same time not so comfortable in his own skin.

The Concrete Wilderness

> A boy and a dog story with a difference.
> —*Kirkus*'s book review of Jack Couffer's *The Concrete Wilderness* (1967)[19]

Before he made *Medium Cool*, Wexler had directed only two short films, both documentaries: *The Living City* (an "industrial" produced for the *Encyclopedia Britannica* in 1953) and *The Bus* (a film account of a 1963 civil rights protest in Washington, DC, released in 1965). He was far better known at the time as a cinematographer; he won his first of two Oscars for *Who's Afraid of Virginia Woolf* (Mike Nichols, 1967) and had an enviable list of DP (Director of Photography or Cinematography) credits including *The Loved One* (Tony Richardson, 1965), *In the Heat of the Night* (Norman Jewison, 1967),

Figure 4.3 Kids on the street in Bronzeville, around 35th and State Streets, on the South Side of Chicago in *Medium Cool* (Wexler, 1969)

racial profile as it was for its desperate poverty as most of the city's educated, successful African Americans, even those who had grown up in Bronzeville, had by the late sixties left for safer neighborhoods. (See Figure 4.3.)

In the film, Gus (Bonerz), John's sound man, stands in for most white filmgoers at the time; while on the South Side, he worries about the car, the audio and video equipment, and his own safety. For a vignette early in their visit to the neighborhood, Wexler asked Bonerz and Forster to stay in character while they went to a store to buy cigarettes. Wexler shot the scene with a telephoto lens from across the street. A young man happens upon the scene, does not see the camera across the street, and accosts Bonerz/Gus who is waiting outside the store on the sidewalk. The dialogue is recorded at a low level, but what is audible—what is clear from the exchange—is an explicit threat.

> YOUNG MAN: What you doing 'round here, man?
> GUS: (nervous) Buying some cigarettes.
> YOUNG MAN: You ain't got no right comin' 'round here buyin' no cigarettes.
> Gus shifts his feet.
> YOUNG MAN: Don't come back here for no cigarettes . . . know what I mean?

Filming on the South Side was made possible by the longtime Chicago resident, civil rights activist, and writer Studs Terkel, who brokered a peace between Wexler and local denizens.[26] Absent Terkel's assurances, the assumption among many residents would have otherwise matched another part of Wexler's script, when John realizes that the footage he's shot for the news station has been commandeered by the FBI. Such a practice was indeed employed at the time, as the FBI's COINTELPRO program targeted Communists and after that the Black Panthers, SDS, and other progressive groups.[27] As Wexler reveals, political activists in the African American community in Chicago in the late 1960s suspected all white men with cameras and would have suspected Wexler—and his screen surrogate John—had he not had Terkel's help.

In the fictional story, John and Gus are assigned a public interest piece focusing on an honest cabbie named Frank Baker who turns over to the cops $10,000 he's found in his cab. The newsmen pay a visit to Frank's South Side Chicago apartment, and there they meet the cabdriver and several of his more militant friends, all played by African American Chicagoans.[28] Working mostly without a script, Wexler let the actors (the pros and the folks more or less playing themselves) improvise. The result is suitably uncomfortable and awkward, the very effect Wexler was going for.[29]

The scene ends as John gets the footage he needs and tries to exit Frank's apartment. Before he reaches the door he is intercepted by a young woman who wants to know why so few people of color are on TV. John tries to put her off. Her boyfriend intercedes, mostly to look good in front of her. Soon enough harsh words give way to a couple of angry shoves. Frank asks a friend to break it up. He does, but then this friend stops John from leaving:

> FRANK'S FRIEND: You came down here for some kind of jive interview. You did that. You came down here with fifteen minutes of a black sensibility. Now you don't understand that. You came down here to shoot fifteen minutes of what has taken 300 years to develop. Grief, you know. And all we're trying to explain to you is that you don't understand.
> JOHN: I do something. See, I do it well. That's my job.
> FRANK'S FRIEND: But you don't do it black enough. You can't. Because you're not black. We are.

The confrontation between Frank's friend and John is shot in medium-close-up, including the two-shot master and the shot/reverse shots of the dialogue and reaction. Just as Frank's friend delivers the line, "We are," we cut abruptly to a close-up on another of Frank's friends, who looks directly into the camera and in direct address offers the scene's payoff:

> FRANK'S OTHER FRIEND: You come in here and you say you've come to do something of human interest. It makes a person wonder—

whether you are going to do something of interest to other humans or whether you consider the person human in whom you're interested. And you have to understand that, too. You can't just walk in out of your arrogance and expect things to be as they are because you brought LaSalle Street with you, City Hall, and all the mass communications media. And you are the exploiters. You are the ones who distort, and ridicule, and emasculate us. And that ain't cool.[30]

The sophistication of the racial politics of this scene was for 1968 remarkable, a matter acknowledged by the notoriously cantankerous New York film critic John Simon in his 1969 review of the film:

[This scene] is perhaps the only instance in the American commercial film of racial tension caught root and branch. These blacks are intelligent and confused, decent yet terrifying, sequestered in their righteous indignation. The whites are nervously apologetic or defiantly logical, and neither attitude works . . . here as in many other scenes, a Hollywood film for the first time faces up to the wretchedness beneath our prosperity; dares to give us a political America, and one whose politics are not suffused with health.[31]

In addition to the visits to Uptown and the South Side, which use real locations to set fictional sequences, as part of the documentary portion of the film, Wexler shot a "man on the street" interview sequence in which we meet a handful of white college students outside a Robert Kennedy campaign office under the ever-familiar "L." (See Figure 4.4.) The vignette, recorded before Robert Kennedy was assassinated, offers an impromptu commentary delivered by one of the students on the government cover-up of the assassination of Robert's brother, President John F. Kennedy, in November 1963. The scene proves to be significant as throughout the film Wexler subtly insists on the complex way things connect, neighborhood to neighborhood, cause to cause. The scene also sets up Wexler's later imaginative staging in the film of the June 5, 1968, assassination of Robert Kennedy, which focuses on the reaction to the news by a handful of African American food service workers in a Chicago hotel. Here, Wexler uses a montage of settings to connect white college kids to black hotel workers and the Robert Kennedy assassination to the riot on the streets in Chicago two months later. The montage conflates and confuses live, documentary footage (the on-the-street interviews) with a staged re-creation (the hotel kitchen scene, shot in

Figure 4.4 White college students supporting Senator Robert Kennedy in a vignette near the beginning of *Medium Cool* (Wexler, 1969), and, later in the film, the Democratic National Convention inside the International Amphitheater

a real hotel kitchen featuring real hotel workers, is staged after the fact). Wexler began working on the film and shot the interview with the college students anticipating Robert Kennedy's successful nomination at the convention; his assassination was, of course, not in the script. But like a good documentarian, Wexler simply went where the story took him. And it took him to a realization that, even though the city was hopelessly segregated— his location work on the South Side proved that—those with a stake in this next election were somehow brought together by Kennedy. The assassina-

Figure 4.5 Location footage of real demonstrations and riots in Chicago, August 1968, from *Medium Cool* (Wexler, 1969)

tion, Wexler understood, promised to further disenfranchise the African American community (as dramatized in the Chicago hotel kitchen).

For the location work capturing the demonstrations and riots, Wexler's crew moved with relative ease even when the TV crews were bullied into retreat.[32] (See Figure 4.5.) The demonstration scenes, including the terrifying footage of police brutality, were picked up by the two cameramen, Wexler and Michael (Mike) Margulies, who appeared to authorities on the scene to be demonstrators who just happened to have cameras rather than professional filmmakers making a feature for Paramount Pictures. For most of the street action, sound was recorded live by Chris Newman, but it was not always or easily synched on location to the image track. The sound was in several scenes synchronized to the images in post-production. So, even when we hear the line: "Look out Haskell, it's real," we understand that the off-screen audio comments on the on-screen image, the disembodied voice is a reminder that the events we are watching are real, that they are not planned or staged. However, the dramatic structure here is complex: the disembodied voice is a narrator inside the text caught by surprise as events unfold around him. But like much of the sound in the film, the "voice-off" technique concealed that it was synchronized and, in this instance, that the remark itself was subsequently devised. It was uttered only after the fact.[33]

The interplay between fictive and documentary footage, sound, and narrative became a key issue in the newspaper and magazine reviews of the film. With the exception of art house screenings of Jean-Luc Godard's films, the interplay of real and fictive footage was not a technique or strategy American filmgoers had seen much before.[34] Ebert, for example, applauded the film's hybrid docudrama: "There are fictional characters in real situations (the woman searching for her son in Grant Park). There are real characters in fictional situations (the real boy, playing a boy, expressing his real interest in pigeons). The mistake would be to separate the real things from the fictional."[35] Far less flatteringly, Andrew Sarris, writing for the *Village Voice*, argued that the technique distracted from and diminished the film's political impact: "*Medium Cool* parades its innocence, clumsiness and simplemindedness as civic virtues while it confronts the Chicago charivari (shivari) of 1968 with footage, some documentary, some simulated, stuck together with the band-aid of broken-hearted liberalism."[36]

The key here, which both Ebert and Sarris miss, is not the contrivance of appearance versus reality, the overlaps between narrative and documentary. Instead, for Wexler, the direct cinema style had a fundamental and practical function; it afforded him and his crew easy access to contested sites whether he was shooting documentary or narrative scenes. For example, Wexler covered the action in Grant Park and Lincoln Park before and during the riots. When we first see Lincoln Park it is in a scene that reestablishes the increasingly thin narrative frame; at this point, the story of a mother looking for her son. First we see a bit of the Yippie "festival of life"—a guy with a snake, a hippie or two—but our eyes quickly turn to the background in which Wexler's camera spies a paddy wagon surreptitiously entering the park. A subsequent tracking shot through the park begins with the hippies but ends with orderly lines of police in riot gear—a sequence that without a single line of dialogue tells us what is about to happen, even though what is being shot is not scripted and is being recorded live. Whatever Wexler's goal is here—and that's a matter of conjecture at this point—at least part of the function of this location sequence is to set a fictional scene (of Harold wandering off . . . of Eileen frantically searching for him). But what he gets additionally is the unique capture of a live, real event as it unfolds before his camera.

Wexler later tracks past the Field Museum to counterpose the enduring image of Chicago as one of the great industrial age American cities with what current events and his film are about to do to that image. The Field Museum evolved out of the Columbian Exposition assembled for the World's Fair held in Chicago in 1893. Located at 1400 S. Lake Shore Drive, the neoclassical building is today, as it was in 1968, a monument to Victorian era classicism. What we see, however, what obstructs our view, looks quite like a military invasion: jeeps, trucks, and armed young men poised for riot. In the background after dark in another scene, we see the Wrigley Building and

Tribune Tower, but again the site is undercut by the marching throng out after curfew. Throughout the film we see familiar streets suddenly contested: black vs. white; young vs. old; dove vs. hawk. And finally, there are the provocative detours to parts of the city tourists and film crews seldom visited: Uptown and the South Side. Wexler leaves it to the viewer to connect the various stories and settings, but he nonetheless frames his travelogue: we are in Chicago, a city we at once recognize and do not recognize; a city that quite suddenly seems central to something big, awful, and irrevocable. He makes clear that what happens to folks in one part of the city relates to what happens to very different people in another. The net effect is a picture of not only what Chicago is noted for (the "L," the Lake, the museum, etc.) and what it's really like (the ghettos, the poverty) but also what the city would become in the American imaginary after the convention week.[37]

The riots are compelling but are situated within the larger context of Chicago: the real and the imagined city. Here again the critic John Simon applauds Wexler's resolve: "Wexler is an artist more than a polemicist . . . [which is] demonstrated by his having shot hours and hours' worth of riot footage, but [he] included only a chaste minimum, as severely pared down as if Aristotle had been looking over his shoulder at the movieola."[38]

Playing (with) the Media: Getting Played by the Media

> Just as Che needed Fidel and Costello needed Abbot, Jerry Rubin and I were destined to join forces. We both had a willingness to go beyond reason.
> —ABBIE HOFFMAN[39]

Hoffman and Rubin's plan to "bring hordes of freaks to the 1968 convention" was hatched during Christmas week 1967. Although the convention was still eight months away, the Yippie founders started putting out provocative press releases: "Join us in Chicago in August for an international festival of youth, music and theater . . . making love in the parks, singing, laughing, printing newspapers, making a mock convention and celebrating the truth of a FREE AMERICA in our own time."[40] What Rubin and Hoffman proposed was to remake the city from a built environment serving corporate and political power to a site for social protest, a public space in which to express at once a celebration of a counterculture lifestyle and political opposition to the war and to whomever the party nominated to perpetuate it. Rubin and Hoffman's press release seemed to promise a sort of Woodstock, itself a year away. But it also introduced into the media discourse the possibility of conflict, a conflict that, given Daley's later pronouncements also run in the press, promised a violent spectacle for Wexler's film.

In the months leading up to the convention, the New Left activists used the press to call attention to their plans for Chicago. What they didn't fully apprehend was how their bold pronouncements would be interpreted by the majority of the American public, especially the folks (like Daley) who felt most threatened by them. Many of the mainstream news sources blithely printed Rubin's outrageous claims that as many as five hundred thousand people were prepared to descend upon Chicago for the festival and demonstrations. Throughout the spring and early summer of 1968, the mainstream press found Rubin a particularly colorful character and ran his Yippie itinerary in full, including a simple handwritten plan for Wednesday, August 28: "riot."[41] This bit of boastful provocation on Rubin's part complicated things after the convention when he and seven others were indicted for breaking the so-called H. Rap Brown Act, the addendum to the Civil Rights Act that made it illegal to cross state lines with the intention of inciting a riot.[42] The alternative press, which was closely monitored by COINTELPRO, was steeped in provocation. The lead article in the August 5, 1968, issue of *New Left Notes*, for example, quoted SDS National Secretary Mike Klonsky's modest proposal: "Let's light the fuse and see what happens."[43] Writing for the *Realist*, America's oldest underground paper, Yippie founder Paul Krassner, in a variation on a theme from the B-movie *Wild in the Streets* (Barry Shear, 1968),[44] claimed that there were plans afoot to contaminate the Chicago water supply with LSD.[45]

Hoffman, Rubin, Klonsky, and Krassner posted a surfeit of boasts and provocations. And Mayor Daley responded in kind. In his "welcoming remarks" at the microphone at the amphitheater on August 27, Daley made clear what he thought of the threats posed by the counterculture leaders: "As long as I am Mayor of this city, there's going to be law and order."[46] In doing so, Daley laid claim to *his* city streets. And he used the confrontation to make a larger statement about law and order in the United States. Like Rubin and Hoffman, Daley had a political as well as a practical narrative in play when the demonstrations and riots ensued.

Point-of-fact: nothing like the five hundred thousand protestors Rubin had promised showed up. All told there were between ten thousand and fifteen thousand protestors on the streets. Assembled to meet this largely disorganized throng was the twelve-thousand-member Chicago Police Department, riot-ready thanks to the serial grandstanding of Hoffman, Rubin et al. In addition to the cops, almost six thousand regular army troops were airlifted into the area and six thousand Illinois National Guardsmen were mobilized. The underground newspaper editor Abe Peck posed a discomfiting parallel between Chicago during the convention and the Warsaw Pact invasion of Czechoslovakia, which had suppressed the Prague Spring just the week before: "Daley dozers—national guard jeeps with concertina wire laced to their hood furnished the proper motif for the image of Czech-ago."[47]

Chicago 1968: Now and Forever

> To you, the great silent majority of my fellow Americans, I ask for your support, for the more divided we are at home, the less likely the enemy is to negotiate at Paris. Let us be united for peace. Let us also be united against defeat because let us understand: North Vietnam cannot defeat or humiliate the United States. Only Americans can do that.
>
> —RICHARD NIXON, November 3, 1969[48]

If Daley indeed delivered the 1960 election to John Kennedy by mobilizing and maybe even rigging the vote in Illinois as many believed at the time, his handling of the protest on the streets in Chicago contributed significantly to Nixon's election in 1968. Indeed, Nixon used the disconcerting events in Chicago as ground zero for his law and order campaign. In his history of the American sixties, *Coming Apart*, William O'Neill put the post-Chicago '68 fallout in an appropriately Nixonian context: "Law and order could hardly be too viciously applied to suit people demoralized by years of war, protest, and youthful contempt for the bourgeois life."[49] The punch lines to very uncomical events in Chicago were that Nixon won the presidency and Mayor Daley got a lot of fan mail.

In December 1968, Dan Walker, a Montgomery Ward executive and former staffer for the Illinois Governor Adlai Stevenson, published *Rights in Conflict*, a.k.a. the "Walker Report." This study of the events in Chicago 1968 was culled from over three thousand eyewitnesses and compiled at the behest of the National Commission on the Causes and Prevention of Violence.[50] The report coined the apt term "police riot" to describe the events on the streets and blamed Daley for refusing to grant permits, a decision that forced demonstrators into confrontation with law enforcement. But blame seemed quickly beside the point after Nixon's stunning victory. What emerged after Chicago 1968 was a new American zeitgeist; the age of aquarius had unraveled all too quickly and what Hunter S. Thompson glibly termed the "doom-struck era of Nixon" began.[51] Chicago 1968 proved for many Americans that it was time to stop talking to these kids and start cracking some heads.

Wexler's film captures that impatience, that "end of the line" vibe. You see it in the hostility to even the best of intentions in the scenes in the African American ghetto on the city's South Side where the notion of "human interest" regards an impossible duality: a duality between a story interested in other humans and a story interesting to other humans . . . a duality that Wexler, the human interest filmmaker, struggles to sort out on screen. You see it in the willingness to suspend basic freedoms: the freedom to express political arguments, to congregate and demonstrate, and to carry on a public debate in front of a free press. The chant "the whole world is watching" accompanies not the political activity of a dedicated opposition, nor the full freedom of the so-called fourth estate, but instead the forced exit of network television cameras.

Much as the counterculture journalist Abe Peck re-dubbed his city "Czech-ago" to highlight the similarities between Chicago and Czechoslovakia in 1968 there were also confluences and similarities between the events in Chicago in August and another urban protest that same year, the general strike and ensuing civil unrest in Paris in May.[52] As Gitlin affirms, Paris, May 1968, was a signpost for many of the younger members of the American Left, at once an affirmation of possibility and a reminder of the complexity and risks inherent to an organized protest rooted in the radical politics routinely discussed on university campuses at the time: "In the radical imagination, the university, easily shaken by relatively small numbers, became a prototype for society as a whole—or at least raised the question: What if students and their allies threw themselves into all the gears? Couldn't they bring the entire works to a crashing halt? Hadn't they come close enough in France?"[53]

Gitlin's comparison between Paris and Chicago is apt in part because both protests identified the city in and of itself as the site of oppression and targeted said urban space for demonstration, occupation, and riot. In an edition of the *Internationale Situationniste*, published nearly seven years before the May events in Paris, Attila Kotanyi and Raoul Vaneigem foregrounded the Situationist critique of urbanism that so influenced the French students in May 1968, highlighting the seizure or occupation of urban space with regard to some future recalibration:

> ALL SPACE IS already occupied by the enemy, which has even reshaped its basic laws, its geometry, to its own purposes. Authentic urbanism will appear when the absence of this occupation is created in certain zones. What we call construction starts there. It can be clarified by the *positive void* concept developed by modern physics. Materializing freedom means beginning by appropriating a few patches of the surface of a domesticated planet.[54]

Further foregrounding urban protest in his 1967 Situationist manifesto, *The Society of the Spectacle*, Guy Debord concluded that the built environment "safeguards class power" and thus an attack on its security and safety, on its very organization of space, people, and money could be effective.⁵⁵ "The atomization of workers ... dangerously brought together by the urban conditions of production," Debord maintained, rendered political conflict (and class warfare) inevitable.⁵⁶

How well Wexler knew the work of the Situationists is a matter of conjecture. (The intellectual leaders of the New Left certainly did.) But he was familiar with the events in Paris in May and the films of the French New Wave, Godard in particular, and Godard was very much engaged in and by the events in Paris. Some of the references to Godard in *Medium Cool* are very much on the surface: Cassellis has a photograph of Jean-Paul Belmondo, who starred in Godard's 1960 film *Breathless*, on the wall in his apartment. When he is visiting Eileen and is listening with her to the TV broadcast of King's "I Have a Dream" speech, an unlikely network promo can be heard touting ("coming up next") Godard's 1963 film *Contempt*. Less obvious textual allusions abound. The penultimate scene of John and Eileen driving seems lifted right out of *Breathless*. The crash that ends the film is quite like the scene that ends *Contempt* and includes a flash forward that alludes to Godard's *Week End* (1967), a film that, like *Medium Cool*, complexly mixes and matches documentary footage, direct-address speeches, and a fictional story line. As he intercut documentary with fictional footage Wexler no doubt considered Godard's famous quip that "the cinema is truth at 24 frames per second."⁵⁷

The final shot of *Medium Cool* is an allusion to the Russian formalist documentarian Dziga Vertov and his 1929 film *Man with a Movie Camera*, an allusion that in 1968 was also a nod to the newly formed Dziga Vertov Group in France, founded in May 1968 by Godard and Jean Pierre Gorin. The camera points at us just as a teenage tourist's camera points at the wrecked car in which John and Eileen are killed: "When I say the whole world is watching," Wexler mused on a recent DVD commentary track, "what I'm saying is that someone else is taking a picture of us taking a picture."⁵⁸ Perhaps it is that simple, that *Medium Cool* is less a film that records an event and tells a story than a rumination on the process of gathering and then sifting through the wealth of footage that we come in contact with every day. In a media culture committed to the rule "if it bleeds, it leads," what Wexler reluctantly apprehends is that footage had by late 1968 become an end in itself.

Two car accidents frame the film, both of which feature mangled bodies, both of which are impassively photographed. Wexler wants to insist on the value of these images precisely because the fictive Chicago news agency that employs and summarily fires John does not. The anonymous death that opens the film is part of a little joke about cameramen as ambulance chasers. The latter accident kills off the male and female leads in the picture, but it too has a muted impact; the untimely death of two random people is dismissed with a line or two on the radio. It has been a big news day in Chicago after all, what with riots on the streets.

NOTES

1. The history recounted here was culled from a variety of sources. Foremost among these sources: David Farber, *Chicago '68* (Chicago: University of Chicago Press, 1988); Todd Gitlin, *The Sixties: Years of Hope, Days of Rage* (New York: Bantam, 1987); and Frank Kusch, *Battleground Chicago: The Police and the 1968 Democratic Convention* (London: Praeger, 2004). More general histories: William O'Neill, *Coming Apart: An Informal History of the 1960s* (Chicago: Ivan R. Dee, 1971); William Leuchtenburg, *A Troubled Feast: American Society since 1945* (Boston: Little, Brown, 1973); Marty Jezer, *The Dark Ages: Life in the United States, 1945–1960* (Cambridge, MA: South End Press, 1999); and Abe Peck, *Uncovering the Sixties: The Life and Times of the Underground Press* (New York: Citadel Press, 1991). Also useful, the following Internet sources: "Chicago '68: A Chronology," http://chicago68.com/c68chron.html; and "Federal Judicial Center: The Chicago Seven Conspiracy Trial," http://www.fjc.gov/history/home.nsf/page/tu_chicago7_doc_13.html. For a terrific bibliography on Chicago 1968, see http://chicago68.com/c68bibli.html.

2. The Chicago Seven included Rennie Davis, David Dellinger, Tom Hayden, Jerry Rubin, Abbie Hoffman, John Froines, and Lee Weiner. Bobby Seale was indicted as well—hence, the initial press headlines referring to the "Chicago Eight." However, the Black Panther activist so disrupted the proceedings (after being denied a postponement to enable his attorney, Charles Garry, time to recover from gallbladder surgery) that he was bound and gagged in the courtroom and, then, after being handed an astonishing four-year sentence for contempt of court, had his case severed from the others. The seven were defended by William Kunstler and Leonard Weinglass. The trial became one of the key events in the struggle between the anti-war counterculture and the so-called establishment. In February 1970, the defendants accused of crossing state lines to foment riot were found guilty after a trial that was easily as exciting and frightening to watch as the riots the defendants were accused of planning. The seven were sentenced to five years in prison and fines totaling $5,000. Judge Julius Hoffman issued numerous contempt citations during the trial to the defendants and their attorneys. Sentences for these offenses ranged from two-and-a-half months to four years. In 1972, most of the charges were dropped on appeal and then in October 1973, District Court Judge Edward T. Gignoux formally waived sentencing for the remaining offenses, citing "judicial error, judicial or prosecutorial misconduct." By then, the war was over and the Nixon presidency was unraveling as millions of Americans watched the Watergate hearings on TV.

3. See: David Farber, *Chicago '68* (Chicago: University of Chicago Press, 1988), 73–75, 82–83, 98–99, 100, 112, 165. That plans for demonstrations in Chicago were discussed so far in advance contributed to the case against Davis, Dellinger, and Hayden for violating the new antiriot law.

4. Douglas O. Linder, "The Chicago Seven Conspiracy Trial," *Famous American Trials*, http://law2.umkc.edu/faculty/projects/ftrials/Chicago7/Account.html.

5. The title of and a repeated lyric in a song made popular by Frank Sinatra in 1964. The Oscar nominated song was written by the composer Jimmy van Heusen with lyrics by Sammy Cahn for the Rat Pack musical *Robin and the Seven Hoods*, directed by Gordon Douglas.

6. Norman Mailer, *Miami and the Siege of Chicago* (New York: Plume, 1986), 223.

7. Todd Gitlin, *The Sixties: Years of Hope, Days of Rage* (New York: Bantam, 1987), 317–318.

8. Roger Ebert, "Haskell Wexler: See, Nothing Is 'Real,'" *Chicago Sun-Times*, August 10, 1969, http://www.rogerebert.com/interviews/haskell-wexler-see-nothing-is-real/.

9. Lewis Mumford, *The Urban Prospect* (New York: Harcourt, Brace, 1968), 184.

10. Roger Ebert, "Haskell Wexler."

11. In the Ebert interview, Wexler notes the importance and influence of Jean-Luc Godard to his juxtaposition of both the real and the fictive and documentary style and fictive narrative. Although Wexler does not explicitly mention *Easy Rider*, a huge box office hit released a month before *Medium Cool*, it is hard not to see the confluence between Wexler's and Dennis Hopper's fluid overlaps between types or styles of footage and their exploitation of real settings to set (and render realistic) fictional scenes. Wexler does mention Francis Ford Coppola's road picture *The Rain People*, released on the same day as *Medium Cool*, a film that also uses real settings and interactions with unprofessional actors to create something akin to an American neorealism.

12. Roger Ebert, "Haskell Wexler."

13. Vincent Canby, "*Medium Cool* (1969)," *New York Times*, August 28, 1969, http://www.nytimes.com/movie/review?res=9F05E4DF1031EE3BBC4051DFBE668382679EDE/.

14. Roger Ebert, "*Medium Cool*," *Chicago Sun-Times*, September 21, 1969, http://www.rogerebert.com/reviews/medium-cool-1969.

15. Wexler in an interview with the film director Paul Cronin in the "making-of" documentary *Look out Haskell, It's Real* (2001).

16. Acknowledging the camera, and sometimes the cameraman as well, was an aspect of the direct cinema style. In *Grey Gardens* (Ellen Hovde, Albert and David Maysles, Muffie Meyer, 1975), for example, one of the subjects in the film carries on a conversation with David Maysles, one of the filmmakers. The "truth effect" here is that the filmmaker acknowledges his framing of the story, his involvement with the participants, and his role in the true story he is telling.

17. Wexler went to Chicago anticipating a riot, but precisely what sort of riot is subject to some debate. My view is that the provocations serially placed in the media by publicity savvy anti-war activists along with Daley's hardly tempered media response to these provocations rather set the stage for trouble. So, whether Wexler got what "what he came for" may well be a matter of degree (it was worse than he expected). In an excellent essay on the film, Jonathan David Kirschner argues that Wexler anticipated something that might further highlight Chicago's racial divide and Daley and the CPD's violent reaction to civil rights activism: "[In] *Medium Cool*, as [he] was shooting, [Wexler] anticipated a race riot, not a police riot. Given what had happened, and what would happen, in American cities, this was not a bad guess, and would have more tightly linked

together several elements in the movie. Lines like 'do you realize how much guns and ammunition $10,000 would have bought,' and 'people are afraid the Negros are going to tear up their stores, burn neighborhoods,' not to mention the cut from black anger to white ladies at a shooting range (featuring a nice turn by Peter Boyle as the outfit's manager, interviewed for the news), would have seemed, if anything, too obvious in retrospect." See Kirschner, "The Whole World Is Watching," *Bright Lights*, no. 81 (2013), http://brightlightsfilm.com/81/81-medium-cool-counterculture-DVD-criterion-kirschner.php#.VJSxWue5Q.

18. The film is available on vimeo: http://vimeo.com/20546520. Also available on vimeo is Cronin's 2001 "making of" documentary, "Look out Haskell, It's Real": http://vimeo.com/64142316.

19. "*The Concrete Wilderness*," *Kirkus*, September 1, 1967, https://www.kirkusreviews.com/book-reviews/jack-couffer-2/the-concrete-wilderness/.

20. Wexler tells this story on a commentary track on the 2001 Paramount home video DVD.

21. Little Appalachia was a poor, white slum in Chicago that formed briefly in the 1950s and 1960s as middle-class whites moved out of Uptown and so-called white trash from Appalachia and the South moved in. The squalor on exhibit in *Medium Cool* was short lived, thanks in part to the work of SDS, which organized in the community in the early 1960s, and was followed by various other urban renewal projects. More recently, gentrification dramatically changed the neighborhood. For more on this neighborhood during the 1950s–1960s, see Todd Gitlin and Nancy Hollander, *Uptown: Poor Whites in Chicago* (New York: Harper and Row, 1970). For a powerful photographic study of Uptown in this era, see Danny Lyon, *Memories of Myself* (London: Phaidon Press, 2009).

22. J. R. Jones, "The Lost Chicago of *Medium Cool*," *Chicago Reader*, July 10, 2013, http://www.chicagoreader.com/chicago/medium-cool-haskell-wexler-studs-terkel-robert-forster-uptown/Content?oid=10298605. Relevant here: the presumptive nominee Robert Kennedy had in the months before the convention visited Appalachia and had made a point in the run up to the convention to talk about poverty as something of a "color blind" issue.

23. J. R. Jones, "The Lost Chicago of *Medium Cool*."

24. See: Clarus Backes, "Poor People's Power in Uptown," *Chicago Tribune*, September 29, 1968, I46.

25. For more on the history of Chicago's South Side, see Arnold R. Hirsch, *Making the Second Ghetto: Race and Housing in Chicago 1940–1960* (New York: Cambridge University Press, 1983).

26. Terkel is listed in the screen credits as "our man in Chicago" and his contributions to *Medium Cool* included his help in securing sites (including the scenes on the South Side) and casting. Verna Bloom, who plays Eileen in the film, had appeared in one of Terkel's plays, *Amazing Grace*. Bloom studied recordings of Little Appalachian residents to get Eileen's accent right. She was so successful that after the film's release she had difficulty finding work as casting directors assumed the accent was real. See: J. R. Jones, "The Lost Chicago of *Medium Cool*."

27. See: Todd Gitlin, *The Whole World Is Watching: Mass Media in the Making and Unmaking of the New Left* (Berkeley: University of California Press, 1980), 5–6. COINTELPRO was an acronym derived from COunter INTELligence PROgram. The

program was run by the FBI from 1956 to 1971. See Nelson Blackstock, *COINTELPRO: The FBI's Secret War on Political Freedom* (New York: Pathfinder, 1988).

28. Baker was played by the professional actor Sid McCoy, who by 1968 had appeared in episodes of *Mannix, The Wild West, Dragnet,* and *The FBI*. Others on hand for the partly scripted, partly improvised scene were Kuumba Theatre founder Val Grey Ward, *Soul Train* announcer Sid McCoy, the jazz musicians Muhal Richard Abrams and John Shenoy Jackson, and the visual artists Jeff Donaldson and Barbara Jones-Hogu.

29. Much as Wexler was aware of and likely viewed himself as a kindred spirit to the direct cinema documentarians of the era—his inside joke trying to cast the director D. A. Pennebaker as a journalist and later calling the Robert McAndrew character Pennebaker makes that clear enough—this stylistic gesture to direct cinema is complicated. Many among the Drew Associate Group—the former LIFE magazine editor Robert Drew, Pennebaker, Richard Leacock—and others prominent in the new documentary style (that eschewed narration, for example, and built upon new camera and sound technologies that enabled mobile, location production) was rather rooted in television news and nonfiction programming, the very medium and genre the partygoers at Frank Baker's apartment suspect. This is likely another bit of autocritique on Wexler's part, or, at least, a rumination on the ambivalence and ambiguity inherent in the project he is undertaking in *Medium Cool*.

30. LaSalle Street is a major north-south thoroughfare in Chicago. The reference here is to LaSalle Street's historical role as the site of the city's financial district.

31. John Simon, "*Medium Cool,*" *New Leader,* September 1969, http://www.thestickingplace.com/film/films/look-out-haskell-its-real/reviews/john-simon/

32. In addition to the footage in the film that captured the forced exit of a TV crew, see: Farber, 129, 182, 185–188, 201, and 204; and Kusch, *Battleground Chicago,* 75–78.

33. Wexler's commentary track on the 2001 DVD edition is the source here and elsewhere for production details.

34. Here again it is significant to note that *Easy Rider* and *The Rain People,* two films that similarly introduced the juxtaposition and interplay of documentary and fictive filmmaking techniques, were also released in the summer of 1969. *Easy Rider* premiered on July 14. *The Rain People* was released on August 27, the same day as *Medium Cool*.

35. Roger Ebert, "*Medium Cool,*" September 21, 1969, http://www.rogerebert.com/reviews/medium-cool-1969.

36. Andrew Sarris, "Arlo Guthrie: More Nowness Than Newness," *Village Voice,* 14, 46, August 28, 1969, http://blogs.villagevoice.com/runninscared/2010/08/arlo_guthrie_mo.php.

37. I can speak to this latter point directly; I was thirteen in 1968 and the images I have of Chicago are still very much a product of what I saw on television in the summer of 1968 and then again nearly a decade later in my first look, as a college student, at Wexler's film.

38. Simon, "Medium Cool." Also reprinted in Joseph Morgernstern and Stefan Kanfer, eds., *Film 69/70: An Anthology by the National Society of Film Critics* (New York: Simon and Schuster, 1970), 167.

39. Hoffman as quoted by Allen J. Matusow, *The Unraveling of America: A History of Liberalism in America* (Athens: University of Georgia Press, 2009), 412.

40. Rubin and Hoffman as quoted by Abe Peck, *Uncovering the Sixties*, 100.

41. Peck, *Uncovering the Sixties*, 100–114.

42. Bruce D'Arcus, *Boundaries of Dissent: Protest and State Power in the Media Age* (New York: Routledge, 2005), 64. See also: D'Arcus, "Protest, Scale, and Publicity: the FBI and the H. Rap Brown Act," *Antipode* 35, no. 4 (2003): 718–741. The act is officially known as the Federal Anti-Riot Act (1968).

43. Peck, *Uncovering the Sixties*, 111.

44. In *Wild in the Streets* (Barry Shear, 1968), after the voting age is dropped to 14, a rock star, Max Frost, becomes president. To please his constituents, Frost puts everyone over 30 into concentration camps and doses them with LSD. The film was produced by the B-movie impresario Samuel Z. Arkoff for American International Pictures (AIP).

45. O'Neill, *Coming Apart*, 383.

46. Kusch, *Battleground Chicago*, 74. See also: "Chicago '68: A Chronology," http://chicago68.com/c68chron.html and the *Chicago Sun Times*, August 27, 1968, 3.

47. Peck, *Uncovering the Sixties*, 113. The Warsaw Pact invasion of Czechoslovakia took place on August 20–21, 1968.

48. For full audio/video and a transcript of the speech, see: http://www.nixonlibrary.gov/forkids/speechesforkids/silentmajority.php.

49. O'Neill, *Coming Apart*, 387.

50. See: Daniel Walker, *Rights in Conflict: The Walker Report* (New York: Bantam, 1968).

51. Hunter S. Thompson, *Fear and Loathing in Las Vegas: A Savage Journey to the Heart of the American Dream* (New York: Vintage, 1998), 178.

52. See, Gitlin, *The Sixties: Years of Hope, Days of Rage*, 241, 243, 288, 345–346, 350, 372.

53. Gitlin, *The Sixties*, 345.

54. Attila Kotanyi and Raoul Vaneigem, "Basic Program of the Bureau of Unitary Urbanism," *Internationale Situationniste*, no. 6 (1961), translated by Ken Knabb, http://www.cddc.vt.edu/sionline/si/bureau.html. For a fuller picture of the Situationist International, see: *Situationist International Anthology*, ed. Ken Knabb (Berkeley: Bureau of Public Secrets, 1995).

55. Guy Debord, *Society of the Spectacle* (Detroit: Black and Red, 1977), 122.

56. Debord, *Society of the Spectacle*, 121.

57. A line of dialogue from Godard's film *Le Petit Soldat* (1963) and routinely attributed to the film's author.

58. Wexler's observations here are taken from his excellent commentary track on the Paramount Widescreen Collection edition of the DVD of *Medium Cool* (2001).

# 5

New York, 1968

STANLEY CORKIN

This chapter looks at three films of disparate origin and mode of production for their representation of, and participation in, the historical moment of 1968 and in particular that moment in New York City. I examine the underground documentary film *Columbia Revolt* (1968) by the Newsreel filmmaking collective, along with two theatrically released fictional films—*Greetings* (Brian De Palma, 1968) and *Midnight Cowboy* (John Schlesinger, 1969)—to locate images and narratives of New York City at that time. As I develop a sense of the historical moment, I also point to what I see as its ephemerality and note how the ways in which we read it are a matter of an embedded historical narrative. As we reach back through the sediment of the various salient descriptions and explanations of the late 1960s to attempt to see these films as documents that reelucidate a cultural moment, it is important to recognize that all narratives of that moment—and indeed any moment—are a matter of our own temporal/spatial/cognitive perch as we fix our eyes on the past. Indeed, if we look at New York, and the United States more generally, it is difficult not to see the limits of the radical political coalitions of the late 1960s—coalitions that included students from a range of racial and economic backgrounds and a multiracial/multiethnic/multigendered working class.

As I watch these films now, I know that Richard Nixon will soon be president, and that he will develop brilliant and nefarious strategies for disrupting such possible radical coalitions through his repeated pushing of the buttons of racial and class resentment.¹ My essay on 1968 is then one of both historicity and historiography, but my choice of films pushes my analysis toward a recognition of a multiplicity of perspectives and elaborates dissonance, rather than harmony, as I form the idea of "1968" from my evidence. *Columbia Revolt, Greetings,* and *Midnight Cowboy* are each distinctive in scale, emphases, and genre, and each emanates from a different point of origin in the era and provides a different point of access to its complexities. As such, the films resist being neatly tied together in a narrow elaboration of a historical zeitgeist. Although at the time of their release they were all very clearly part of the moment of historical change that we know as 1968, that moment becomes increasingly varied and complex retrospectively.

Indeed, it is the conjoining of these three films for the purpose of this historically grounded essay that allows for a reading of the complexity of the moment. These films are all, more or less, of 1968 but each presents and lends itself to a particular narrative of that year. For Schlesinger, in *Midnight Cowboy*, his Academy Award–winning film, 1968 in New York City was distinctive for its cultural fluidity, expressed by its dramatization of tensions between social classes, spaces, sexual mores, and values. *Greetings* offers a similar vision of cultural change but is a kind of wry comedy instead of Schlesinger's drama. Because of the international success of his films *A Kind of Loving* (1962), *Billy Liar* (1963), and *Darling* (1965), Schlesinger was already a significant filmmaker who could command a relatively large budget, but Brian De Palma was considerably younger and new to directing features, and *Greetings* provides an on-the-ground view of a slice of youth culture. *Columbia Revolt*, by contrast, is a work of political filmmaking by a group that was deeply involved in the New Left politics of the day and a film with much lower production values, made in 16mm and black-and-white where Schlesinger and De Palma worked in 35mm widescreen and in color. The disparities in modes of production among these three films allow us to see New York City in 1968 as a place in the midst of social and physical change that requires us to consider a number of salient topics, including the definition and scope of the student Left, the politics of culture, and the nature of the built environment.

New York and the 1968 Moment

Not only was 1968 the year in which Robert Kennedy and Martin Luther King were assassinated and mourned by millions, it was also the year in which George Wallace ran a very successful right-wing populist campaign for president, attracting millions of disaffected white voters. It was also the year in which Richard Nixon, advised by the young Roger Ailes (who would go on to fame and fortune as the CEO of Fox News), was elected president with the slogan "Bring us together," a line that sought to marginalize those who had torn "us" apart—those who visibly and doggedly resisted the status quo.

Not one of the films I examine in this essay falls into the reaction accessed and fomented by the likes of Nixon and Wallace; yet in many ways the distinction between the two commercial features and the documentary *Columbia Revolt* takes us on a tour of the fault line between 1960s liberalism and radicalism, between those focused on changes at the cultural level and a more involved and telling critique of the social and economic hierarchies that were—and are—definitional for life in the United States. This is not to separate absolutely the domain of the cultural and the social. Raymond Williams long ago updated Marx's definitions of base and superstructure by examining those apparently distinctive concepts in the form of "society" and "culture," respectively.[2] Williams's efforts were to show how culture is categorically *not* remote from society, though each is definitionally separate. In Williams's view, society—and the ways in which people concretely structure their means of interaction, including their class affinities and alliances—is subject to modification by aspects of culture, and culture is subject to redefinition by social formations.

By this token, the Newsreel film aims primarily at social critique, while the features have more broadly cultural intentions. For example, both *Greetings* and *Midnight Cowboy* give a prominent place to representations of and commentary on sex and sexuality, an emphasis distinctly connected to their time and place, as we see them engaging the now well-worn narrative trope of looking at New York as a place of sexual licentiousness.[3] Such explicit emphases were not possible in U.S. commercial films prior to the late 1960s as a result of the constraints of the censorship regime known as the Production Code, and the economic system of centralized film production that underpinned it.[4]

Columbia Revolt also documents a time and place and offers a distinctly alternative point of view connected to youth culture as it burgeoned in the late 1960s, but its intervention is far more explicitly political, as it attempts to develop a praxis of cinema that shifts away from Hollywood and moves toward the legacy of leftist documentary filmmakers such as the Film and Photo League of the 1930s.[5] The feature films offer an attempt at altering the dominant mode of commercial film production in the United States (Hollywood), while *Columbia Revolt* seeks to affect both political and motion picture praxis fundamentally. It is no accident that the Newsreel film features no individual credits. Where Hollywood foregrounds the consumable image and the star presence of individuals, *Columbia Revolt* is a paean to a kind of collectivism and images that derive power not from their craft or beauty but from their service to a revolutionary idea and political movement.

New York's 1968 was not the same as that of London, and certainly not Rome or Paris, in that the city's rebellion was largely campus based, but events in New York did possess a kind of resonance in a wide range of places. Tom Hayden, a principal figure in Students for a Democratic Society (SDS), has explained: "I think this strike at Columbia was a strike heard around the world. There were student strikes in, of course, Mexico, all across Latin America, all across Asia, Africa, Europe. Columbia might have been more famous, because it touched the nerve endings of the *New York Times* and the media capital of the United States."[6] And yet, though the Columbia events were noted throughout the world, they lacked the broader base and synergistic impact of other radical actions. For example, in Paris, almost concurrent with the Columbia demonstrations, a coalition of workers and students resulted in massive street confrontations across the city, a general strike, and a military response by the French government.[7] In March in London an anti–Vietnam War protest led to hours of street battles outside the U.S. embassy on Grosvenor Square; in April in Berlin student protesters engaged the police in protest at the shooting of one of their leaders, Rudi Dutschke; and in Mexico City on October 2 between twenty and three hundred twenty-five student protesters were killed by military snipers.[8] The events on the Columbia campus, while noteworthy, never reached this scale of violence or impact. Indeed, if we look for a comparable event in the United States, it occurs in Chicago at the Democratic National Convention in late August, when thousands of protesters clashed with police, resulting in mass arrests, widespread violence, and a televised spectacle of chaos.

New York City, as a center of U.S. commerce and culture since the early nineteenth century, is a place that, despite its ostensibly liberal politics—a politics that is broadly a matter of a centrist liberal consensus—tends as a polity to eschew radical positions. Chicago, for example, with its considerable leftist and organized-labor presence, was a greater hotbed of radicalism in the 1930s, when it was one of the central locales in the organization of the Congress of Industrial Organizations, and remained so into the 1960s, when its radical labor politics at times coalesced with the student movement. In 1968, it was also the home of the SDS national headquarters.[9] San Francisco, with its militant dockworkers, also had a stronger leftist presence in the 1930s—one that became visible in the 1960s because of the Berkeley Free Speech Movement and the founding of the Black Panther Party in Oakland. New York City also had a proportionately smaller student population than the San Francisco Bay Area or a city like Boston. This is not to say that New

York did not have its own radicals and radical activities but that those activities tended to be dwarfed by the scale of the city and its reformist political system. In 1968, moreover, the city was in the midst of a period of decline, largely as a matter of its ongoing deindustrialization, a process that had begun in the 1950s. The result was a loss of jobs and population, and a reduced tax base that led to a decline in amenities and significant middle-class flight. As the city's population became poorer, demands for social services increased, leading to a fiscal crisis that culminated in the city's 1975 default on its bond repayments.[10]

This decline had real implications for the city's infrastructure and appearance—a fact we can see in the films of this era. Subways worked erratically; streets were particularly dirty; buildings showed age and neglect. In 1965, as though to fix these structural problems by employing a new face and attitude, the city's electorate chose the young, attractive, and dynamic liberal Republican John Lindsay as mayor, a remnant of the ideological wing of that party that has gone the way of the dodo. With the beginning of the regime of Mayor Lindsay in January 1966 city government took on a more liberal cast, but that orientation must be understood within the context of U.S. government and politics. Indeed, much of Lindsay's "leftist" disposition is best understood as stylistic. Images of the young and attractive mayor with his African American constituents in decaying urban locales were well circulated in the local and national press. Lindsay was antiwar and positioned on many issues to the left of the national Democratic Party, which was largely prowar and also contained old-guard labor bureaucrats such as the AFL-CIO's George Meany and the residue of the profoundly conservative and segregationist Dixiecrats. Vincent Cannato explains in his meticulous study *The Ungovernable City: John Lindsay and His Struggle to Save New York*, "From education to police to budget policy, Lindsay's reform administration sought to root out inefficiency, bureaucratic plodding, racial inequality, and other urban sins and create a new progressive city government."[11] And it is important here to note that Cannato accurately employs the term "progressive" not to align Lindsay with the residue of the American Communist Party but to show his connection to the early twentieth century party of Theodore Roosevelt and the good-government Republicans that defined the Progressive movement.[12]

True to his bureaucratic disposition, as an aspect of a broader strategy for attracting nonindustrial jobs, in 1966 the newly elected Lindsay created the Office of Film, Theatre, and Broadcasting to encourage location production in the city. This initiative succeeded almost immediately, and New York of 1968 is well documented in films such as *Funny Girl* (1968), *Where Were You When the Lights Went Out* (1968), *Popi* (1969), *Rosemary's Baby* (1968),

Coogan's Bluff (1968), *Cactus Flower* (1969), *Midnight Cowboy*, and approximately twenty more.[13] And while the city we see varies according to emphasis, for the most part the cinematic New York of this era is depicted as dirty, gritty, and downtrodden. But this emphasis, at least in narrative fiction film, does not translate into a cinema of engagement, by which I mean films that have at the center of their presentations a compelling political and economic critique. Rather, New York as a city in decline is treated as incidental, or even made metaphoric, and employed as a further means of defining characters.

Though New York, as an aggregate, is not like San Francisco or New Orleans in its predominance of alternative lifestyles, Greenwich Village did serve as one of the significant U.S. sites for countercultural activity in the twentieth century; and in the 1960s it was one of the most important urban centers of bohemian lifestyles, while the East Village was home to Dadaist types, such as the Yippies Abbie Hoffman and Jerry Rubin. Christopher Mele writes about the relative quiet of 1967 in the East Village being replaced by an increasing police presence and violence in 1968, as young residents of that neighborhood actively resisted what they felt was police harassment and numerous drug raids—a resistance in which Hoffman and Rubin were instrumental.[14] The West Village was a visible center for an increasingly coherent gay population during the mid- to late 1960s, and in 1969 it was the site of the Stonewall rebellion, an event in which the denizens of a gay bar on Christopher Street fought police harassment in an assertion of sexual freedom—an act often described as a starting point for the gay rights movement.[15]

Representing the Built Environment

Important in these films is the discrete view of New York City and its built environment that each provides. Architectural and spatial definitions of Manhattan are central. In *Columbia Revolt*, this is true notwithstanding the fact that out of focus and shaky images mark the production, as do shots that are inadequately or imprecisely lit. In its opening scene we are provided a slow pan up the neoclassical columns of Columbia University's Low Library, which in 1968 housed that institution's administration. (See Figure 5.1.) As the voice of President Grayson Kirk drones on, giving a long-winded commencement speech about the university's role in contemporary life, our tour continues in the atrium, featuring statues of Demosthenes, Euripides, Sophocles, and Caesar Augustus accompanied by Kirk's words, "The modern university is the cradle of the nation's future. It preserves and transmits knowledge and values: the chief force of our social system." In the context of the Newsreel film, this is a kind of self-indictment. We are given a camera's

Figure 5.1 The architecture of Columbia University in *Columbia Revolt* (Newsreel, 1968)

eye tour of the building's entrance, atrium, and statuary, which Kirk implicitly lauds in terms of the glory of "liberal education." The camera pauses and pans to show the face of a statue of Pallas Athena, patterned after one in the Louvre, which celebrates Athena as the goddess of truth and wisdom, creating a kind of visual emphasis that we can only see as ironic. But only minutes into the film it cuts from the neoclassicism of the Low Library to the utilitarian modernism of student dorms and the voice over of a student impugning the university's participation in the military industrial complex, its "servicing of the corporations and servicing of the war machine." This juxtaposition of commentary and building styles looks behind the "ivory tower" and visually critiques the humane front of the modern university, affirming its utilitarian role in an international regime of repression.

The two feature films also prominently feature images of the built environment, though in *Midnight Cowboy* they are more telling than in *Greetings*. In *Midnight Cowboy*, we first see the Manhattan skyline from the New Jersey Turnpike, as our protagonist Joe Buck approaches by bus. (See Figure 5.2.) The shot shows us the signature mass of high-rise buildings in the distance, and then briefly centers the spire of the Empire State Building before cutting to Joe looking out on the street from his cheap Times Square hotel.

Figure 5.2 The built environment in *Midnight Cowboy* (Schlesinger, 1969): Manhattan skyline, Times Square, Joe Buck (Jon Voight) on Park Avenue, and the abandoned apartment building that serves as a home for Joe and Ratso (Dustin Hoffman)

Below is the low-slung and tawdry Times Square of the late 1960s. Joe's room features a coin-operated television. Soon, accompanied by Harry Nilsson singing the film's hit country pop theme song, "Everybody's Talking," Joe is walking on Fifth Avenue, a street that is replete both with wealth and despair.[16] A street-level tracking shot finds him encountering a man in a suit passed out on the sidewalk in front of the Tiffany building. The camera pans up to show Joe stopping and looking down in concern, as other pedestrians ignore the immobile body. These shots show us a New York of economic extremes and personal callousness, a view that defines this film as Joe attempts his life as a male prostitute. Those features are definitional for U.S. capitalism of the moment, but that definition is not part of a systematic social critique.

The opening shot of *Greetings* shows a television newscast detailing the Tet offensive in Saigon, and then President Lyndon Johnson proclaiming the necessity of the Vietnam War, a position we now know he did not believe himself.[17] This scene establishes the war as a focal point, providing a vision of the ongoing carnage in Vietnam, with a map in the background, and a subsequent news item about Johnson meeting with a group of prowar labor leaders.[18] We next see the film's protagonist walking up Sixth Avenue near Greenwich Village. The avenue is wide, littered, and clearly of New York—we can just spy the Empire State building in the depth of the frame—but largely nondescript. We hear the film's theme song, "Greetings," a folk rock song by The Children of Paradise, which was not a major hit but provides a further sense of the countercultural moment. Our character enters an unprepossessing building under a sign that says "BAR" but that seems to have no other name, after which we find him in a hippie boutique looking at clothes and then at the bear cage in the recently refurbished Central Park Zoo. Throughout these scenes, the character is being instructed by his friends on how to convince his draft board he is gay, and thus receive a deferment.

In these visions of New York's built environment in 1968, the viewer is provided with resonant images of the place and the moment: conflict, callousness, and whimsy in each case, respectively. Similarly, the sound of the city narrates a mode of analysis: *Columbia Revolt* offers live street noise and speeches that indict the dominant strains of U.S. politics and education. The two feature films—*Midnight Cowboy* and *Greetings*—offer fairly conventional film soundtracks that imbue them with a further sense of melancholy and whimsy, respectively. Each of these films focuses on the central social problems of the moment—war, inequality, and urban ennui—though in varying degrees. Yet, after their opening scenes, the two features slide into narratives that offer an indirect address of the issues, whereas *Columbia Revolt*, true to its initial images, continues to focus on the role of education in the reproduction of a ruling class and the question of institutional racism.

Creating Narratives of the Moment

In each incarnation 1968 is a related entity but clearly distinct. Part of this distinction relates to the scale of production of each film, which has a corollary in scale of reception, and those scales have political valence. *Midnight Cowboy* was budgeted at $3.6 million—a fairly substantial production featuring Dustin Hoffman, who had been Oscar-nominated for his lead role in *The Graduate* (1967). *Midnight Cowboy* earned over $44 million worldwide, making it the second largest grossing U.S. release of that year, and it would go on to win several Academy Awards, including those for Best Picture, Best Actor, and Best Screenplay.[19] *Greetings*, on the other hand, was shot for an estimated $43,000 by the then unknown Brian De Palma with a cast of then unknowns including Robert De Niro, and the film's earnings were miniscule.[20] *Columbia Revolt* was shot on a shoestring budget—probably no more than a few thousand dollars—and not intended to make a profit, playing mostly at festivals and universities.[21] It was the work of the leftist Newsreel collective and a work not just *about* political activism but also a work *of* political activism.[22] Despite their limited box office, *Greetings* and *Columbia Revolt* have developed a kind of cult status over time: *Greetings* for its eventually famous principals and

Columbia Revolt for engaging a significant event from the days of student activism, as well as its status as a film by a notable group of radical filmmakers involved in a form of media experiment, employing cinema to "build an adversarial culture," as Michael Renov has argued.[23] Such a stated political intention positions this film as distinct from the other two in a manner that goes beyond scale of production but that has implications for its scale. It is clearly a work embedded in a movement that would be unlikely to galvanize an audience that was not already inclined to see the events it depicts in a particular light. A reviewer in the *New York Times* noted in early October 1968: "Like all propaganda, the film will be most effective among the faithful. They will (as who wouldn't?) relish reliving their role as embattled resistance heroes, an impression heightened by the ragged camera work—one might almost be watching newsreels smuggled out of Poland in 1938."[24]

Despite these major distinctions in scale, all three films define an oppositional culture. This is obvious in the documentary, but less clearly so direct in the two features. Even as *Midnight Cowboy* was both profitable and much honored, it stands as the only X-rated film ever to win an Academy Award for Best Picture. It is a brave depiction of a would-be male prostitute in a city that is both hostile and decayed. *Greetings* takes on the issue of the military draft from the point of view of a character who has been called and whimsically takes us through his disquiet and limited resistance.

All of these films point to innovations in film production in the United States. *Columbia Revolt* is a signature product of a group of politically engaged filmmakers who coalesced in 1967 with the intention of disrupting what they felt was the monolithic voice of the U.S. media. Its principals were mostly political activists, often connected to SDS. One of them, Roz Payne, has explained, "As Newsreel grew we spread out, opened offices and distribution centers across the country. We had offices in San Francisco, Detroit, Boston, Kansas, Los Angeles, Vermont, and Atlanta. We made films and distributed our films in the hope that the audiences who saw them would respond to the issues they raised. We wanted people to work with our films as catalysis for political discussions about social change in America and to relate the questions in the films to issues in their own communities."[25] Thus, we can see *Columbia Revolt* as part of a broader network of production with the intention of creating a structure of alternative political discourse. In addition to its relationship to leftist documentary filmmakers of the 1930s, Newsreel also drew part of its inspiration from the burgeoning underground film movement of the 1960s, which featured figures such as Bruce Baillie and Kenneth Anger in the San Francisco area, and Adolfas and Jonas Mekas, and Lionel Rogosin, among many others in New York. This was also a period when nontheatrical releases could find an audience in places like the Bleecker Street Cinema in New York. But by the early 1970s, independent theaters were teetering financially and Newsreel was riven by political disagreements over class, gender, and race.[26] And though the political shifts of the 1970s and 1980s further pushed this film culture to remote portions of the political landscape, certain works of the late 1960s did have galvanizing effects on some audiences, including a case at the New York State University at Buffalo in 1969, where *Columbia Revolt* triggered a campus march and assault on the ROTC building.[27]

The two theatrical films are distinctive as edgy productions shot on location that were connected to the new wave of U.S. cinema that was beginning to coalesce in the late 1960s. They were director- and producer-driven and had as their object the youth market—and in the late 1960s that market was both growing and appreciative of unconventional filmmaking. They index a sea change in the U.S. film industry that marks the explosion of youth culture—even as they offer a world view that retains a residual social and cultural conservatism. In their relation to a broader industrial history, they also suggest the incipient auteurism of the New Hollywood, which was not located in Hollywood necessarily but increasingly in other places—and notably in New York.[28] Indeed, between the avant-garde world of the Mekases and the business-driven model of the New Hollywood, there lodged a domain of independent films, in which filmmakers like John Cassavetes and the very young Martin Scorsese exercised complete artistic control over very small productions. And while these films found funding and audiences during the 1960s, many young directors, including De Palma and Scorsese, ultimately gravitated toward the Hollywood system as it was being reconfigured in the 1970s. Schlesinger's *Midnight Cowboy* is a somewhat larger effort than their early films, but it remains a director-driven project by a filmmaker who had already enjoyed considerable acclaim as a British and European auteur. *Columbia Revolt*, on the other hand, is very much an unsigned canvas, one that has a distinctive style but that resists the bourgeois ethos that informs the auteurist valorization of particular film directors.

As a documentary, *Columbia Revolt* engages with the events of late April and early May 1968, when students at Columbia University occupied administrative offices and other buildings on the campus and went on a general strike. This action was a response to the university's plan to build on several acres of Morningside Park—a public park abutting the campus and bordering the substantially African American and overwhelmingly poor neighborhood of Harlem—and the action was brought to an end only when New York City police were called in by the university's administration, restoring order with

Figure 5.3 Two locations from *Columbia Revolt* (Newsreel, 1968): Morningside Park, top, and the student occupation of Columbia University, below

alacrity and some violence. (See Figure 5.3.) After the opening scenes, which foreground the university's neoclassical architecture and last about four minutes, the rest of the film documents the protests, specifically addressing the issue of the gym. A sequence of shots shows a crowd in the park—both students and neighborhood residents—amid a mass of construction machinery, dump trucks, and bulldozers. One shot is from above so that we can see the extent of the excavation, as the heavy machinery and despoiled land look like a war zone—again, an apt visual metaphor. But seven minutes into the film, we return to campus, and the event becomes not a community matter, but a campus ruckus. The visuals show us students—many well dressed in sport coats and ties—milling in large and somewhat random crowds. Most shots of these crowds provide a wide and long view, and often from above. It is as though the filmmakers further their documentary claims by emphasizing the quasiobject of the camera. Such a perspective also provides much visual information for a viewer interrogating these compositions from a fairly distant historical perspective. Even when they repair to the streets of New York—to the part of Broadway that borders the Columbia campus—it appears as though this is a world of and for privileged Columbia students. As the film goes on, it becomes more a paean to youth culture and the efforts of the striking students, bound by its documentary form and by the limits of the student movement in the United States in 1968. The campus focus of the strike also suggests the relative insularity of the U.S. wing of the international student movement as well as the ways in which this important aspect of dissent could be both physically repressed—we see the police marching into campus to dislodge the strikers—and ideologically repressed, as the class-based and the institutional affiliations of the dissidents suggest at least a familial affiliation with the mainstream of U.S. society. In his treatment of the film, David James rightly seizes upon its singularity of focus and purpose, arguing that "the film is unequivocal in celebrating the rebellion."[29] Indeed, *Columbia Revolt* offers a polemic that affirms a certain social critique but which does not necessarily move beyond a particularist view, leaving the prospect of ideological synergy and coalition politics largely forestalled. James explains, "What self-consciousness there is in *Columbia Revolt* is largely a matter of the propagandistic single-mindedness that proceeds from its moment in the history of New Left theory."[30]

Reading out from *Columbia Revolt* to *Greetings* and then to *Midnight Cowboy*, we are able to see a kind of narrative of place and moment that is historically revealing. In *Columbia Revolt*, we see the culture of students and their distinctive social formation, but in the end there is no merging of that culture and society with that of the African American population in the surrounding community, nor is there an alliance formed with other members of the working class. Indeed, in Harlem in 1968 the impact of the Black Power movement was affecting local politics, and its sense of power and solidarity was involved in community responses to the building of the Columbia gym. But that formation was always distinct from the politics of the white Columbia University students.[31] In *Columbia Revolt* the predominance of white faces is striking. About eight minutes into the film we find that the white students and black students have split up, with the African American group maintaining control over one building and the white students occupying several others. A white student leader explains, "The two groups [black and white] realized that we had two different political identities. The blacks wanted to stop the gym.... The whites, on the other hand, saw, and still see, that our goal is to radicalize other white people." This seems somewhat reductive of the intentions of the black students, as if lacking concern for interracial solidarity. The film presents a few minutes of footage and voice-over comments of black protestors, barricading the Hamilton Hall administrative building against the police, highlighting the symbolic importance for the larger black community of revolt by black students at such a prestigious university, showing a rally of

Harlem high school students in sympathy with their action, and a black student leader reading a list of demands. These seem to emphasize the greater degree of radicalization of black students, but the film soon moves on and barely returns to the subject.

Indeed, Columbia's strike featured a significant SDS presence, and included various individuals who were later involved in the far-left Weatherman splinter group. In strike leader Mark Rudd's memoir, there is little mention of workers or community groups being much involved in the action, even though he does affirm "support from the Harlem community."[32] As two major historians of the period have written, "In the two years after the Columbia event, similar confrontations occurred on hundreds of campuses. But, with each takeover, the prospect of building a movement as socially broad as it was tactically daring receded further into the realm of wishful thinking."[33]

The racial landscape of the city in the two theatrically released films remains overwhelmingly white. In *Midnight Cowboy*, Joe Buck does have a passing relationship with a fellow dishwasher in Texas who is African American and there is a black character we meet in an early scene in a Times Square bar where Joe meets Ratso, but he proves relatively invisible in the subsequent narrative. *Greetings* is even whiter. Such omissions speak to both the city's demographics in this period as well as the conceptual limits of the filmmakers. In 1970, the city's African American population was around 21 percent and its Latino population was over 16 percent. Manhattan's population was 25 percent African American, but due to spatial segregation, an overwhelming majority of African Americans and Latinos lived north of 96th street, which partially explains the absence of people of color from the features, which dwell on locations well south of that line.[34] And the relative whiteness of *Columbia Revolt* reinforces the students' concern regarding the racist and classist nature of U.S. higher education.

About twenty minutes into *Columbia Revolt*, in a move that James notes as central, the film turns to the blossoming communalism which emerges among the occupying students. Soon, we are witnesses to a wedding in one of the occupied buildings. At this moment the tone becomes less belligerent and less overtly political, as social critique seems to elide into cultural effect. This is extended about five minutes later, when we see a rally on the campus featuring the iconic counterculture band the Grateful Dead. In this phase, the film blends more easily into the kind of terrain developed by *Greetings*.

Greetings and *Midnight Cowboy*, both of which are clearly fiction, engage the broader city as a place, showing us shots of Midtown, Uptown, the East Village and the financial district. But unlike *Columbia Revolt*, which explicitly engages the domain of politics, these films engage culture. *Greetings* and *Midnight Cowboy* are also temporally of 1968, as both were shot in the city that year, but analytically, as entertainments, they require a great deal of contextualization and a strong interpretive frame. It is their narratives that are most apparent to the viewer, but as "documents" of a moment, they need to be carefully embedded both in time and place.

In *Midnight Cowboy*, to which I will return, the emergence of the downtown arts scene and its role in gentrification is invoked, as is the broader vision of New York as a place of potential danger, squalor, and deep division among classes and races. In *Greetings*, as I suggested earlier, the Vietnam War is at the forefront, as the film opens with footage from a newscast showing the Tet offensive and the alliance of President Johnson with prowar labor leaders. That alliance partially explains the lack of intergenerational and interclass solidarity visible in *Columbia Revolt*, especially given the well-known hostility to leftist students of AFL-CIO president George Meany. But after its opening clip, *Greetings* places its central emphasis on an individual narrative: trying to define a strategy for getting out of the draft. The initial idea is for Jon (Robert De Niro) to convince the psychiatrist that he is a homosexual. The succeeding strategy is to convince the doctor of his more general and psychotic bigotry. The film becomes a series of vignettes around his attempt to avoid the draft. But it also defines its characters, within its fairly loose plot, as figures of the 1960s counterculture. Many of these situations involve some expression of sexuality: a fairly sophomoric description of an encounter with a woman, an encounter with a man selling pornographic post cards, and a computer date.

As the film goes on, one of Jon's friends, Lloyd, becomes obsessed with the Kennedy assassination and the presumed lies of the Warren Commission Report, but his concern is treated in an antic manner. This thread takes up a significant portion of the latter part of the movie. But rather than expressing a broader streak of resistance to authority, it is difficult to link with the potential and expression of late 1960s radical politics. And while we are well aware of the energy and innovation at work here, the world we see looks, in hindsight, so anarchic and so lacking a sustained analytical center, it is very difficult to see a broader idea of social change at work in the film. Nor is the physical city represented in a coherent way. Many scenes are shot in Central Park, with some showing us the zoo, an enclave built in 1860 as the park was opening, but significantly rebuilt by Robert Moses in 1934. (See Figure 5.4.) And while there were countercultural gathering places in the park in the late 1960s, they were far from the zoo, in the Sheep Meadow virtually on the other side of the enclave. In 1966 the park was the site of a major antiwar protest,

Figure 5.4 Selected locations in *Greetings* (De Palma, 1968): Sixth Avenue near Greenwich Village, Central Park Zoo, Isamu Noguchi's Red Cube outside the Marine Midland Bank (1967), lower Broadway, and the adjacent One Chase Manhattan Plaza building (1961)

the first such use of the park since 1914, and then again in 1967 it served as the site for the beginning of a mass march to the United Nations headquarters on First Avenue. In *Greetings*, however, the park's Victorian auspices are to the fore. Similarly, in an early scene we see three main characters out gamboling around lower Manhattan. The scene lingers for a moment at the Marine Midland Bank building at 140 Broadway in lower Manhattan, where we see Isamu Noguchi's *Red Cube*, a major piece of that era's public art, that was installed in 1968. This sculpture offers a vision of the new, but it is so unrelentingly formalist that it is difficult to see it as anything but a corporatist play on modernist architecture. Its whimsy replicates the whimsy of the characters, as does its lack of engagement. It also suggests precariousness, which is indeed a metaphor for the generation represented. Indeed, Noguchi himself has said it represents the "rolling of the dice."[35]

The film's penultimate scene offers another news story, featuring De Niro's character with a rifle in a rice field in Vietnam. Unlike the opening shot, however, this is a faux documentary moment, and one that suggests the futility of resisting the draft. The film ends whimsically with the character deciding not to shoot a Vietnamese woman and instead taking her picture as the scene morphs back—apparently through the device of his fantasy—to another woman he has photographed in New York. The opening newscast of Lyndon Johnson returns in the closing moments, suggesting that no action can be fully transformative, even as change seems to pervade every moment. This vision is further elaborated by a pervasive sexism, a just-below-the-surface racism, and a lack of gravity in the film's portrayal of its characters. This New York is a playground in which there is much motion but little change. *Greetings*, ultimately, is a film that participates in the cultural changes of the 1960s even as its commentary—through its narrative—places those changes at a distance.

Midnight Cowboy is a far less whimsical film and offers a distinctive view of the city at its moment of production, even as it replicates some of the embedded moralism we find in the DePalma film. Here, however, it is more explicit. Unlike *Greetings* and *Columbia Revolt*, Schlesinger's film offers a far more focused view of the city in decline. It is ostensibly the despairing story of a young man's migration to New York City from Texas, and his efforts to make money as a male prostitute. Needless to say, this is not an easy endeavor, and it is particularly difficult for one as unsophisticated as Joe Buck. But here, unlike in *Greetings*, where New York as it exists in 1968 is something of a given, Joe's migration and lack of savvy allow us to locate New York as a place with distinctive environs and cultural mores. His experience is a heightened version of the traditional coming-to-the-city narrative, for which he is underprepared and by which he is overwhelmed and alienated. But it is in the details that we locate 1968. Unlike *Columbia Revolt* and *Greetings*, *Midnight Cowboy* leaves the most compelling national event of the time—the war in Vietnam—substantially out of the narrative. There are a few brief references, but it is far from a focal point. Early on, what seems to be a screaming Vietnamese girl is seen briefly on the TV while Joe has sex with a woman he meets in the street, and later, in a flashback, Joe appears in an Army uniform sitting on his grandmother's stoop. But these are fleeting moments that are never enlarged to occupy a significant space in the film's dramatic narrative. We also see some men singing in Veterans of Foreign Wars regalia on the bus to New York City, but they have clearly fought in a different war, likely World War II. And while it is true that the source material for the film, a novel, was written in 1965, Schlesinger's film updates that narrative considerably and strategically employs the 1968 streetscape.

The shooting style of this film is far more character-based than the other two, so we are to some degree bound by Joe's experience and point of view. Yet, there are moments when we do get a shot that allows for more context, whether defined by its height, distance, or both. Unlike *Greetings*, *Midnight Cowboy* features no distinctive period architecture. Its buildings are mostly those built in the early twentieth century and its ethos is more about decay or stasis than renewal. In these first scenes, Joe clumsily propositions a woman on Park Avenue and 70th Street; and after she rejects him, he stands embarrassed on the median strip as the camera moves away, revealing him isolated in a deep focus shot of Park Avenue as an urban tunnel defined by the Pan-Am Building in the distance. Joe's first sexual encounter ends with *him* paying a woman who clearly is taking advantage of his lack of sophistication. The encounter takes place in a postwar high rise on East 72nd Street, notable for its garish modern furnishings, suggesting the vulgarity of the new. As they have sex, they roll on the remote control, producing a montage of crass TV shows. As Joe leaves, poorer but no wiser, we see him in a rare long shot, looking small on the sidewalk, seen from a nearby roof.

After Joe is evicted from his Times Square Hotel, our view of the city, and of the moment, moves into a spiral of decline. Times Square becomes, rather than benignly seedy, more abjectly so. One of Joe's first acts of hustling after his displacement is to allow an adolescent male to perform oral sex on him in a movie theater, but the young man then tells Joe he has no money. Joe does not beat him, and even as he begins to take the young man's watch, finds himself unable to do so. Joe is something of a victim, marked by his innocence in a city that is a hostile environment for those without means. However, it remains for us to extrapolate the film's politics, since Joe's story, and that of his companion Ratso, are so much a matter of their individual experiences. As Joe's fortunes decline, we see him spend more and more time in the trash-laden and threatening subway, traversing its tunnels and subculture. These contrast with the image of lavish New York defined by what the film calls the "Berkeley Hotel for Women," but that was actually the Gotham Hotel (now the Peninsula Hotel) at Fifth Avenue and 55th St. Ratso sends the naive Joe into the hotel to find his clientele and begin to make his fortune, only to be summarily evicted.

Just over forty-eight minutes into the film, we see where all previous actions have led. Joe, accompanied by Ratso, moves to Ratso's home in an abandoned apartment building on the Lower East Side. The building is marked with an *X* since it is condemned and due for demolition—a building typical of the regional decay of that era, before the prospect of gentrification emerged.[36] Again, this is a tale of despair and a quite affecting one, but not necessarily in a politically cathartic way. The New York of 1968 is a city defined by the *haves* and *have nots*, but it is also a place that seems to envelop its poorer residents, forcing them into increasingly dire situations, from which it is impossible to escape. Perhaps most definitional of the moment is the appearance of young, sexually ambiguous bohemians, who find Joe and Ratso at a downtown coffee shop and invite them to a party at "Broadway and Harmony Lane," a nonexistent address but one that apparently leads to an exterior shot of a building on Mercer Street, which runs through Soho. The reference is clearly to Andy Warhol and the social scene that he defined, although Warhol's "Factory" was never any further downtown than Union Square, where it moved in 1967 from East 47th Street.[37] Still, by 1968 the Fillmore East had opened on Second Avenue near East 6th Street, providing rock impresario Bill Graham with a New York complement to his successful San Francisco rock and roll venue.[38] This converted movie theater was something of an anchor for the alternative downtown New York scene, and built upon Warhol's 1967 use of a space on St. Marks Place as a site for a multimedia show.

Clearly the reference to the downtown avant-garde in *Midnight Cowboy* is more general than specific, but it suggests the existence of a viable subculture, making the world of Joe and Ratso less a matter of rich and poor. They are invited to the party for the visual spectacle they present, standing out for Joe's clearly un–New York dress and manner and its contrast with the club-footed Ratso's swarthy and down-and-out visage. The party is replete with psychedelic costumes, characters, drugs, and music, and Joe ends up going home with a woman through whom he finally achieves his goal of getting money for sex. This shift in narrative and in fortune suggests that there is a New York that might be welcoming for these characters. But even in good fortune, the city fails to deliver, resulting in Joe assaulting a man in order to get bus fare to remove his dying friend from the city.

1968 and 2018

Joe's resolution in his flight from Manhattan to Miami is that he would like to find work other than hustling. In this assertion and in his tender devotion to Ratso, Joe is transformed. Indeed, if we look back at the film as a whole—and to some degree also to *Greetings*—New York is articulated as a culturally open space, an area where behavior one might consider fringe has a place. This includes a range of sexual expressions, which, in 1968, were not "normative" in the United States. These films participate in that moment in their depiction of these various acts—unmarried sex, gay sex, prostitution, etc.—but in each case, the treatment of those behaviors is marginalized and made garish. That Joe and Ratso take some solace from an incipient counterculture, but are never really part of it, is revealing in itself. *Midnight Cowboy* situates its characters in a world that is whirling past them, and in which all they seek is some money, a few creature comforts, and a trip to Florida.

Upon their release in December 1968 and May 1969, respectively, both *Greetings* and *Midnight Cowboy* looked like films that would define their moment as one that was decidedly different from that which came before.[39] Certainly they reveal that prior limits on expression had loosened. Both films are somewhat explicit for U.S. feature presentations of that time, featuring nudity and explicit sexual encounters. But both films also assert a critical distance from those acts, offering them as either debased or as acts of commerce. In *Midnight Cowboy,* there is not a single occasion in which Joe seems to fully enjoy himself in a sexual situation, while *Greetings* is informed by an adolescent sexual imaginary with misogynistic overtones. So even as these films usher in a new era of frank representations of sex, they also police those representations in neo-Victorian fashion. And while the politics of *Columbia Revolt* are certainly distinct from the ultimate cultural commentary of *Midnight Cowboy* and *Greetings,* its use of locations (mostly the Columbia campus) and its triumphal tone tend to isolate its critique, both temporally and geographically. As we look at the New York of 2018, with its gloss of wealth and plethora of new structures, it is difficult to look back on the 1968 moment as other than a lost historical opportunity. But—in hindsight, of course—the rationale of that lost opportunity emerges from these films.

NOTES

1. See Rick Perlstein, *Nixonland: The Rise of a President and the Fracturing of America* (New York: Scribner's, 2009).

2. Raymond Williams, *Keywords: A Vocabulary of Culture and Society* (New York: Oxford University Press, 1983), 87–93, 291–295.

3. New York as a place of rampant sin and sexuality has been a staple of film, literature, and news stories since the late nineteenth century, with examples ranging from Stephen Crane's *Maggie, A Girl of the Streets* (1893) to Theodore Dreiser's *Sister Carrie* (1903) to Hubert Selby's *Last Exit to Brooklyn* (1964); the films *Strictly Dishonorable* (1931), *The Apartment* (1960), and *The Bad Lieutenant* (1991) to name just a few in each medium.

4. See Thomas Doherty, *Hollywood's Censor: Joseph I. Breen and the Production Code Administration* (New York: Columbia University Press, 2007), 313–350.

5. See David E. James, *Allegories of Cinema: American Film in the Sixties* (Princeton, NJ: Princeton University Press, 1989), 171–175. See also Russell Campbell and William Alexander, "Film and Photo League Filmography," *Jump Cut*, no. 14 (1977): 33.

6. See Tom Hayden in http://www.democracynow.org/2008/4/25/forty_years_after _historic_columbia_strike.

7. See Angelo Quattrocchi and Tom Nairn, *The Beginning of the End: France, May 1968* (London: Panther Books, 1968; London: Verso, 1998) and Kristin Ross, *May '68 and Its Afterlives* (Chicago: University of Chicago Press, 2002) for two very good considerations.

8. See Mark Kurlansky, *1968: The Year That Rocked the World* (New York: Random House, 2005); Martin Klimke and Joachim Scharloth, *1968 in Europe: A History of Protest and Activism, 1956–1977* (London: Palgrave Macmillan, 2008); Elena Poniatowska, *Massacre in Mexico*, trans. Helen R. Lane with an introduction by Octavio Paz (Columbia: University of Missouri, 1991), 207.

9. See James Miller, *Democracy Is in the Streets: From Port Huron to the Siege of Chicago* (Cambridge: Harvard University Press, 1987), esp. 246–250; Peter B. Levy, *The New Left and Labor in the 1960s* (Urbana-Champaign: University of Illinois Press, 1994), 145–146; and see also Carol Quirke, "Reframing Chicago's Memorial Day Massacre, May 30, 1937," *American Quarterly* 60, no. 1 (March 2008): 129–157.

10. This was memorialized in the October 1975 New York *Daily News* headline, "Ford to City: Drop Dead."

11. Vincent Cannato, *The Ungovernable City: John Lindsay and His Struggle to Save New York* (New York: Basic Books, 2001), xiv.

12. For illuminating discussions of U.S. Progressivism in the early century see Morton Keller, *Regulating a New Society: Public Policy and Social Change in America, 1900–1933* (Cambridge: Harvard University Press, 1994); Kenneth Finegold, *Experts and Politicians: Reform Challenges to Machine Politics in New York, Cleveland, and Chicago* (Princeton, NJ: Princeton University Press, 1995); James Weinstein, *The Corporate Ideal in the Liberal State, 1900–1918* (Boston: Beacon Press, 1968); Robert H. Wiebe, *The Search for Order, 1877–1920* (New York: Hill and Wang, 1967).

13. The Mayor's Office of Film Production does not have an archive of the films it has supported. On New York feature filmmaking in the 1960s, see, for example, James Sanders, *Celluloid Skyline: New York and the Movies* (New York: Alfred Knopf, 2003), 345–398.

14. Christopher Mele, *Selling the Lower East Side: Culture, Real Estate, and Resistance in New York City* (Minneapolis: University of Minnesota Press, 2000), 178–179.

15. See David Carter, *Stonewall: The Riots That Sparked the Gay Revolution* (New York: St. Martin's, 2010).

16. This song was a major hit for Harry Nilsson in 1969. Initially, Bob Dylan had been contracted to write the film's theme song, but his "Lay, Lady Lay" was ultimately rejected because, according to Dylan, it was submitted too late, as was Harry Nilsson's "I Guess the Lord Must Be in New York City." Nilsson's cover of Fred Neil's composition then became the film's celebrated song. See Jann S. Wenner, "Bob Dylan Talks: A Raw and Extensive First Rolling Stone Interview," *Rolling Stone*, November 29, 1969. http://www.rollingstone.com/music/news/bob-dylan-talks-a-raw-and-extensive-first-rolling-stone-interview-19691129; and Sean Fennessey, "Deconstructing Harry: Remembering Harry Nilsson: American Beatle, Filthy Drunk, and the Great Lost Music Genius of the 1970s," *Grantland*, August 6, 2013. http://grantland.com/features/the-legacy-harry-nilsson/.

17. See Robert Caro, *The Passage of Power; The Years of Lyndon Johnson* (New York: Knopf, 2012), 530–550.

18. See Frank Koscielski, *Divided Loyalties: American Unions and the Vietnam War* (New York: Routledge, 1999).

19. See William J. Mann, *Edge of Midnight: The Life of John Schlesinger* (New York: Billboard Books, 2005), 312.

20. See Geoff Mayer, *Historical Dictionary of Crime Films* (Scarecrow Press: Lanham, Toronto, 2012), 112.

21. There is very little available documentation of this film's costs or proceeds. However, filmmaker Christine Choy, who was active in the student movement and joined Newsreel in 1970, has recalled that she directed *Teach Our Children* (1972) and other Newsreel films in the early 1970s on a typical budget of $2,000–$2,500 per picture. See "Christine Choy," interview by Scott MacDonald, in *A Critical Cinema 3: Interviews with Independent Filmmakers* (Berkeley: University of California Press, 1998), 196–217, 202.

22. For revealing discussions of the Newsreel Collective and radical documentary more generally, see Jonathan Kahana, *Intelligence Work: The Politics of American Documentary* (New York: Columbia University Press, 2008), esp. 172; Michael Renov, "Newsreel: Old and New: Towards an Historical Profile," in *Film Quarterly, Forty Years: A Selection*, ed. Brian Henderson and Ann Martin, with Lee Amazonas (Berkeley: University of California Press, 1999), 268–289; first published in *Film Quarterly* 41, no. 1 (Fall 1987): 20–33.

23. Renov, "Newsreel: Old and New," 22.

24. Dan Sullivan, "Review of Columbia Revolt," *New York Times*, October 8, 1968.

25. http://documentaryisneverneutral.com/words/roznewsreel.html.

26. Newsreel's descendants, Third World Newsreel and California Newsreel, took on a new shape after 1975, offering a far more modest agenda, though one that remains resolutely leftist and political. Renov, "Newsreel: Old and New," 24.

27. Renov, "Newsreel: Old and New," 25.

28. See my *Starring New York: Filming the Grime and Glamour of the Long 1970s* (New York: Oxford University Press, 2011) for an analysis of the cultural/spatial/historical meanings of a large group of films set in New York City.

29. James, *Allegories of Cinema*, 226.

30. James, *Allegories of Cinema*, 228.

31. See Stefan M. Bradley, *Harlem vs. Columbia University: Black Student Power in the Late 1960s* (Urbana-Champaign: University of Illinois Press, 2009).

32. Mark Rudd, *Underground: My Life with SDS and the Weathermen* (New York: William Morrow, 2009), 83.

33. See Maurice Isserman and Michael Kazin, *America Divided: The Civil War of the 1960s* (New York: Oxford University Press, 1999), 238.

34. U.S. Census Bureau, "Table 33. New York—Race and Hispanic Origin for Selected Large Cities and Other Places: Earliest Census to 1990," accessed April 27, 2016, http://www.census.gov/population/www/documentation/twps0076/NYtab.pdf. See also Martha Biondi, *To Stand and Fight: The Struggle for Civil Rights in Postwar New York City*. (Cambridge: Harvard University Press, 2003); Douglas S. Massey and Nancy A. Denton, *American Apartheid: Segregation and the Making of the Underclass* (Cambridge, MA: Harvard University Press, 1993).

35. Noguchi quoted in Masayo Duus, *The Life of Isamu Noguchi: Journey without Borders* (Princeton, NJ: Princeton University Press, 2006), 6.

36. Neil Smith, *The New Urban Frontier: Gentrification and the Revanchist City* (New York: Routledge, 1996). Ratso's squat seems to be located somewhere around Avenue B and 11th Street, but it is difficult to pinpoint its definite location.

37. Caroline A. Jones, *Machine in the Studio: Constructing the Postwar American Artist* (Chicago: University of Chicago Press, 1996), 189–267.

38. Richard Kostelanetz and Raeanne Rubenstein, *The Fillmore East: Recollections of Rock Theater* (New York: Schirmer Books, 1995).

39. Release dates retrieved from American Film Institute, ProQuest AFI Catalog: *Greetings* (1968), http://search.proquest.com/docview/1746185544; and *Midnight Cowboy* (1969), http://search.proquest.com/docview/1746216713. Accessed April 28, 2016.

6

"It's a Big Garage." Cinematic Images of Los Angeles circa 1968

Mark Shiel

Los Angeles in 1968 did not witness mass political insurrection on the dramatic scale of events in that year in Paris or Chicago, nor did it produce any single cinematic master work on urban revolution to rival Jean Luc Godard's *La Chinoise* (1967) or Haskell Wexler's *Medium Cool* (1969). However, a history of LA in 1968, and of its cinematic representation as a contested urban terrain, can be pieced together that amounts to more than the sum of its parts. If the turbulent events of 1968 were the culmination of a long twentieth century crisis of the modern city and its social and physical fabric, as Marshall Berman has suggested, that revolutionary moment was all too soon followed by the setting in place of a new postmodern gestalt of which Los Angeles in its post-Fordist, simulacral glory was and remains arguably the greatest exemplar.[1]

Following exponential growth after World War II, by the late 1960s Los Angeles was emerging for the first time as a genuine "global city" to rival New York, Chicago, London, and Paris, with a metropolitan population of nearly 10 million, booming aerospace, high technology, and cultural industries, and a physical size only slightly exceeded by the combined urban agglomeration of New York and New Jersey.[2] But the most visible manifestations of the city's expansion—freeways, automobiles, and suburban sprawl—did not hide its tumultuous social unrest. The era was marked by the social, physical, and economic degradation of many long-established neighborhoods, which frequently resulted in violence. Downtown had been in a seemingly terminal decline as a commercial and social hub since the early 1950s, its beaux-arts, art deco, and streamlined moderne commercial buildings predominantly given over to low-rent activities or derelict, and its Victorian residential enclave, Bunker Hill, razed to the ground for a new wave of skyscrapers that would come in the 1970s and 1980s. Hollywood was no longer the business and symbolic center of the film industry it had been in the studio era and was becoming what *Los Angeles Times* columnist Jack Smith called "a rut of pornography and decadence," populated by fast-food outlets, porno theaters, prostitutes, and stores selling movie memorabilia for tourists.[3] Watts in South Central LA was torn apart by riots in 1965 which claimed thirty-four lives and caused tens of millions of dollars' worth of property damage. The Latino communities of East LA exploded in an unprecedented wave of mass protest beginning in 1968 and culminating in the Chicano Moratorium demonstration of August 29, 1970, during which three people were killed, including the journalist Ruben Salazar.[4]

Los Angeles's best-known underground newspaper, the *Los Angeles Free Press*, reported extensively throughout 1968 on the political activism and demonstrations then gripping Paris and many other cities worldwide, reflecting and strengthening connections between New Left and countercultural groups in Los Angeles and elsewhere. For example, on May 24, the French artist and activist Jean Jacques Lebel contributed the front-page report "Diary of the French Revolt," which dramatically reported "smoking barricades, overturned cars everywhere..." and presented a detailed account of confrontations between protesting students and police. (See Figure 6.1.) On September 13, the front page headline of the *Free Press* announced "LA City and County declare war on young people and subversives" over an account of local efforts to resist draconian policing of young people socializing on the Sunset Strip, a social and political conflict that was presented in spatial terms:

> Essentially the Strip is the scene of a clash between two very different life styles: the young people represent the new style of the future in which, more and more, people will be out on the sidewalks talking to each other. The police and the businessmen represent the old style of people who lock themselves in their houses at night and hate the man next door and the people across the street. But in a more immediate and tangible sense, it is a confrontation between the young, who need a place to go, and, on the other hand, the old men in banks and real estate offices, clutching desperately at crumbling myths—corrupt, greedy little men who care nothing about young people in need of a place to go.[5]

Figure 6.1 "Diary of the French Revolt," cover story reporting the events of May 1968 in Paris in the *Los Angeles Free Press*, May 24, 1968

At this time, urban planners in Los Angeles slowly recognized that the city was not only in a social but also a physical crisis, and that the two were inseparably linked. For example, in one of an increasing number of high-profile calls for urban reform, in January 1970, the Los Angeles Department of City Planning report *Concept for the Los Angeles General Plan* sternly warned of the city's "air pollution, traffic congestion, inadequate public transportation . . . blight and obsolescence, limited choice of housing types, poorly designed apartment buildings, intrusion of residential neighborhoods . . . , inefficient strip patterns of commercial development, hillsides scarred by excessive grading, poor access to beaches, inadequate park lands, and the drab and cluttered appearance of older commercial and residential areas."[6] Above all, it added, "the ghetto condition must be a top concern in the planning and future of Los Angeles."[7] Meanwhile, working on the scale of the neighborhood, the Department of City Planning produced the *Hollywood Motion Picture, Television, and Communication Industry Study*, following an April 1967 initiative led by Mayor Sam Yorty to respond to film industry concerns about the relative decline of Los Angeles as a filmmaking center because of "runaway" production—feature films shot on location abroad or in other parts of the United States such as New York City.[8] That study called for tax incentives, land use studies, rezoning, and better traffic planning to reassert Los Angeles primacy as "a totally integrated entertainment industry center" not only for the sake of the local economy but for the good of "the American way of life."[9]

The increasing social tension and infrastructural crisis of Los Angeles was matched by an increasing politicization of its film culture. From February 26–29, 1968, Jean-Luc Godard took part in four panel discussions at the University of Southern California's Hancock Auditorium organized by Charles Lippincott, USC professor and filmmaker, and programmed together with the first screenings in Los Angeles of *La Chinoise*, *Les Carabiniers* (1963), and *Two or Three Things I Know about Her* (*Deux ou trois choses que je sais d'elle*, 1967).[10] These discussions were extensively and enthusiastically described by Gene Youngblood in the *LA Free Press* as "an event of major significance, especially to students of cinema whose lives have been so influenced by the art form that grew out of the French New Wave," although Youngblood also noted that while audiences for the talks were respectably large they might have been even bigger but for "[an] apparent lack of concern for Godard of the nearly 600 students in the combined film departments of USC and UCLA."[11] On February 26, Godard praised Andy Warhol's *Chelsea Girls* (1966), new Brazilian cinema, and North Vietnam, declaring that "the underground is to the cinema of Hollywood what the new revolutionary politics is to the established order."[12] He lamented the decline of Hollywood cinema, including formerly great directors like Hitchcock, Hawks, and Wilder, as well as the fact that others like Demy, Polanski, and Renoir "have come to Hollywood, and I think it's tragic."[13] On February 27, he appeared with Lippincott and Agnès Varda who would soon shoot *Lions Love . . . and Lies* (1969) on location in Hollywood, a sympathetic portrait of Los Angeles's hippie scene starring both Andy Warhol protégé Viva and the independent New York–based filmmaker Shirley Clarke, with each actress playing her real self. On February 28, Godard spoke in an atmosphere of mutual admiration with a panel comprising Samuel Fuller, Roger Corman, King Vidor, and Peter Bogdanovich, although the American directors spent much of the time talking Hollywood business among themselves while Godard, according to Youngblood, "sat staring at the ceiling."[14]

Godard's final appearance at USC saw him share ideas and lessons with a panel and audience of young LA-based filmmakers, including Lewis Teague, manager of the experimental film theater Cinematheque 16, based on the Sunset Strip. As David James has explained, this was one of the key venues in the region's thriving alternative film exhibition circuit, having opened to great success in June 1966 to cater for youth audiences' hunger for European art cinema, American avant-garde film, and their shared artistic experimentation and progressive social values.[15] Film exhibition in LA was also liberalized in law—for example, in July 1968, the *Los Angeles Free Press* provided a lengthy and approving report when the absolute control of movie theater licensing exercised by the Los Angeles Police Department's Board of Commissioners was successfully challenged in the California Supreme Court by an action by Sawyer Theaters, against the City of Los Angeles.[16] Previously, city ordinances had assumed the authority to revoke an exhibitor's license when, for example, the screening of an objectionable film "will not comport with the peace, health, safety, convenience, good morals, and general welfare of the public" or when a particular theater owner was "unfit . . . or had a bad moral character, intemperate habits, or a bad reputation."[17] According to the Court, these ordinances granted an unconstitutionally sweeping power to the LAPD at the expense of citizens and tended to encourage "censorship under the cloak of regulation of business activity."[18]

Although James has thoroughly and movingly documented the rich and dynamic experimental film culture that thrived in Los Angeles at this time, the ways in which the increasing social and political turmoil of LA was and was not represented in narrative fiction film remain underexplored. After the city's heyday as a setting in film noir ran out of steam in the late 1950s, it achieved a new currency in films that did not invert its sun-drenched iconography in a world of murderous darkness, as film noir had done, but which foregrounded its sunshine and openness as the basis of a new image. In *Sex and the Single Girl* (Richard Quine, Warner Bros, 1964), *The Swinger* (George Sidney, Paramount Pictures, 1966), and *Don't Make Waves* (Alexander Mackendrick, MGM, 1967), romantic comedies with all-star casts, the Hollywood majors characterized LA as a place of sex-obsessed suburban frivolity. That characterization had its counterpart for teen audiences in beach party movies by independent exploitation film companies, from *Beach Party* (William Asher, American International Pictures, 1963) to *It's a Bikini World* (Stephanie Rothman, American International Pictures/Trans American Films, 1967). In the late 1960s, in films associated with the so-called New Hollywood, such as *The Graduate* (Mike Nichols, 1967), and *Bob and Carol and Ted and Alice* (Paul Mazursky, 1969), LA was described in terms of a much graver suburban alienation which even sex could not relieve. Hard-edged urban thrillers such as *Point Blank* (John Boorman, 1967) and *Targets* (Peter Bogdanovich, 1968) pointed to a deeply disturbed masculinity and obsessive gun violence as the true fault line of Southern California. Biker films such as *Hells Angels on Wheels* (Richard Rush, 1967) and *The Angry Breed* (David Commons, 1968) ambivalently drew attention to youth alienation by heroically striking out from the city and suburbs onto the open road, both in their narratives and location shooting, although ultimately the films framed rebellion in sensationalist and moralistic terms.

Many of these films presented stylistically and thematically challenging explorations of Los Angeles. Some demonstrated what Fredric Jameson has described as a "political unconscious," exploring dynamics of "oppressor and oppressed," but within the restrictive codes and conventions of genre film, by which their politics were largely "repressed and buried."[19] Representation of the highly charged issue of race in LA, for example, received scant attention until the following decade when independent films such as the "blaxploitation" thriller *Sweet Sweetback's Baadasssss Song* (Melvin Van Peebles, 1971) and neorealist studies of black working-class life such as *Bush Mama* (Haile Gerima, 1976) and *Killer of Sheep* (Charles Burnett, 1977) achieved new critical insight in their depictions of urban poverty, manual labor, institutional racism, and police brutality, especially in Watts and other parts of South Central LA. Moreover, *Bush Mama*, *Killer of Sheep*, and other films associated with the "L.A. Rebellion" school of filmmakers trained in UCLA's film department emerged, after a time lag, as a function of the upheavals of the late 1960s: for example, Charles Burnett, the first member of the school to graduate, enrolled at UCLA in 1967, benefited from new affirmative action policies designed to improve racial minorities' access to higher education, and was involved in founding the university's first black studies program.[20] Circa 1968, however, in the geographic imagination of Los Angeles in narrative fiction film, largely African American South Central LA constituted what Pierre Macherey might have called a huge "structured absence," as did largely Latino East LA as well, where Chicano cinema first emerged in a cluster of important documentary films about the Chicano Moratorium demonstration of August 29, 1970—that is, Thomas Myrdahl's *Chicano Moratorium* (1970), David Garcia's *Requiem 29* (1970), and Francisco Martinez's *August 29, 1970* (1971).[21]

In the remainder of this chapter, I examine a little more closely some of the most interesting cinematic responses that emerged at this time in relation to three specific places in Los Angeles—Century City, the Sunset Strip, and Venice—in which there was a critical mass both of political contestation of urban space and of motion picture representation, whether in Hollywood feature films, art cinema, exploitation film, or documentary. In all of these, mass protest or other forms of antiauthoritarian dissent by the New Left, Black Power, and hippie counterculture will be the constant thread. My aim here is to extend our understanding of the "spatial history" of Los Angeles and its moving image culture in the transformative moment of the late 1960s by applying what Edward Soja called "historical-geographical materialism" to the analysis and interpretation of particular films, with an emphasis on their site-specific representation of precise and heterogeneous locales.[22]

Century City

Almost entirely absent from narrative fiction films set in Los Angeles, despite their decisive influence on real-world events, was representation of the political activism of the New Left and Black Power movements. One index of this omission can be found in the cinematic history of Century City, the 176-acre site just west of Beverly Hills that underwent an almost complete transformation in the late 1960s as the legendary back lot of Twentieth Century Fox movie studios was redeveloped as the region's premier purpose-built commercial center and shopping mall. Mostly designed by the leading Los Angeles architectural firm of Welton Beckett and Associates, but with the important addition of the luxury Century Plaza hotel by Minoru Yamasaki, the development was billed as the largest and most high-profile rationalist intervention in the Los Angeles landscape, with the exception of the freeways themselves. Typifying what Sylvia Lavin has called "the cool and neutral spaces of modernism" and its "perfected abstraction of space," Century City nonetheless soon became the site of a telling contradiction.[23] On the one hand, because it was adjacent to the remaining, though much-reduced, studio buildings of Fox, it became a favored location for the filming of that studio's typically sumptuous genre films, most of which were romantic comedies joking about sexual liberation but ultimately attached to marriage, family, and the suburban single-family home, and conforming to the dominant capitalist and patriarchal order—for example, *A Guide for the Married Man* (Gene Kelly, 1967), *Caprice* (Frank Tashlin, 1967), and *Live a Little, Love a Little* (Norman Taurog, 1968). On the other hand, because the Century Plaza became a favorite venue for visiting dignitaries, it hosted President Lyndon Johnson during a visit to Los Angeles in June 1967, during which the streets outside witnessed the largest antiwar demonstration and the most violent confrontation between protestors and police in Los Angeles history to that point in time. (See Figure 6.2.)

Cinematic Images of Los Angeles circa 1968   171

Figure 6.2 *Demonstration, Century Plaza, 1967*, 16mm film by the Los Angeles Police Department of the protest against the Vietnam War that marked the visit to Century City, Los Angeles, by President Lyndon Johnson on June 23, 1967

A photojournalistic account of these events published by the American Civil Liberties Union described police management of the ten thousand to fifteen thousand strong crowd in terms of "indiscriminate violence, of relentless intolerance, of a careless indifference to the civil liberties which they were sworn to uphold."[24] The *Los Angeles Free Press* reported graphically what it called the LAPD's "wave after wave of remorseless sadism" in which "the rationalization and self-deception that insulates the lives of those in WASP society from the violence of American wars and racist programs was stripped away.... the Asian War that had been so far off was coming home."[25] Meanwhile, police and government accounts, arguing that the protest posed a security risk to the president, asserted their determination not to allow a repeat in Los Angeles of what had happened to President Kennedy in Dallas in 1963.

Feature films presented little direct response to such events, just as they neglected Watts and other calamities—indeed, it would appear that the only extant motion picture records of the Century Plaza protest are twelve minutes of color 16mm footage filmed by officers of the Los Angeles Police Department, a twenty-seven minute training film compiled by the U.S. Secret

Service from the same LAPD footage intercut with other footage from television news, and a KCET public television broadcast of the subsequent public hearings into the policing of the event, held at Los Angeles City Hall in October 1967.[26] In subsequent social histories, the police response to the Century Plaza demonstration has developed a reputation for having had a chilling effect. According to a report over twenty years later in the *Los Angeles Times*, it left "an indelible mark on politics, protests, and police relations. It marked a turning point for Los Angeles, a city not known for drawing demonstrators to marches in sizeable numbers."[27] The repression of the demonstration may well be the reason mass protest was less frequent and usually lower key in Los Angeles in and after 1968 than it was in other cities of comparable size.[28]

Surely the most important example of a feature film that *did* depict mass protest in LA is Michelangelo Antonioni's *Zabriskie Point* (1969), whose partial treatment of the subject very loosely echoes the actual January 1969 shootings of the black activists John Huggins and Bunchy Carter on the campus of UCLA and the political controversy that led to the firing of the radical black assistant professor, Angela Davis.[29] Although the action of *Zabriskie Point* takes place mostly in the Mojave Desert and Death Valley, its first thirty minutes are dominated by a visually striking student protest sequence, although Antonioni had difficulty finding a university campus that would allow him to shoot on location. Making a big-budget film that *Show* magazine aptly described as a "$6 million volcano" and that became a huge commercial failure for its backer, MGM, Antonioni was originally slated to film at California State College at Long Beach until turned away by student leaders who distrusted the Hollywood film industry.[30] Hence, the sequence was shot not in Los Angeles but in the San Francisco Bay Area, on the campus of Contra Costa College, whose student leaders apparently took a different view out of respect for the involvement in the film of the antiwar activist Fred Gardner, the Open Theater experimental theater company, and members of the Black Panther Party. (See Figure 6.3.) Throughout principal photography, from September 1968 to April 1969, and even when Antonioni left the city for the desert, the production was embroiled in high-profile controversy, as wild rumors circulated about the film's politics. These were noted with concern by executive producer Harrison Starr: "Suddenly, in the rabid right-wing sections of Hollywood and Southern California, the word was on the vine that we were making 'a filthy anti-American flag-desecrating film' with hippies making love all over everything."[31] Starr and MGM received numerous concerned phone calls from the Los Angeles County Sheriff's office and lawyers for the Mobil Oil corporation whose building in downtown

Figure 6.3 Contra Costa College, San Pablo, California, standing in for a Los Angeles university in *Zabriskie Point* (Antonioni, 1970)

Los Angeles was being used as a location for the offices of the film's rapacious Sunny Dunes Real Estate company. Indeed, in 1969, the film was even investigated by the U.S. Justice Department and the Federal Bureau of Investigation, allegedly at the instigation of the newly installed administration of President Richard Nixon. MGM came close to canceling the film's release.

Although *Zabriskie Point* was primarily a road movie set in rural space, in which mapping the city of Los Angeles was not Antonioni's main concern, films that were consistently interested in urban space and counterculture tended to focus on zones within the city dominated by an extended struggle for access and control between young people and the police and business owners. Two of the most prominent of these locales, not only in reality but in cinema, were the commercial Sunset Strip on Sunset Boulevard in West Hollywood and the bohemian beach community of Venice.

The Sunset Strip

The so-called Riot on the Sunset Strip, like other protest events circa 1968 in LA, consisted of a drawn out series of confrontations—in this case, between the LAPD and LA County Sheriffs, on the one hand, and thousands of young people, many under 18, who since the early 1960s had taken to gathering along the 8000 and 9000 blocks of Sunset Boulevard, especially on weekend nights. The Strip, originally famous for the glamour of movie stardom, nightlife, stage shows and big bands at such clubs as Ciro's and the Trocadero in the 1930s and 1940s, had often featured in Hollywood cinema, from the musical *A Star is Born* (1937) to the film noir *The Strip* (1951), but it had subsequently declined, or been transformed, into the region's most important cluster of countercultural coffee houses such as The Fifth Estate and Pandora's Box, and of rock music venues such as the Whisky-A-Go-Go and Gazzari's. From the summer of 1966 through the fall of 1968, police harassment of young people aimed to clear the neighborhood of unsavory elements on behalf of conservative local interests, using mass arrests and old-fashioned curfews for the minors, and leading to occasional open street fighting. The resistance of youth to the police was celebrated by Stephen Stills and Richie Furay in the Buffalo Springfield hit single "For What It's Worth," but it received scant attention in feature films with the exception of Arthur Dreifus's *Riot on Sunset Strip* (1967).[32]

Released in March 1967, that film opens with striking location-shot footage of the Sunset Strip, composed mainly of long and medium shots of police and protestors in opposing ranks, bemused or concerned passersby, police lights piercing the night, and slow-moving traffic outside Pandora's Box and other venues. (See Figure 6.4.) As a historical document, these are compelling, but their dynamic effect is undercut when, after just a few minutes, the film switches to an almost entirely studio-based mise en scène, in which not only the interiors of clubs but also the street and sidewalks are re-created on a soundstage. A prominent pop-rock music soundtrack is interspersed, often concentrated in nightclub scenes of dancing that vaguely attempt a psychedelic style (handheld camera, colored lights) while inviting viewers to enjoy the sight of pretty young women gyrating. From the outset, the film characterizes a not altogether plausible difference between hipsters who just want to dance and get stoned and others, more zealous and less appealing, who want to march and protest for freedom. The brief social realism of the opening footage is soon constrained by a melodramatic narrative in which a weary but benevolent, paternal police chief finds his efforts to mediate between youth and conservative local business owners complicated by the fact that his own daughter is a hipster on the Strip, damaged by her parents' broken marriage and her mother's drinking, all presented in a moralistic tone reminiscent of the much earlier *Rebel without a Cause* (Nicholas Ray, 1955). Indeed, not only is the narrative spatially specific in its focus on the Strip, it surprisingly contains no reference to any larger civil rights movement, to Black Power, or the Vietnam War. Instead, it concentrates on white, suburban, middle-class kids in trouble, their frequent fistfights suggesting the irrational propensity of teenage youth for delinquency and violence, and leading to a sensationalistic ending in which the police chief's daughter has her drink spiked with LSD and is gang raped by five of the guys she hangs out with in a party at a plush Beverly Hills mansion they have broken into (though the film leaves open the possibility she is intentionally promiscuous

Figure 6.4 The Sunset Strip re-created in studio, top, and shot on location at night, bottom, in *Riot on the Sunset Strip* (Dreifus, 1967)

in order to get back at her parents). Notwithstanding its pretense to hipness in subject, soundtrack, and visual style, this ending, capped by a voice-of-god narrator warning of society's need for responsible parenting, seems calculated to cater to conservative stereotypes of youth rebellion.

Such a film is indicative of the sensationalist and moralizing way social protest was generally treated in narrative fiction film and, prior to 1968, mostly by independent companies.[33] Other genres presented somewhat more sympathetic views, although they were rare: for example, the youth culture documentary *Mondo Mod* (Peter Perry, 1967) featured a short but relatively respectful location-shot segment of demonstrators on the Strip and the much-loved local television news show *Ralph Story's Los Angeles*, on KNXT, reported wryly, if not wistfully, on the closure of Pandora's Box, which was forced out of business in October 1967 when the City of Los Angeles condemned the building to subdue its unruly clientele.[34]

Venice

Like the Sunset Strip, by the late 1960s Venice Beach had also become a prominent enclave of countercultural resistance to mainstream culture and society and, like the Strip, it too was the subject of a struggle with police. Alex Apostolides reported in the *Los Angeles Free Press* of April 12, 1968, on what he called "a 72-hour display of official violence" carried out by police against Venice's hippie community:

> During the course of the blitz, one man's neck was broken. Many peaceful people were beaten bloody by over-eager fuzz. Business places were entered without warrant, proprietors and clients subjected to verbal and physical abuse. Displays were torn from walls, merchandise destroyed—or taken—as the Metro Squad romped through its field day of destruction. Police cars, marked or plain, hot-rodded down the pedestrian-filled boardwalk, careless of the people there. Cameras and film were confiscated when people dared take pictures of the fuzz in action. . . . The town experienced, for a short time, what it's like to live in a police state.[35]

Established as a seaside resort in the early 1900s, and partly modeled on the Italian original, Venice had quickly become famous for its Italianate colonnades, canals, boardwalk, pier, and funfair, but fell into decline during the Great Depression, when the discovery of oil transformed much of the adjoining area into an ugly field of derricks. Subsequently, its increasing dilapidation earned it roles in film noir from *He Walked by Night* (Alfred L. Werker, 1948) to *Touch of Evil* (Orson Welles, 1958) while combining with its low rents to produce a burgeoning artists' colony. In the late 1950s and early 1960s, Beatnik writers were drawn to live and work in Venice by what Reyner Banham called its "romantically blighted" landscape, focusing their critiques of Cold War conformity in poetry readings and jazz sessions at the Gas House café, a flashpoint of controversy over freedom of expression made world famous by the publication of Lawrence Lipton's portrait of the Venice beatnik scene, *The Holy Barbarians* (1959).[36] Meanwhile, though the City of

Los Angeles threatened to modernize Venice by building a freeway through its heart, the district's light industrial decay and chintzy commercialism richly rewarded what Cecile Whiting has called the "taste for the decrepit" of Ed Ruscha and other painters and sculptors in LA's rapidly emerging school of Pop Art.[37]

Venice's renegade reputation also took cinematic form through low-budget exploitation films about Beatniks such as *A Bucket of Blood* (Roger Corman, 1959) and *The Beat Generation* (Charles F. Haas, 1959), as well as avant-gardist films sympathetic to, or made by, Beatniks or hippies—from Curtis Harrington's occult feature *Night Tide* (1961) to Dan McLaughlin's experimental short *Brucemas* (1968). In 1968, in the art film *Model Shop*, by French director Jacques Demy, Venice provided a downbeat start and end point for the action and several intervening scenes, in a narrative that mapped a series of journeys from Venice to West Hollywood, and a series of subcultural and countercultural spaces, including the protagonist's Venice beach hut, a pool hall, a seedy candid photographers' model shop on Melrose Avenue, the office of the real underground newspaper *Open City* on Santa Monica Boulevard, and a Queen Anne–style mansion occupied by the LA-based rock group Spirit. With the exception of the interiors of the model shop and an apartment set featured briefly near the film's end, both of which were filmed on a Columbia Pictures sound stage, all of the film's settings were found on location around the city and, Demy explained, filmed exactly as they were found for the sake of authenticity.[38] As such the film stands out as an example of the rediscovery of the real city by filmmakers at this time, which stemmed from a rejection of studio contrivance in favor of the street and its immediacy—Demy explained that he worked quickly, with a twenty-five day shoot, low budget, small crew, and a minimum of equipment.[39] Anouk Aimée, recently the star of Claude Lelouch's international hit romance *A Man and a Woman* (1966), plays Lola, a French divorcée who has been traveling for a number of years in order to find herself and who now pays her bills by working as a model for amateur candid photographers, hoping to earn enough money for the journey back to Paris. Gary Lockwood, who had played in Stanley Kubrick's *2001: A Space Odyssey* (1968), plays George Matthews, an angst-ridden young architect who has only black humor, a few hippie friends, and a brief liaison with Lola to protect him from the fact that he is just days away from being drafted to serve in Vietnam.

Demy, who was known for three previous films—*Lola* (1961), *The Umbrellas of Cherbourg* (*Les Parapluies de Cherbourg*, 1964), and *The Young Girls of Rochefort* (*Les Demoiselles de Rochefort*, 1967)—was one of those foreign filmmakers who found relatively easy access to the Hollywood film industry in the 1960s because of the popularity then of European art cinema in the United States, together with Hollywood's increasing reliance on overseas markets and the search by the major studios for new creative ideas.[40] Indeed, many of the most perceptive and critical representations of LA of the era were by foreigners, including the aforementioned *Lions Love . . . and Lies* by Varda, who was Demy's wife and also in LA at the time, as well as Antonioni's *Zabriskie Point* and the slightly later *The Outside Man* (*Un homme est mort*, Jacques Deray, 1972). As an outsider, Demy explained that he first visited Los Angeles when he was invited to the San Francisco Film Festival of October 1967, not intending to make a film but becoming fascinated with Los Angeles and determined to bring its distinctive physical character to the screen because, it seemed to him, Hollywood films were not doing so and European audiences, who were largely unfamiliar with LA, were likely to find it compelling.[41] Crucially, for Demy, LA provided him with something he had been missing at home in France in recent years: he explained to the *Los Angeles Times* that "When I left Paris it was dead. Now I've missed the revolution [of May '68]. . . . But I had been so depressed, so discouraged. I said I must go someplace where something's happening. I don't want to be pretentious, but I want *The Model Shop* to be 'Los Angeles, 1968.'"[42]

Surely one of the era's most representative political and ethical characterizations of the city, in this image of "Los Angeles, 1968," there is no cataclysmic revolt, but rather a low-level oppression and resistance shapes the film's narrative and its mise en scène.[43] The protagonist George exists in a state of suspended animation because the draft hangs over his head and, as he puts it succinctly, "it's kinda hard to plan anything, you know." In Venice, this state is poetically evoked in several shots in which oil rigs tower over his beach hut, their metallic bulk, slow, repetitive movement, and monotonous drone literally and figuratively hemming him in. George is not a protagonist in control of his actions, but rather an enigmatic man of few words who spends the bulk of his time haphazardly driving or sometimes walking through the city, from incident to incident, in the vain hope of navigating his way out of a dead end. As such, the film contributes to the crisis of classical narrative that asserted itself in American cinema from *Bonnie and Clyde* (1967) to *Taxi Driver* (1976) as the young adult audiences upon which Hollywood came to rely demanded more self-reflexive and questioning modes of storytelling and representation, often drawing on new wave cinemas from outside Hollywood and outside the United States. That crisis, which Gilles Deleuze characterized as a crisis of "the action-image" typified by classical Hollywood cinema, entailed a collapse of the strong and coordinated "sensory-motor links" that had characterized the narrative agency of the heroic protagonist in the studio era.[44]

Figure 6.5 The heavily commercialized streetscapes of Los Angeles in *Model Shop* (Demy, 1968)

Indeed, films set in LA, like *Model Shop*, had a natural advantage when it came to disarticulating the unities of space and time not only because of that city's relatively dispersed and decentered geography, in which each neighborhood becomes a micropolitical habitat, but also because of its hypercommodified street-level environment.[45]

When asked by an audience member during one of his talks at USC, "What is your impression of Los Angeles?" Jean Luc Godard was heard to reply simply, "It's a big garage."[46] Demy's *Model Shop* does not present as biting a critique of automobile culture as that of Godard's *Weekend* (1967)—indeed, when it was released in the spring of 1969, Demy's film was often praised for its originality in capturing what many critics described as the unconventional beauty of LA. Demy spoke of his affection for the place, explaining that he "learned the city by driving from one end of Sunset to the other, down Western all the way to Long Beach. LA has the perfect proportions for film. It fits the frame perfectly."[47] Reviewer Charles Champlin, in the *LA Times*, praised *Model Shop* because "it's a film which understands that ours is a pneumatic, nomadic culture," while Richard Gertner, in the *Motion Picture Herald*, argued that "Demy deserves a citation from the LA Chamber of Commerce. By photographing it with the eye of a poet he has often made that not-too-attractive city look positively beautiful."[48]

Demy's film does indeed contain several extended driving sequences along the length of Santa Monica Boulevard, Melrose Avenue, or other thoroughfares in which medium shots of George through the windshield of his car, accompanied by the edifying strains of Bach, Schumann, or Rimsky-Korsakov, discern a kind of beauty in LA's raucous urban landscape. (See Figure 6.5.) In some ways, therefore, *Model Shop* parallels the observations of the British architectural historian Reyner Banham. His groundbreaking book *Los Angeles: The Architecture of Four Ecologies* (1971), which had its roots in a series of BBC radio talks that he delivered in the spring of 1968, was among the first sustained analyses of the city's geography, planning, and architecture to take a decidedly positive view of its "instant architecture in an instant townscape," embracing its populism, visual noise, and eccentricity.[49]

Streetscapes

However, the driving sequences of *Model Shop* are at least as melancholic as they are beguiling, always undercut by the long-term threat of war and death and the short-term threat that George's car will be repossessed because he is way behind on his monthly installments—an important subplot in the film insists on George's constant financial precarity in this ultimate consumer environment. Outside Venice, and especially in the film's equally significant pedestrian sequences, Demy's Los Angeles consists of never-ending heavily commercialized streetscapes presented mostly in bright sunlight, with a preponderance of natural eye-level perspectives, and dominated by crisscrossing cars, outsized billboards and signage, and the reflective glass of store front windows. The existentialist crisis of the protagonist owes much to this built environment that is utilitarian, commodified, and excessive and that is also increasingly difficult to find one's way around because it is constantly expanding. The result is a semiotically confused streetscape in which human scale seems diminished and devalued. Many of the film's reviewers missed (or chose to overlook) this, although Vincent Canby in the *New York Times* neatly evoked its "solid state grid of boulevards, parking lots, two-story loft buildings, drugstores, supermarkets, and beach houses. Demy is almost right. In '*Model Shop*' you don't experience Los Angeles as often as you read it, on billboards and neon signs, in a freeze-dried vocabulary of words like Sale, Eat, Wash, Service."[50]

That Los Angeles's built environment was excessive in a bad way was a sensation increasingly felt by Angelenos at this time, and was apparently shared by Demy. Indeed, his approach seems to coincide with the LA Department of City Planning study of *The Visual Environment of Los Angeles* (1971), an innovative project that borrowed the methodology of "cognitive mapping" from Kevin Lynch's *The Image of the City* (1961). *The Visual Environment of Los Angeles* opened with a blunt assertion that "People are angry about their environment . . ." before going on to argue that:

> Seen from the air [LA's] development seems quite clear. However, when seen at ground level by people going about their daily activities it can produce a confusing mental image which may impede purposeful action. . . . Many streets in Los Angeles are difficult to identify due to their similar appearance [and are] so "busy" with signs, billboards, utility poles and lines, and gaudy structures that they are confusing and discomforting to the observer.[51]

As Lynch had argued in *The Image of the City*, the rampant growth of Los Angeles had resulted in an overabundance of architecturally nondescript, low-cost, low-rise, and cluttered strip development, a dehumanizing type of built environment of which Los Angeles was increasingly recognized as an unfortunate exemplar. Hence, Los Angeles's built environment was especially lacking in "legibility," and that problem was compounded by atmospheric problems due to smog and noise, insufficient government regulation of construction, and an overreliance on freeways, which divided and damaged communities as often as they brought them together.[52]

Reviews of *Model Shop* and interviews with Demy in the French press tended to draw attention to the issues of Vietnam and capitalist excess more often and more pointedly than did their American counterparts, and in them Demy showed somewhat more political awareness than he is usually given credit for.[53] For example, in *Le Monde* he explained his desire "to talk about certain problems of American youth that are not talked about," presenting "a subjective and necessarily limited point of view" but based on "a very large number of young Americans that I met: they told me their worries, they explained to me their refusal to integrate into society, to take part in the war in Vietnam. Their attitudes recall somewhat those of young French men during the Algerian War."[54] This aspect of *Model Shop* made the film different from his previous work—"I am tackling a situation which excludes all sentimentality and which examines solitude and fear"[55]—although French critics too acknowledged that George's response to his predicament is not protest or some other form of political engagement but a kind of "detached sadness" that pervades the film.[56] This moral sincerity contrasts with the unfortunately cavalier tone of Banham in relation to urban conflicts in LA: "Yet these extremes contrive to coexist with only sporadic flares of violence—on Venice Beach, in Watts, or whatever is the fashionable venue for confrontations."[57]

Demy's Los Angeles in *Model Shop* takes some pleasure from the city's populist built environment, but without neglecting its dehumanization, a strategy that places him politically to the left of Banham, and of most American directors, but not quite so much as Antonioni or Godard. The film's analysis of Los Angeles's new urban geography concludes in a very downbeat manner. Having befriended and slept with Lola, but knowing nothing lasting can come of it, George gives her his last hard cash so that she can fly back to Paris while his car is repossessed and he awaits shipping out to Southeast Asia. Social relations in the city are shaped not only by its geography and architecture but by the hidden violence of war, the constant threat of the draft, and a near state of emergency that is only slightly relieved by the city's abundant sunshine. In this sense, Demy's movie, rather than matching Banham, anticipates the ambivalent critiques of LA that would be presented by French sociologists and philosophers, a significant number of whom came for extended visits or to live in Southern California shortly after 1968, and who saw it as new terrain literally and metaphorically, a respite from the culturally and ideologically moribund status quo of France under Charles de Gaulle and Georges Pompidou. These included Edgar Morin, Louis Marin, Alain Touraine, Jean Baudrillard, and Jean-François Lyotard, all of whom had been members of the faculty at the University of Nanterre or other Parisian universities during the events of May that year.[58]

Hence, Morin, in his book *California Journal* (1970), described LA as "a strange bio-cybernetic organism," sensed in a hippie love-in at Griffith Park that "a great religion is struggling to emerge," praised the *Los Angeles Free Press* as "the reflection and mouthpiece of this exuberant movement, which is at once formless and multiform," and sympathized with Angela Davis and the Black Panther Party while cautioning against their identification with "the Marxist vulgate" in China, Vietnam, and Cuba.[59] In 1969, Alain Touraine taught at UCLA, providing his students with what J. W. Freiberg has called "the most powerful intellectual experience of our graduate career ... a theoretical model that would add together for us all that we experienced so poignantly—Vietnam, the student movement, the Black rights movement, the new values on patterns of interpersonal relations, the repressiveness of the military, espionage and police machinery of the United States, and so on."[60] Touraine himself recalled with passion the October 1969 Moratorium demonstration against the Vietnam War at UCLA when liberals and radicals joined together in "a huge gathering in the evening, speeches by Hollywood stars, and an almost religious silence when, at the end of the evening, everyone lit a candle and sang 'We Shall Overcome.'"[61] Louis Marin, in *Utopics: The Semiological Play of Textual Spaces* (1973)—a work Marin explained was directly inspired by the recent events of May 1968—presented a study of utopianism in art and literary history since ancient Greece, and building to a critique of the planning and iconography of Disneyland as "a degenerate utopia ... ideology changed into the form of myth ... a fascinating image of the past and the future, of what is estranged and what is familiar: comfort, welfare, consumption, scientific and technological progress, superpower, and morality. These are values obtained by violence and exploitation ... projected under the auspices of law and order."[62] Jean Baudrillard, in 1970, made the first of a series of visits from which he often identified Los Angeles as the *ne plus ultra* of the simulacrum, as in *Simulacra and Simulation* (1981), in which he claimed that "Disneyland is presented as imaginary in order to make us believe that the rest is real, whereas all of Los Angeles and the America that surrounds it are no longer real but belong to the hyperreal order and to the order of simulation."[63] And Lyotard, first arriving in 1972, described Los Angeles in his semiautobiographical novel *The Pacific Wall* (1979) as "the absolute West: the source of American capitalism ... the capital of the world," heir to the mantle of ancient imperial Rome, but not so much for beauty and grandeur (which Lyotard admits it often has) as for its inherent violence—Lyotard's book hinges on an appreciation and analysis of LA Pop artist Edward Kienholz's installation *Five Car Stud* (1969–1972), a shockingly violent depiction of a lynching.[64]

For these observers, as for Jacques Demy, the aftermath of 1968 was a time of regret and reassessment in which Los Angeles offered a striking social and political novelty and strangeness. They had seen the high hopes of May '68 dashed in a violent confrontation in the historic core of Paris in which radical students, though heroically defiant, had been eventually outmaneuvered and overwhelmed by superior state forces. In the aftermath of such a showdown in the modern city, it is easy to understand why LA's lack of any such center might have suggested the possibility of endless, nomadic resistance. But, as these filmmakers and philosophers soon learned, LA's lack of a center did not mean that authority had gone away—only that it now took different forms.

NOTES

1. On 1968, see Marshall Berman, *All That Is Solid Melts into Air: The Experience of Modernity* (New York: Verso, 1983), 163. Berman argues for 1968 as an artistic and political high point in the history of modernism, although he expresses skepticism of the value of "post-modernism" as a descriptor or analytic concept. I find his account of modernism compelling, though I do not share his skepticism of the need for a different term for the subsequent era.

2. LA was also assuming a new world cultural significance at this time beyond mass media and popular entertainment. See *Birth of the Cool: California Art, Design, and Culture at Midcentury*, ed. Elizabeth Armstrong (New York: Prestel Publishing/Orange County Museum of Art, 2007); and Janet Abu-Lughod, *New York, Chicago, Los Angeles: America's Global Cities* (Minneapolis: University of Minnesota Press, 1999), 237–268.

3. Jack Smith, "Hollywood Boulevard," in *The Big Orange* (Pasadena: Ward Ritchie Press, 1976), 15–22, 15. This decline was matched by an increase in nostalgia for the studio era and for Hollywood as a lost community, which intensified in the early 1960s. See Charles Higham, "Hollywood Boulevard 1965," *Sight & Sound* 34, no. 4 (Autumn 1965): 177–179, and *Hollywood at Sunset* (New York: Saturday Review Press, 1972), 180–181.

4. Abu-Lughod, *New York, Chicago*, 264–266.

5. Jean Jacques Lebel, "Diary of the French Revolt," *Los Angeles Free Press*, May 24–30, 1968, 1, 3. See also Roy L Walford, "French Set France on Fire," *Los Angeles Free Press*, June 7, 1968, 5, 8; Roy L. Walford, "Paris: Faces Dull and Hard Become Tender and Beautiful," *Los Angeles Free Press*, July 5, 1968, 3, 6, 13–14.

6. Los Angeles Department of City Planning, *The Concept for the Los Angeles General Plan*, Los Angeles, January 1970, 4–5.

7. Ibid., 5.

8. Los Angeles Department of City Planning, *Hollywood Motion Picture, Television, and Communication Industry Study*, Los Angeles, 1969.

9. Ibid. 6 and 30.

10. Gene Youngblood, "Jean Luc Godard: No Difference between Life and Cinema," part one of a four-part Godard roundtable discussion, with Mark Woodcock, Charles Lippincott, and Toby Mussman, February 26, 1968, published in *Los Angeles Free Press*, March 8, 1968, 15, 20. There was often a significant time-lag between the theatrical release of Godard's films in France and in the United States—*La Chinoise* was released in the United States in March 1968, *Les Carabiniers* in September 1967, and *Two or Three Things I Know about Her* in September 1970, although the latter was screened at USC in February 1968 and again at the New York Film Festival in September that year. Some of Godard's films were released and marketed in the United States under their original French titles, others with titles in English; I name them in this essay as they were named in LA at the time.

11. Ibid., 15, and Gene Youngblood, "Jean-Luc Godard: Hollywood Should Shoot in 8mm," part two of the four-part Godard roundtable discussion, with Mark Woodcock, Charles Lippincott, and Agnès Varda, February 27, 1968, published in *Los Angeles Free Press*, March 15, 1968, 5.

12. Youngblood, "Jean Luc Godard: No Difference between Life and Cinema," 15.

13. Ibid.

14. Ibid. According to Youngblood, Jacques Demy was supposed to participate, with Michel Legrand, in the February 27 event with Agnes Varda, but he did not show.

15. David James, *The Most Typical Avant-Garde: History and Geography of Minor Cinemas in Los Angeles* (Berkeley: University of California Press, 2005), 225.

16. Paul Eberle, "LAPD Loses Theater Control," *Los Angeles Free Press*, July 19, 1968, 5. On parallel developments across the United States in 1968, see Paul Monaco, *The Sixties*, History of the American Cinema, vol. 8 (Berkeley: University of California Press, 2001), 64.

17. Eberle, "LAPD Loses Theater Control."

18. Ibid.

19. Jameson, *The Political Unconscious: Narrative as a Socially Symbolic Act* (London: Routledge, 1989), 20.

20. See Allyson Field, Jan-Christopher Horak, and Jacqueline Najuma Stewart, eds., *L.A. Rebellion: Creating a New Black Cinema* (Berkeley: University of California Press, 2015), 15, 87, 209; Paula Massood, "An Aesthetic Appropriate to Conditions: *Killer of Sheep*, (Neo)Realism, and the Documentary Impulse," *Wide Angle* 21, no. 4 (1999), 20–41, 23; and Ntongela Masilela, "The Los Angeles School of Black Filmmakers," in *Black American Cinema,* ed. Manthia Diawara (New York: Routledge, 1993), 107–117. See also Brian Puser, *Burning Down the House: Politics, Governance, and Affirmative Action at the University of California*, (Albany: SUNY Press, 2012), 25–28.

21. Pierre Macherey, *The Theory of Literary Production* (New York: Routledge, 2012); originally published as *Pour une théorie de la production littéraire* (Paris: Maspero, 1966); Marcia Eymann and Charles Wollenberg, *What's Going On? California and the Vietnam Era* (Berkeley: University of California Press, 2004), 126.

22. On the "spatial history" of Hollywood cinema in the 1910s–1950s, see my *Hollywood Cinema and the Real Los Angeles* (London: Reaktion Books, 2012), 15. Soja discusses "historical-geographical materialism" in *Postmodern Geographies: The Reassertion of Space in Critical Social Theory* (London: Verso, 1989), 70, 131.

23. Sylvia Lavin, *Form follows Libido: Architecture and Richard Neutra in a Psychoanalytic Culture* (Cambridge, MA: MIT Press, 2004).

24. American Civil Liberties Union of Southern California, *Day of Protest, Night of Violence: The Century City Peace March, A Report of the American Civil Liberties Union of Southern California* (Los Angeles: Sawyer Press, 1967), 33.

25. H. Lawrence Lack, "The Asian War Is Coming Home," *Los Angeles Free Press*, June 26, 1967, 5.

26. Los Angeles Police Department Film and Video Unit, *Demonstration, Century Plaza, 1967,* 16mm color footage, June 23, 1967, LAPD Film Can 133, City of Los Angeles, City Archives and Records Center; U.S. Secret Service, *Century Plaza Demonstration (President Johnson, June 1967),* 16mm training film, captioned "Century Plaza,

June 23, 1967, Compiled from footage and sound tracks of the Los Angeles Police Department and Local Television Stations," item USSS #18502, National Archives and Records Administration, Washington, DC; *Los Angeles City Council hearings on the Century Plaza demonstration*, KCET Department of Public Affairs, producer-director, Tom Burrows, reporter, Leo McElroy, recorded October 10 and October 13, 1967, UCLA Film and Television Archive item VA3909T.

27. Quoted in David McBride, "Death City Radicals: The Counterculture in Los Angeles," in *The New Left Revisited*, ed. John Campbell McMillian and Paul Buhle (Philadelphia: Temple University Press, 2003), 110–138, 134.

28. The aforementioned Chicano Moratorium of August 1970 is the key exception here, as it attracted a significant crowd, usually estimated at about twenty thousand to thirty thousand people. See, for example, Lorena Oropeza, *¡Raza Sí! ¡Guerra No!: Chicano Protest and Patriotism during the Viet Nam War Era* (Berkeley: University of California Press, 2005), 145. Numerous estimates of the size of crowds of protestors at various key demonstrations in the late 1960s, internationally, are provided in *1968: The World Transformed*, ed. Carole Fink, Philipp Gassert, and Detlef Junker (Cambridge: Cambridge University Press, 1998)—these numbers range from about three thousand at the first student occupations in West Berlin in 1966 to about eight hundred thousand at the mega-rallies of the Japanese Beheiran antiwar group in 1970. See Fink et al., *World Transformed*, 330, 451, passim.

29. See Laura Pulido, *Black, Brown, Yellow, and Left: Radical Activism in Los Angeles* (Berkeley: University of California Press, 2006) and Joshua Bloom and Waldo E. Martin, *Black against Empire: The History and Politics of the Black Panther Party* (Berkeley: University of California Press, 2013), 216–225.

30. Louise Sweeney, "*Zabriskie Point* Lives," *Show* magazine, February 1970, 41–43, 41.

31. Sweeney, "*Zabriskie Point* Lives," 42.

32. The *Hollywood Community Plan* specifically called for improvement and beautification of the Sunset Strip. See Los Angeles Department of City Planning, *Hollywood Community Plan: Implementation Report*, Los Angeles, September 1970, 12.

33. For histories of the respective responses of Hollywood cinema and U.S. independent filmmakers to political protest in the 1960s, see Mark Shiel "The American New Wave, Part 1: 1967–1970," in Michael Hammond and Linda Ruth Williams, eds., *American Cinema Since World War Two* (New York: McGraw-Hill, 2006), 12–28; J. Hoberman, *The Dream Life: Movies, Media, and the Mythology of the Sixties* (New York: The New Press, 2005); and David James, *Allegories of Cinema: American Film in the Sixties* (Princeton, NJ: Princeton University Press, 1989).

34. *Ralph Story's Los Angeles*, "Demolition of the Pandora's Box Night Club-Coffeehouse," KNXT, Los Angeles, October 29, 1967, archival copy, UCLA Film and Television Archive, video item VA13900 T. For an evocative account of the Sunset Strip protests, see Mike Davis, *In Praise of Barbarians: Essays against Empire* (Chicago: Haymarket Books, 2007), 312–328.

35. Alex Apostolides, "Venice Survives," *Los Angeles Free Press*, April 12, 1968, 34.

36. See Lawrence Lipton, *Holy Barbarians* (New York: Julian Messner, 1959); also John Arthur Maynard's *Venice West: The Beat Generation in Southern California* (New Brunswick, NJ: Rutgers University Press, 1993).

37. Cecile Whiting, "Los Angeles in the 1960s," in *Time and Place: Los Angeles, 1957–1968* (Moderna Museet: Stockholm/Steidl: Gottingen, 2008, 10–35), 29; see also Whiting, *Pop L.A.: Art and the City in the 1960s* (Berkeley: University of California Press, 2006). As late as 1978, the *Free Venice Beachhead* alternative newspaper campaigned against plans for a Venice Freeway, which had been at the planning stage since the 1940s, reminding its readers that the threat of "the construction of a major highway through Venice has long hung like a cloud over this community." Ultimately, the Venice Freeway was one of a number of similar routes—such as the Beverly Hills Freeway and the Pacific Coast Freeway—whose construction was under serious consideration during LA's rapid growth in the 1960s but which were never actually built. For contemporary accounts of the planning of the Venice Freeway and community resistance to it, see Los Angeles Department of City Planning, *Venice Community Study CPC14311*, Los Angeles, July 1968, and Horst Schmidt-Brummer, *Venice, California: An Urban Fantasy*, trans. Feelie Lee (New York: Grossman Publishing, 1973).

38. "J'ai été en Amérique pour apprendre, pour comprendre," Jacques Demy, interviewed by Yvonne Baby, *Le Monde*, May 23, 1969, press clipping file on Jacques Demy, Cinémathèque française, Paris.

39. Interview by Gerard Langlois, *Lettres françaises*, May 7, 1969, press clipping file on Jacques Demy, Cinémathèque française.

40. *Model Shop* is a kind of angst-ridden sequel to Demy's earlier romance *Lola*—Aimee reprising her lead role in the first film, but disillusioned and displaced after the breakup of her marriage.

41. *Le Monde*, May 23, 1969; see also "Jacques Demy à propos de *Model Shop*," television interview, *Monsieur Cinéma*, ORTF, May 5, 1969, available at l'Institut National de l'Audiovisuel, online video archive, http://www.ina.fr/video/I00014251.

42. Kevin Thomas, "Demy, Anouk Meet Again—in LA, of All Places," *Los Angeles Times*, July 21, 1968, C14. Some press coverage of the film's production prior to its release referred to it as *The Model Shop*, though the official title on release was *Model Shop*.

43. Demy's Venice seems quiet and underpopulated, although Varda's *Lions Love . . . and Lies* does include a few brief shots of documentary footage of a music festival during which hippies defy police orders to disperse. But the sequence is fleeting and not developed in narrative terms.

44. Gilles Deleuze, *Cinema I: The Movement Image* (Minneapolis: University of Minnesota Press, 1986), 206–207.

45. Ibid. For Deleuze, these films typify what he calls "the crisis of Hollywood and its old genres."

46. Youngblood, "Jean-Luc Godard: Hollywood Should Shoot in 8mm," 25.

47. Thomas, "Demy, Anouk Meet Again."

48. Charles Champlin, "*Model Shop* May Leave Scene Unseen," *Los Angeles Times*, March 25, 1969, H1; *Motion Picture Herald*, February 19, 1969, unpaginated press clippings file on Jacques Demy, Margaret Herrick Library, Academy of Motion Picture Arts and Sciences, Beverly Hills.

49. Reyner Banham, *Los Angeles: The Architecture of the Four Ecologies* (London: Allen Lane, 1971), 3.

50. Vincent Canby, "Screen: *Model Shop* Looks Out on Los Angeles," *New York Times*, February 12, 1969, 30.

51. Los Angeles Department of City Planning, *The Visual Environment of Los Angeles*, 1971, 2, 23. See also Kevin Lynch, *The Image of the City* (Cambridge, MA: MIT Press, 1960).

52. *Visual Environment of Los Angeles*, 6.

53. Many scholarly and popular accounts of Demy and his work emphasize his bittersweet fascination with the musical genre, fantasy, dream, and myth. See, for example, Darren Waldron, *Jacques Demy* (Manchester: Manchester University Press, 2015); Mathieu Orléan, ed., *Le monde enchanté de Jacques Demy* (Paris: Skira-Flammarion, 2013); and Jean-Pierre Berthomé, *Jacques Demy: Les racines du rêve* (Nantes: l'Atalante, 1982). Waldron's analysis is distinctive for acknowledging the philosophical complexity masked by Demy's preoccupation with fantasy, but his analysis does not extend to *Model Shop*.

54. *Le Monde*, May 23, 1969.

55. *Le Monde*, May 23, 1969.

56. Michel Capdenac, *Lettres françaises*, May 14, 1969, press clipping file on Jacques Demy, Cinémathèque française.

57. Banham, *Los Angeles*, 7.

58. See Edgar Morin, *California Journal* (Eastbourne: Sussex Academic Press, 2008); originally published as *Journal de Californie* (Paris: Le Seuil, 1970); Alain Touraine, *The Academic System in American Society* (Piscataway, NJ: Transaction Publishers, 1974); originally published as *Université et société aux États-Unis* (Paris: Le Seuil, 1972); Alain Touraine, *The Post Industrial Society*, trans. Leonard F. X. Mayhew (New York: Random House, 1971); originally published as *La Société Post-industrielle* (Paris: Éditions Denoël-Gonthier, 1969); J. W. Freiberg, Foreword, in Alain Touraine, *The Self-Production of Society*, trans. Derek Coltman (Chicago: University of Chicago Press, 1977); originally published as *Production de la société* (Paris: Seuil, 1973), xi–xvi; Louis Marin, *Utopics* (Atlantic Highlands, NJ: Humanities Press, 1984); originally published as *Utopiques: Jeux d'espaces* (Paris: Éditions de Minuit, 1973); Jean-François Lyotard, *The Pacific Wall* (Los Angeles: Lapis Press, 1990); originally published as *Le mur du pacifique* (Paris: Éditions Galilée, 1979); Jean Baudrillard, *Symbolic Exchange and Death* (Thousand Oaks, CA: SAGE Publications, 1993); originally published as *L'Échange symbolique et la mort* (Paris: Gallimard, 1975); Jean Baudrillard, *Simulacra and Simulation* (Ann Arbor: University of Michigan Press, 1994); originally published as *Simulacres et simulations* (Paris: Éditions Galilée, 1981); Jean Baudrillard, *America* (New York: Verso, 1988); originally published as *Amérique* (Paris: Grasset, 1986); Jean Baudrillard and Philippe Petit, *Paroxysm: Jean Baudrillard, Interviews with Philippe Petit* (London: Verso, 1998), 79–88.

59. Morin, *California Journal*, 42, 44, 13.

60. Freiberg, Foreword, xi–xii.

61. Touraine, *The Academic System in American Society*, 227.

62. Marin, *Utopics*, 239–240.

63. Baudrillard, *Simulacra and Simulation*, 12.

64. Jean-François Lyotard, "Passages from 'Le Mur du Pacifique' (1979)," trans. Pierre Brochet, Nick Royle, and Kathleen Woodward, *SubStance* 11, no. 4, issue 37–38, A Special Issue from the Center for Twentieth Century Studies (1983): 89–99, 94–95.

7

Cinema and the Mexico City of 1968

JESSE LERNER

By any reckoning, October 1968 was a milestone in modern Mexican history. That month Mexico City hosted the summer Olympic Games, making it the first city of the so-called "third" (or "developing") world to do so. The XIX Olympiad and building projects associated with it marked the culmination of a series of ambitious efforts by the Mexican state to transform and showcase the capital city as a modern and prosperous metropolis. Any number of Mexican films from the era, as well as a smaller number of foreign productions, make use of the city's new buildings, public spaces and neighborhoods as representative of an emphatically Mexican modernity, at once cosmopolitan and explicitly nationalistic. But October 1968 also has much darker resonances. It saw a violent repression of a broad coalition of leftists—primarily students, though joined by significant numbers of workers affiliated with labor unions independent of state control.[1] These were perceived by the state as a threat to the nation's moment in the international spotlight and were misrepresented in the press as a subversive influx of foreign agitators.

On October 2, ten days before the opening of the Olympic Games, government forces massacred an unknown number of leftist protesters—probably in the hundreds—in the district of Tlatelolco.[2] Survivors understood that if peaceful protests would be brutally suppressed with impunity, they then faced a stark range of alternatives, including exile, guerrilla insurgency inspired by the Cuban model, or a switch in focus from advocating political change to the creation of an alternative society through a counterculture, or "la onda." As I explain, small-gauge filmmaking, especially by the so-called "superochero" movement, was one vehicle for politicized youth to imagine alternative futures and critique existing conditions. For them, the city became either an oppressive and traumatic space from which to escape, a potential site of violent acts of insurgency and terrorism, or an open playing field in which to envisage utopias, all in response to the events of 1968. In this chapter, I contrast the countercultural city of the *superocheros* with mainstream filmic celebrations of the city's modernist architecture and urban planning, focusing on three highly charged sites within Mexico City—Tlatelolco, the campus of the National University (officially, the Universidad Nacional Autónoma de México, or UNAM), and the Palacio de Lecumberri jail. Mexico City was not a key center for the production of a political modernist cinema such as the "Third Cinema" called for by the Argentine filmmakers Fernando Solanas and Octavio Getino, or the "Imperfect Cinema" championed by Cuba's Julio García Espinosa, in their famous manifestos of 1969. However, as I explain, the repression of the student movement in 1968 did foster an important and dynamic range of radical cinemas in Mexico, distinct in their historical development but in dialogue with international trends.[3]

The Modernist City

Given its long history of human settlement and the enduring quality of much of its ancient and colonial architecture, Mexico City's constructed environment is strikingly diverse and filled with dramatic juxtapositions. In this environment, the Le Corbusier–style clean slate has been an impossibility for urbanists, with the exception of some developments at what were once the city's outermost edges—for example, the Jardines de Pedregal residential neighborhood and the National University campus, known as the Ciudad Universitaria, dating from the late 1940s and early 1950s, respectively. In most cases, modern architecture has had to coexist in close quarters with many earlier styles, to make do with or adapt to an infrastructure inherited from former times, when the city had a small fraction of the current population.[4] The introduction of principles of modern urban planning—from Emperor Maximilian's construction of the Haussmann-inspired Paseo de la Reforma in the 1860s to the construction of the axial boulevards known as *ejes vials* in the 1970s—has periodically updated some of the city's infrastructure. But it has remained an eclectic landscape. In the U.S. documentary film *Architecture of Mexico* (1952), for example, over a traveling shot of the *zona rosa,* past a grab bag of 19th and early 20th century structures in a wide range of architectural styles, the narrator assures the viewer that while "the expansion of Mexico City is still haphazard and illogical . . . the architects of Mexico, though it has not been generally conceded, have led the world in building modern."[5] On the other hand, the city's modernizing efforts have often had to adapt to circumstances and unexpected discoveries. In 1968, for example, while building a connection between the city's first two underground metro lines, workers excavating in the city's historic center uncovered the Pirámide de Ehécatl, an Aztec altar whose discovery necessitated a rerouting of passengers and accommodation of the preserved structure in the design of the new Pino Suarez metro station, opened the following year.[6]

There are particular areas and landmark buildings of the city where the principles of modern architecture and urban planning flourished in distinctively Mexican manifestations, and which today embody the aspirations, triumphs, and disappointments of the urban transformations of the post–World War II era: the aforementioned Jardines de Pedregal, the upper-class housing development in the south of the city, which was designed by Luis Barragán; the middle-class suburb of Ciudad Satélite, founded in 1957, whose master plan was laid out by Mario Pani; and the Museum of Modern Art (1964) and the National Anthropology Museum (1964) in Chapultepec Park, both designed by the late Pedro Ramírez Vázquez. However, arguably the most indicative of such locales is Tlatelolco, the scene of the massacre of October 2, 1968. The zone is dominated by the modernist office tower built in 1965 for the Secretaría de Relaciones Exteriores (Ministry of Foreign Relations). Today the home of a university cultural center and a memorial to the victims of the massacre, it shares a plaza with a colonial church and the ruins of the pre-Columbian settlement, market and ceremonial complex known as Tlatelolco. In the early sixteenth century this was the site of one of the final, decisive battles in the Spanish Conquest. The juxtaposition of Aztec, colonial, and modern structures has given it the name of the *Plaza de las tres culturas* (Plaza of the Three Cultures).

In the decades following the Mexican Revolution, rural migrants to the city arriving by train had settled in Tlatelolco and the neighboring Nonoalco, building informal and improvised residences with low-cost or recycled materials, characteristically covered with corrugated metal roofs. This rural to urban migration transformed the metropolis, feeding expansion to the point that the city's mayor, Ernesto Uruchurtu, came to characterize the city as a "macrocephalic capital" whose growth and size were lamentably uncontrolled.[7] The city's central districts gained a reputation for being inhospitable to the middle class and often dangerous. This was true of Tlatelolco, in particular, given its proximity to the central railroad terminal, its reputation for vice and lawlessness, and its characteristically modest homes, typically built without architects or plans. These traits made the area a preferred setting for filmic tales of urban deprivation. For example, in the melodrama *Víctimas del pecado* (1950), Emilio Fernández imagines the neighborhood as a netherworld of cantinas and criminality, a place where locomotive smoke seeps into sordid interiors, where unwanted newborns are thrown in trashcans, and pimps lacking scruples dictate the law. Juan Rulfo, the modernist writer, photographed brooding abstractions of the shadows in this neighborhood. Luis Buñuel used it to shoot exteriors for his film *Los olvidados* (1950), in which the looming steel skeletons of buildings under construction, such as the Hospital General on Avenida Cuauhtémoc, hint at a contrasting, functionalist urbanism that would soon displace the squatter settlements. For while Tlatelolco had enduring monumental structures, both ancient and colonial, its squatter settlements could be razed without any effective resistance—and so they were, in Mexico City's largest urban renewal project, which saw Tlatelolco remade around the Plaza de las tres culturas, the backdrop for the tragic events of October 1968.

The land on which the squatter community had developed belonged to the National Railway and many of the breadwinners of the community worked in railroading. Without formal titles, however, and with many recent migrants from the countryside who had come to seek their fortunes in the city, most of the residents could only make shaky legal claims to their dwellings. Railroad work had another significance as well: in the 1950s these workers had tried to buck the state-controlled railroad workers' union (the Sindicato de Trabajadores Ferrocarrileros de la República Mexicana, or STFRM), forming an independent union with links to the Communist Party (Partido Comunista Mexicano, or PCM) and Workers' and Peasants' Party (Partido Obrero-Campesino Mexicano, or PO-CM). That effort peaked in 1958 when Demetrio Vallejo led an unauthorized strike of railroad workers, but it was brutally repressed, as were similar attempts by teachers and doctors to organize strikes and escape the control of state-sponsored unions. Hence, the October 1968 repression was not so much an anomaly as it was part of a long history of iron-fisted domination by the post-Revolutionary state, which developed a Machiavellian arsenal of repressive strategies including spying, sabotage, the cynical manipulation of public opinion through the mass media, and, ultimately, brute force.[8] Tlatelolco is thus not simply a site where informal, improvised urbanism was razed to make way for functionalist modern apartment complexes. It is also a place where the histories of state repression, modernist urban planning, the European conquest, indigenous resistance, and the authoritarian control of workers and students all came together in a rapidly changing urban landscape.

The high-rise residences, called *multifamiliares*, were designed on modernist principles by Mario Pani and inaugurated in 1964, displacing the area's unlicensed constructions and requiring the relocation of thousands of people, mostly to neighborhoods farther from the city center.[9] What was once their land became a self-contained haven of the middle class, many of the new residents being mid-level government office staff, like the head of household in the melodrama *A dónde van nuestros hijos* (Benito Alazraki, 1958). Indeed, Tlatelolco's *multifamiliares* were frequently represented in newsreels, documentaries, and fiction films, a fact that reinforces Beatriz Colomina's assertion that "modern architecture becomes 'modern' not simply by using glass, steel, or reinforced concrete, as is usually understood, but precisely by engaging with the new mechanical equipment of the mass media."[10] Conversely, slums of the kind replaced, and the urban poverty associated with them, were notably invisible in the mass media, their representation actively discouraged through a variety of mechanisms.

The Mexican state and its apologists condemned and suppressed filmic, photographic, and written representations of the capital that focused on the poverty and misery of the marginalized working class and poor. The producer of *Los olvidados*, Oscar Dancigers, was by all accounts appalled by Buñuel's film and felt compelled to add a prologue explicitly making the case that the deprivation depicted was by no means exclusively Mexican but just another manifestation of a global condition. A narrator intones in the film's opening sequence: "The great modern cities—New York, Paris, London—hide behind their magnificent buildings miserable homes inhabited by malnourished children . . . Mexico, the great modern city, is no exception to this universal rule."[11] Even then, the film only went into general release in Mexico after winning the Palme d'Or at Cannes. When the Pan American Union in Washington, DC, hosted documentary photographer Nacho López's evocative exhibition *Así es México* in 1956, its striking representations of Mexican poverty led to polemics and censorship.[12] And a scandal was provoked when the anthropologist Oscar Lewis published his best-selling ethnography, *The Children of Sánchez* (1961)—a study of cycles of exploitation, deprivation, and abuse as experienced by a multigenerational family in Tepito, a neighborhood abutting Tlatelolco. The Spanish-language edition cost the publisher's director, Arnaldo Orfila, his job, and was officially denounced as "obscene . . . defamatory . . . subversive and antirevolutionary."[13] By 1979, when Lewis's book was adapted as a film melodrama, the 1976 devaluation of the peso and the economic disaster that followed in its wake left no doubt that Mexico's "economic miracle" had been inequitable and hollow. Significantly, the film originated not in Mexico but in the United States, directed by Hall Bartlett from a screenplay he cowrote with the Italian neorealist veteran Cesare Zavattini. The Mexican state of the 1950s and 1960s, in short, was heavily invested in promoting the new modernist urbanism of the capital city and the mirage of the "Mexican miracle," while actively suppressing representations that troubled or contradicted them. The 1968 Olympics and its media representations were the capstone in that effort.

1960s Mexico City in Cinema

If Mexico City was in the midst of dramatic changes in the years leading up to 1968, so too was Mexican film, both in the commercial industry and in the increasingly vibrant independent sector. The industry's golden age of the 1940s and early 1950s was indisputably over, victim principally of a loss of foreign markets, a stultifying overreliance on formulas, and powerful restrictive unions (the Sindicato de Trabajadores de la Industria Cinematográfica, or STIC) which barred the entry of new talent into commercial film production. The growth of the "Cine Club" movement expanded options for viewing alternative cinemas and the serious discussion of them.[14] In 1961, the New Cinema Group (Grupo Nuevo Cine) published a manifesto in their short-lived periodical of the same name that suggested specific steps to be taken to spur a film revival: the formation of a national film school and of a *cineteca*, an opening up of the film industry, and more public support for cine clubs.[15] The first feature film associated with the group, *En el balcón vacío* (Jomi García Ascot, 1961), demonstrated the viability of this independent, low-budget production model. The union-sponsored Experimental Film Competitions (Concursos de Cine Experimental) of 1965 and 1967 succeeded in identifying new talent.[16] The label "experimental" may be misleading here, however, as most of the films submitted were feature-length, character-driven narratives showing a marked influence of the French New Wave rather than of the interwar European avant-garde, its equivalent in the Americas, or the contemporaneous neo-avant-garde, such as the films of Jonas Mekas or Andy Warhol. But the Experimental Film Competitions nonetheless mark the moment when Mexico's incipient independent cinema movement, struggling in the 1940s and 1950s, came of age. As the union sponsoring the competitions had hoped, several of the new talents who emerged from the competitions were subsequently absorbed into the film industry.

On a few occasions, directors of the emergent, alternative cinema chose to use the new buildings and transformed public spaces of the capital as shooting locations. The Museo de Arte Moderno figures prominently, for example, in *Tajimara* (Juan José Gurrola, 1965), a drama about the romantic entanglements of bohemian youth. More characteristically, however, the city is represented in these films by the decaying historical center or by modest, weathered, typically middle-class neighborhoods like the Colonia del Valle or Narvarte. In contrast, we frequently see these modernist buildings and new locations utilized in a variety of ways in the commercial cinema of 1968 and the immediately preceding years. The sex comedies of Mauricio Garcés, for example, represent much of what the New Cinema Group criticized: formulaic, lightweight, and aspiring merely to entertain rather than to advance what the New Cinema Group manifesto called "one of the most formidable media of expression of our century."[17] In many such films, Garcés plays what is essentially the same character, a dapper, middle-aged man with complicated intimate relations with the most attractive young starlets of the Mexican screen: *Don Juan '67* (Carlos Velo, 1966), *Mujeres, mujeres, mujeres* (José Díaz Morales, 1967), *Click, fotógrafo de modelos* (René Cardona Jr., 1967), *24 horas de placer* (René Cardona Jr., 1968), and *Departamento de soltero* (René Cardona Jr., 1969).[18] The protagonist of these films invariably lives, works, seduces, wines, and dines in the modernist buildings of the era. *Despedida de casada* (Juan de Orduña, 1966), for example, uses Rámirez Vazquez's National Anthropology Museum, one of Mario Pani and Salvador Ortega Flores's apartment complexes, and Acapulco locations designed by Felix Candela and Juan Sordo Madaleno.[19] *Click, fotógrafo de modelos* finds Garcés photographing beautiful women in an expansive modernist home with a generous studio attached. The paradigmatic constructions of mid-1960s Mexican modernity—often pairing distinctive local materials like volcanic rock with a cosmopolitan sensibility—shine in these films, often proving to be more compelling than the films' comedy and innuendo.

The 1968 Olympics demanded an acceleration in Mexico City's program of building and were accompanied by a massive arts festival—nowadays an obligatory sort of cultural extravaganza, but seen for the first time in 1968. The Games required the construction of both sports facilities (Felix Candela's Palacio de los Desportes, Manuel Rossen Morrison and Jesús Montoya Pérez's Alberca Olímpica) and housing for the visiting athletes (Villa Olímpica and Villa Coapa). Indeed, the architect Pedro Rámirez Vázquez took over as director of the Mexican Olympic Committee when ex-president Adolfo López Mateos was forced to step down because of poor health. Simultaneous with the construction of these utilitarian structures, the cultural

Olympics encompassed art exhibitions from around the world, a theater festival, an international poetry festival, and performances by musicians ranging from the pianists Van Cliburn and Claudio Arrau to a percussion ensemble from Ghana, the Mormon Tabernacle Choir, and Duke Ellington and his orchestra.[20] A series of twenty-two monumental public sculptures also transformed the city's landscape in lasting ways. Collectively known as the Ruta de la Amistad (Route of Friendship), these were built along a major artery in the city's southern district, leading to one of the Olympic venues, Ramírez Vázquez's Estadio Azteca (1966). Here the showcase was emphatically internationalist. The expatriate artist Mathias Goeritz, serving here as a curator, selected and coordinated a group that included Herbert Beyer, Alexander Calder, and Gonzalo Fonseca. Goeritz had been instrumental in bringing kinetic sculptures, installations involving projected and reflected light, and other new art forms to Mexico as a key interlocutor in the National University art museum's then recent exhibition of new art forms, *Cinetismo: esculturas electrónicas en situaciones ambientales.*[21] For the Ruta de la Amistad project he corresponded with curators the world over in search of suitable artists experienced with large-scale public sculptures. By limiting the selection to abstract work, Luis Casteñeda has explained, the organizers hoped to avoid potential controversies that might come with propagandistic or explicitly political art while also demonstrating the host country's cultural sophistication and cosmopolitan sensibility.[22]

Another feature of the cultural activities involved an "International Film Festival" in which hundreds of movies were screened. Organized principally around national and genre themes, such as "Fifty Years of Italian Cinema" or "The American Musical Comedy," this event aimed to attract a general audience to "not only filmdom's masterworks, but diverse types of documentaries as well, whose exhibition is usually limited to specialized or so-called art theatres."[23]

Throughout all this, an effort was made to balance the national and the cosmopolitan, to emphasize elements defined as characteristically Mexican while acknowledging an awareness of global trends and tastes. Exhibition stands scattered throughout the city, showcasing the Olympics, were designed to evoke the monumental sculptures, the so-called Atlantes, of the tenth century city of Tula, Hidalgo. The competition events were identified with neo-Mesoamerican pictographs. And the graphic identity of the games, cultural events, stadiums, and other facilities was designed by New Yorkers Lance Wyman and Beatrice Trueblood to blend the pop styles of international modern art with distinctly national—and more specifically indigenous—references.

For example, one ill-chosen logotype for the Olympics, a white dove of peace, evoked both Op Art and the weavings of Mexico's Huichol Indians, rendered in a distinctly psychedelic palette.[24] Reacting to the military repression of their peaceful protests, the artists of the student movement parodied such designs—for example, in their own silk-screened posters of the same stylized dove skewered on the point of a bayonet, with the five interlocking Olympic rings reconfigured as gun barrels pointed at the viewer.

The state's official account of the 1968 Olympics is recorded in the documentary film *Olimpiada en México* (Alberto Isaac, 1968), in the tradition of Riefenstahl's *Olympia* (1938) and Ichikawa's *Tokyo Olympiad* (1965). With eighty-one camera crews, hundreds of technicians, and three quarters of a million feet of film, it was one of the most ambitious Mexican documentaries ever made, and it was honored with a nomination for the Academy Award for Best Documentary Feature in 1970. The Olympic Committee also created a series of six short films showcasing cities of historical and touristic interest: *Acapulco 68* (Salomón Laiter), *Guadalajara 68* (Angel Bilbatúa), *Guanajuato 68* (Nacho López), *Puebla 68* (Rafael Corkidi), *Monterrey 68* (Salomón Leiter), and *México 68* (Rafael Corkidi). (See Figure 7.1.) Additional shorts were commissioned to showcase the everyday life and cultural riches of the host country—*Domingos* and *Eva* (Manuel Michel), *Los escuincles* (Antonio Reynoso), *Imágen 68* (Julio Pliego), and a series of portraits of Mexican poets, writers, and scientists, *Campeones de la cultura* (Julio Pliego). Another series of shorts showcased the preparations and history of the Olympic Games—*Trabajo olimpico* (Felipe Cazals), *400 mil años de deportes* (Juan Guerrero), and *Olimpia 68* (Giovanni Korporaal)—while Paul Leduc and Rafael Castanedo made yet another series of documentaries for television that was broadcast throughout Latin America.[25]

What is striking about the list of names in charge of these projects is that the filmmakers did not come from the crumbling commercial film industry but rather were variously associated with the cinema of the counterculture, of political dissidence, or of the emergent independent sector shortly before or after 1968. For example, Giovanni Korporaal's directorial debut, *El brazo fuerte* (1958), had been censored for its biting satire of the corruption, ignorance, and cynicism endemic to Mexico's political machinery. Corkidi was one of the paradigmatic filmmakers of Mexican psychedelia, albeit less known for his own pop-surrealist cinematic trips than for his contributions as cinematographer to Alejandro Jodorowsky's *Fando y Lis* (1968), *El topo* (1970), and *La montaña sagrada* (1973). Nacho López's lifelong ambition to make films was frequently frustrated, but his documentary photographs, in-

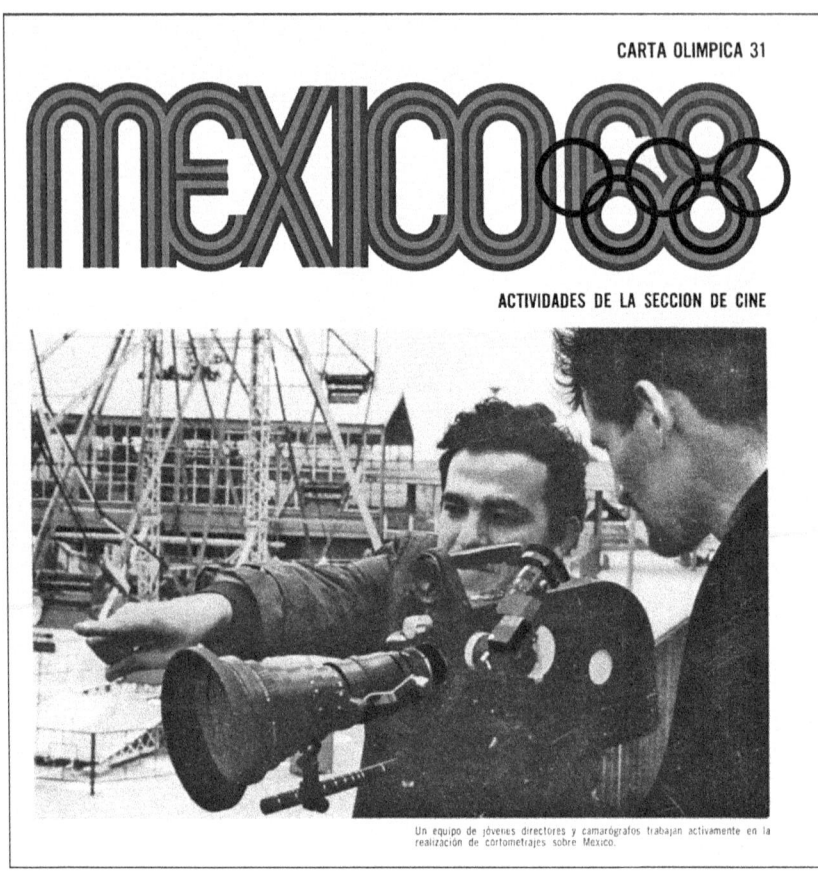

Figure 7.1 Front cover of the official *Mexico 68* magazine, no. 31, Actividades de la seccion de cine, 1968; photo caption reads "A team of young directors and cameramen are actively involved in the production of short films on Mexico"

cluding those in the *Así es México* exhibition that brought condemnation in Washington twelve years earlier, were filled with searing social criticism. Felipe Cazal's *Canoa* (1976) reconstructed a smaller, lesser-known Mexican massacre of 1968 in the town of San Miguel Canoa, Puebla—the killing of a group of university students on a camping trip by a village of peasants whipped into anti-Communist hysteria by the demonical parish priest. Neither simply dissenters nor propagandists, these directors all maintained a delicate professional balance between independent film projects, in which they were free to criticize their society and the state, though always at the risk of censorship, and reliable if compromised work for the government and its affiliates and apologists.

City of Protests

Surely the most ideologically compromised filmmakers in this era were those who, ten days before the inauguration of the Olympic Games, documented the massacre of several hundred demonstrators at the Plaza de las tres culturas by a secret paramilitary security force, the Batallón Olimpia, working in concert with the Mexican military—the massacre of October 2, 1968. In this event, the functionalist apartment complexes of Mario Pani's *multifamiliares* were utilized as gun towers by the state's snipers, and as elevated surveillance posts for the cameramen who filmed the footage, which was subsequently long suppressed. On the orders of interior secretary (and later president) Luis Echeverría, a team of eight camera crews supervised by Servando González Hernández recorded the massacre.[26] Veteran film industry professionals such as Alex Phillips Jr. and Ángel Bilbatúa participated as cinematographers, and the cameras they used were the same ones used a week and a half later to film the official documentary, *Olimpiada en México*.

This pivotal moment in national history has been explored and documented in various ways: in photography, by photojournalists including Enrique Bordes Mangel, Rodrigo Moya, Enrique Metinides, Aaron Sánchez, and Héctor and María García;[27] in literature, especially in Elena Poniatowska's epic documentary collage of testimonials, *La noche de Tlatelolco* (1971); and in a masterfully designed public memorial, the Memorial del 68, on the lower floors of the former home of the Secretaría de Relaciones Exteriores.[28] (See Figure 7.2.) The filmic representations of the massacre, its larger context, and the events leading up to it range from the feature-length compilation of actualities, *El grito* (López Aretche, 1969) and the more allegorical treatment in *La montaña sagrada* (Alejandro Jodorowsky, 1973) to accomplished student films such as *Y si platicamos de agosto?* (Maryse Sistache, 1980), the painstaking historical reconstructions of *Tlatetlolco, verano de 68* (Carlos Bolado, 2012), and notable recent documentaries such as *Ni olvido, no perdón* (Richard Dindo, 2012). In the first mainstream narrative film to address the massacre, *Rojo amanecer* (Jorge Fons, 1989), the city is largely offscreen and the massacre is not shown. Instead, reflecting its theatrical origins, Fons's film reconstructs events taking place just meters from the massacre as it is set almost entirely within a single interior location, an apartment in one of the *multifamiliares*, the Edificio Chihuahua, above the Plaza de las tres culturas. The film uses a fictional, middle-class family as a microcosm to explore the rifts between generations, genders, and ideologies. In spite of some of the characters' passionate declarations of allegiance to the state and condemnations of the protesters, government forces have by the end of the film

Figure 7.2 Student life and student demonstrations at the Ciudad Universitaria campus of the Universidad Nacional Autónoma de México (UNAM), as seen in *El Grito* (López Aretche, 1969)

killed all but one of the family members, regardless of the ideological positions that they espoused.

More vivid than Fons's staged reconstruction, however, are the rough-hewn 16mm films made by participants in the student movement at the time. The six installments of the *Comunicados* (1968) series are urgent dispatches from the students of the National University's Centro Universitario de Estudios Cinematográficos (or CUEC). In these the camera works minimally: footage of marches, newspaper headlines, and zooming and panning shots of still photographs of the repression. Urban landmarks and sites of confrontation between protestors and the repressive forces mark the evolving standoff. Explanations and contextual information are not offered to the viewer—these are films directed at partisans, for whom all this would have been painfully familiar. The soundtrack records the chants of thousands denouncing the authoritarian state and mocks the official justifications of state repression, echoed by the conservative press.

In *Comunicado Número 2*, quotations by military officers repeated uncritically in newspapers (e.g., "nuestro ejercito es de paz," or "our army is one of peace") are accompanied by overblown military choral music and bombastic orchestration. That film also uses the South American protest song *Me gustan los estudiantes* (written by Chile's Violeta Parra, sung by Uruguay's Daniel Viglietti), which is suggestive of hemispheric links that find frequent expression in music. Indeed, the preferred music of the 1968 movement included not only that of Mexicans like Oscar Chávez and Los Folkloristas, but also Argentina's Atahualpa Yupanqui and Mercedes Sosa and Chile's Víctor Jarr and Ángel Parra. The same recording used in *Comunicado Número 2* provides both soundtrack and title to the equally urgent, roughly made Uruguayan short of the same year, *Me gustan los estudiantes*, Mario Handler's tribute to the student protesters that greeted President Lyndon B. Johnson's visit to Punta del Este. This recurrence is suggestive of the musical links that united much of the Latin American Left, in spite of differences in particular circumstances.

Some of the footage and stills that make up the *Comunicados* series reappear in *El grito*, a two-hour documentary chronicle of the movement, which was also a product of CUEC. (See Figure 7.3.) Sometimes working surreptitiously, its students had filmed many of the protests and their repression, and they acquired additional material from a foreign television network, resulting in hastily made dispatches from the barricades. A more reflective and analytic representation, the product of years of research, is evident in the feature-length documentary *Batallón Olimpia: documento abierto* (1998) by the Canal 6 de Julio collective of video activists. Released three decades after

Figure 7.3 The prelude, events, and aftermath of the military massacre of demonstrators at Plaza de las tres culturas, Tlatelolco, Mexico City, October 2, 1968, as depicted in *El Grito* (López Aretche, 1969)

the events depicted, their documentary is assembled from interviews about the massacre on the plaza and testimonials of eyewitnesses together with archival footage of the massacre, slowed down, enlarged, and examined in detail. This allows for a meticulous investigative study, although many details of the massacre remain shrouded in secrecy to this day and not a single government official was ever convicted for the crime.

In 1968, the Ciudad Universitaria was another critical site of confrontations between the state and student movement. It had been under construction for a decade when officially inaugurated in 1954 and it was not fully operational until several years later. Already over four centuries old, and previously scattered across a handful of mostly colonial structures, the university was unified and transformed by the new campus, designed by Enrique del Moral and Mario Pani, with remarkable modernist architecture, iconic public murals, mosaics by José Chávez Morado and David Alfaro Siqueiros, and expansive open spaces. More than Pani's *multifamiliares* at Tlatelolco, the nationalistic adornments on the buildings of Ciudad Universitaria—some of them evoking pre-Hispanic sources—link them to an early generation of state-sponsored, ostensibly revolutionary muralism.

In 1968, Alfredo Joskowicz interviewed fellow university students about the brewing conflict. Echoing events at the Sorbonne in June, soldiers occupied the Ciudad Universitaria campus in September, as well as the National Polytechnic Institute (Instituto Politécnico Nacional, or IPN). The college students in Fons's *Rojo amanacer*, like many real students of 1968, cite the military occupation of the campus as a violation of the autonomy of the National University and a key motivation for their protests. Raul Kamffer's documentary short *Mural efímero* (1968–1971) contemporaneously documents some of the ways in which the student movement laid claim to the campus's central quadrangle.[29] A statue of the former president Miguel Alemán, under whose administration the Ciudad Universitaria campus had been built, stood on a grassy plaza surrounded by some of the campus's most iconic structures—Juan O'Gorman's mosaic-covered central library and the Rector's Tower, designed by Pani, del Moral, and Salvador Ortega Flores, with an exterior relief mural by Siqueiros. In the escalating confrontations between students and the army, the statue was vandalized in September 1968 and the damaged likeness was temporarily covered with laminated metal sheets.[30] Students from the Consejo Nacional de Huelga organized a collective mural project to claim the metal sheets and the grassy expanse surrounding them. This was not an amateur or student art project—nationally noted artists participated, including José Luis Cuevas, Manuel Felguérez, and Adolfo Mexiac. The first part of *Mural efímero* documents the art work and the festive atmosphere of open-air concerts and student activism that characterized the summer before the massacre. Indeed, Kammfer's film represents the suppression of the movement with a few photographs of the corpses, and it memorializes the fallen with a particularly poetic passage of voice-over narration:

> *The youth fought with roses / The youth were buried without flowers*
> *They were burned in military ovens / Castrated / And raped, even after death*
> *But don't think that we've forgotten / We haven't stopped dying*
> *We haven't stopped dying / We haven't stopped dying!*[31]

Following the massacre at Tlatelolco, the survivors who were arrested—many were also beaten and stripped of their clothing—were transported to the Palacio de Lecumberri or "Black Palace" for detention, interrogation, and, not infrequently, torture. Lecumberri is therefore another key location in this history of the city, one that reflects an earlier paradigm of modernization.[32] Inaugurated in 1900 by the pre-Revolutionary dictator Porfirio Díaz, Lecumberri was the first structure in Mexico intended from its inception to function as a jail. It replaced older prisons, structures designed for other functions and subsequently converted, and from which inmates often escaped. The architects Antonio Torres Torija and Miguel Macedo designed Lecumberri on the model of Jeremy Bentham's Panopticon (1787), a prison house in which the inmates are constantly subjected to the inescapable, controlling gaze of guards in the prison's central tower.

However, the protocols at the jail allowed for family visits on Sundays, and this enabled some prisoners to have access to contraband, including Super 8 cameras. Later, shortly before it closed in 1976, Lecumberri became the subject for officially approved documentaries such as *Lecumberri, el palacio negro* (Arturo Ripstein, 1976) and the setting for fiction films like *La otra virginidad* (Juan Manuel Torres, 1975). But *Historia de un documento* (1970) is different, a film shot by Oscar Menéndez, who survived the massacre and was imprisoned. Menéndez's footage was clearly shot surreptitiously within a very confined space and much of it focuses on the logistics of its own production. Comrades outside the jail are able to complete the picture, contrasting the "city of palaces" admired by Alexander von Humboldt with the ring of misery around the city's perimeter, filled with the urban poor and recent migrants from the countryside. Menéndez's camera does not have the freedom of movement that Ripstein's authorized production was granted, but the mere act of filming, of returning the guards' gaze, and of continuing the activist filmmaking that led to his arrest, are themselves significant gestures of defiance. ORTF, the French television channel, provided the postproduction facilities for Menéndez's documentary, but diplomatic efforts by President Echeverría successfully prevented its broadcast. Ironically, since 1980, the former prison has held the National Archive, which did not declassify thousands of boxes of government papers on the student movement until more than three decades later, following the end of the monopoly on power of Echeverría's Partido Revolucionario Institucional (PRI). Historians have yet to fully digest their contents.

Countercultural City

However, the small-gauge filmmaking movement of the *superocheros*—or "super-eighters," named after their preferred film format, Super 8—turned out be the most important political cinema to take stock of the events of Mexico's 1968.[33] Oscar Menéndez had turned to Super 8 out of necessity, when, in the words of one colleague "as was to be expected, his camera and 16mm equipment were confiscated in one of the now familiar incidents of police repression."[34] In 1970, Menéndez, released from jail, along with writer Leopoldo Ayala and the coffee shop owner, countercultural impresario, and artisan Victor Fosada, launched the First National Super 8 Competition.[35] The small-gauge format offered several advantages over 16mm, being lower cost, more mobile, and relatively free from censorship. Unlike 16mm and 35mm, neighborhood camera shops offered a decentralized network for film processing that was not subject to state supervision. The phantom of 1968 repression figured so consistently in the competing films that one critic wrote that all participants were trying to make the same movie.[36] The protagonist of that film was a young, alienated male resident of Mexico City, tortured by memories of the 1968 repression, unsure of his next move, and wondering whether escape from the city, the urban counterculture, guerrilla actions, or despondent drug use would offer the most promising route to relief.

In order to exhibit this small-gauge cinema of protest, the *superocheros* borrowed models of spectatorship from Soviet and Cuban precedents, outfitting Volkswagens to function as mobile projection centers or *Cine móvil* and showing their films in union halls and collective farming communities.[37] The exhibition of the films was never simply that, but a *proyección-debate* that engaged the members of the audience to reflect on their circumstances. The government's own Cineteca Nacional began a program of mobile projections shortly afterward, and in the years that followed, the Super 8 movement transformed, taking on more than 1968. Another massacre, on June 10, 1971, by paramilitary Halcones, emerged as a major theme in activist films like *El año de la rata* (1971), made by the Cooperativa Cine Marginal, which sought to define common ground between the 1958 railroad strike and the massacres of 1968 and 1971.[38] Gabriel Retes, who had been a member of the cooperative, later reflected back on the activism of that era from a distance of twenty years in his feature film *El bulto* (1991), a Rip van Winkle story of a leftist photojournalist emerging from two decades in a coma provoked by the era's violence.

Tlatetlolco and the Ciudad Universitaria endured as spaces of trauma in CUEC student films and Super 8 shorts of the 1970s. In *La libertad es un hombre chiquito con ganas de darle en la madre a todo el mundo, la soledad es el mismo hombre un poco menos politizado* (Rafael Montero, 1973), the protagonist runs past the *multifamiliares* of Pani in anguish. Sergio García, the *superochero* most dedicated to the format and its promise, examines the city as a sort of countercultural playground in *El fin* (1970), *Ah, verda'?* (1973), and *Un toque de roc* (1988). Similarly, in the 16mm and 35mm countercultural cinema made in the immediate aftermath of the Tlatelolco massacre, the same modernist landmarks celebrated in the films made for the Olympics feature time and again but used in strikingly different ways. Consider *Anticlimax* (1969–1973), the only feature film made by painter and theater director Gelsen Gas. A psychedelic tale of urban alienation, the film is indebted to Jacques Tati's *Playtime* (1967) and the work of Gas's occasional collaborator, Alejandro Jodorowsky. When the hipster protagonist walks past the sculptures of Ruta de la Amistad, it is not a celebratory moment, but one of alienation and displacement, far from the playful city of missed romantic glances celebrated in Michel's *Eva*. Alfred Joskowicz's *El cambio* (1971) presents the city as a place to escape from. A young artist finds no positive response to his work there; thugs steal his treasured 35mm still camera while he photographs a homeless man sleeping in the street in a failed effort to make socially committed art. The city is a space filled with trauma, oppression, and entrapment, of bad memories and limited options, from which he flees to a remote beach in Veracruz, but still finds no solace.

It is surprising, given the historical importance of its national cinema, that Mexico participated so little in the tri-continental political modernism variously labeled "Third Cinema" or "Imperfect Cinema." The films of Bolivia's Grupo Ukamau, Argentina's Grupo Cine Liberación and Grupo Cine de la Base, Brazilian Cinema Novo, and postrevolutionary Cuba's ICAIC

(Instituto Cubano del Arte e Industria Cinematográficos) were all widely screened in Mexico.³⁹ In his memoir of the student movement, Paco Ignacio Taibo II recalls animated youth "wailing like Algerian women" in the stairwells of the Cine Roble following a screening of Gillo Pontecorvo's dramatization of the French colonial war, *La battaglia de Algeri* (*The Battle of Algiers*, 1966).⁴⁰ But the dominant direction of Mexico's politically committed filmmaking was quite distinct, in part because of the proximity of the most important commercial film industry in the Spanish speaking world. Although one finds, as elsewhere in Latin America, calls for active spectatorship, for the dissolution of authorship in a collective mode of production, and for a cinema relevant to the most marginalized sectors of the population, the ability of the commercial sector to recruit independent filmmakers meant that radical cinema played out in Mexico in very different ways.

A cinema of denunciatory testimonials was developed by a series of collectives. A group of students from the National University's film school, calling themselves Grupo Cine Octubre, directed documentaries including *Explotados y explotadores* (*The Exploited and the Exploiters*, 1974) and *Los albañiles* (*The Masons*, 1974). Grupo Cine Testimonial made militant documentaries along similar lines, such as *Una y otra vez* (1972–1975) and, in a rural context, *Atecingo* (1973). In these films, the capital city is one network of structures for maintaining the hierarchy of social classes, defined in relationship to the means of production. Other influences in the 1970s pushed Mexican documentary into the testimonial realm as well: Mexican feminism, the arrival of magnetic striped super 8 film, and Jean Rouch's lessons at the CUEC.

Participants in a Latin Americanist small-gauge film movement connected periodically in cities such as Havana, Caracas, and Mexico City through the 1970s and early 1980s. Here they met kindred spirits from other parts of the Spanish-speaking world, and learned what the artist Luis Camnitzer meant when he wrote: "I believe that there were many 1968s in the world, that they were quite different, and that they did not always happen in the same year."⁴¹ All shared a sense of what Alfonso Gumucio Dagrón called "the immense potential [Super 8 film] embodies as a tool in the hands of organized workers."⁴² At other times their reels of film were secretly handcarried or surreptitiously shipped across borders to screen at festivals and alternative venues, laying the foundations of a continental network of committed artists. In these Latin American Super 8 encounters, many of "the children of May '68" came together—a group of which Gilles Deleuze and Félix Guattari noted "you can run into them all over the place, even if they are not aware of who they are. Each country produces them in its own way."⁴³

In Mexico City, the "children of 1968" produced a cinematic reflection of the student movement and its repression equal in power to the photographic, musical, and literary records of this moment. Although, given the repression of student groups, peasants, "Indians," teachers, railroad workers, and others in the years preceding and following October 2, 1968, the Tlatelolco massacre must be understood as a high water mark rather than an anomaly in a bitter history of social conflicts and their suppression, its aftermath still resonates strongly both on the screens and on the streets of Mexico City.

NOTES

1. For most of the twentieth century, most Mexican labor unions were controlled by and answerable to the national government and ruling party. See Dan La Botz, *Mask of Democracy: Labor Suppression in Mexico Today* (Boston: South End Press, 1992), 67.

2. Elena Poniatowska, *La noche de Tlatelolco* (México, D.F.: Era, 1971).

3. The terms "Third Cinema" and "Imperfect Cinema" come from two of the better-known manifestos of the "New Latin American Cinema." Fernando Solanas, Octavio Getino, and the *Grupo Cine Liberación* first published their manifesto "Hacia un tercer cine/Towards a Third Cinema" in 1969. Julio García Espinosa published the manifesto *"Por un cine imperfecto"* that same year. Both are reprinted in *Hojas de cine: Testimonios y documentos del nuevo cine latinoamericano*, 3 vols. (México D.F.: Secretaria de Educación Pública/Universidad Autónoma Metropolitana, 1988).

4. To give an indication of Mexico City's rapid growth, its population grew from 2.9 million in 1950 to 5 million in 1960 and 8.8 million in 1970, by which time it was the fourth largest city in the world. See United Nations, Department of Economic and Social Affairs, Population Division, World Urbanization Prospects: The 2005 Revision, File 14: The 30 Largest Urban Agglomerations Ranked by Population Size, 1950–2015. POP/DB/WUP/Rev.2005/2/F14, http://www.un.org/en/development/desa/population/.

5. *Architecture of Mexico* (Spencer Moore, Prod. Allen-Moore Productions, 1952). See Museum of Modern Art (NY), "Poetics of Development" archive, 2013, accessed May 1, 2016; https://www.moma.org/momaorg/shared/pdfs/docs/calendar/Poetics_of_Development_LAiC.pdf.

6. "Pirámide de Ehécatl," Instituto Nacional de Antropología e Historia (INAH), accessed October 24, 2016; http://www.inah.mx/es/boletines/2051-piramide-de-ehecatl.

7. "Los problemas del Distrito Federal," *Excelsior*, May 7, 1963.

8. See Kevin J. Middlebrook, *Unions, Workers and the State in Mexico* (San Diego: Center for Mexican Studies/UCSD, 1991) and Robert F. Alegre, *Railroad Radicals in Cold War Mexico: Gender, Class, and Memory* (Lincoln: University of Nebraska Press, 2013).

9. Miguel Adriá, *Mario Pani: La construcción de la modernidad* (México, D.F.: CONCACULTA/Gustavo Gili, 2005). Parallel adaptations of functionalism took place elsewhere in Latin America, including contemporaneous housing projects by Venezuela's Carlos Raúl Villanueva and Brazil's Oscar Niemeyer.

10. Beatriz Colomina, *Privacy and Publicity: Modern Architecture as Mass Media* (Cambridge, MA: MIT Press, 1996), 73.

11. The original reads: "Las grandes ciudades modernas—Nueva York, Paris, Londres—esconden tras sus magníficos edificios hogares de miseria que albuergan niños malnutridos . . . México, la gran ciudad moderna, no es excepción a esa regla universal." All translations from the Spanish are my own unless otherwise acknowledged.

12. John Mraz, "Nacho López y la mexicanidad," *Luna Córnea* 31 (2007): 165–177.

13. Claudio Lomnitz, *Deep Mexico, Silent Mexico: An Anthropology of Nationalism* (Minneapolis: University of Minnesota Press, 2001), 258–259. See also Lomnitz's prologue to the 50th anniversary edition of the *Los hijos de Sánchez/Una muerte en la familia Sánchez* (México D.F.: Fondo de Cultura Económica, 2012).

14. Though Mexico's first cine club dated to 1931, these spread in the 1950s and 1960s, following the founding of the *Federación Mexicana de Cine Clubs* in 1955. See Manuel González Casanova, *¿Qué es un cine-club?* (México, D.F.: Dirección General de Difusión Cultural, Sección de Actividades Cinematográficas, Universidad Nacional Autónoma de México, 1961).

15. *Manifesto del Grupo Nuevo Cine* (1961), reprinted in Scott MacKenzie, ed., *Film Manifestos and Global Cinema Cultures: A Critical Anthology* (Berkeley: University of California Press, 2014), 209–211.

16. The two experimental film competitions were sponsored by the *Sindicato de Trabajadores de la Producción Cinematográfica*.

17. *Manifesto del Grupo Nuevo Cine* (1961).

18. These later titles might be translated as *Women, Women, Women*; *Click, Model Photographer*; *24 Hours of Pleasure*; and *Bachelor Pad*.

19. The Canadian artist Terence Gower extracts these and other architectural gems from Garces's *Despedida de casada* in his digital video *Ciudad moderna* (2004). When installed in his 2005 solo exhibition at the Laboratorio Arte Alameda, a sixteenth-century church reconfigured as a contemporary art space, Gower projected the video in the midst of photographs of modernist Mexican architecture of the era, displayed on a pared-down grid of free-standing scaffolding and photomurals, which the artist described as a "modernist make-over" for the colonial building.

20. *The Cultural Olympiad*, 4 (Organizing Committee of the Games of the XIX Olympiad, 1968).

21. The show included the likes of Len Lye, Julio Le Parc, and David Medalla. See Jennifer Josten, "Mathias Goeritz y el arte internacional de nuevos medios en la década de los sesenta" in *Ready Media: Hacia una arqueología de los medios y la invención en México* (México D.F.: Laboratorio Arte Alameda, 2012), 119–132.

22. Luis Casteñeda, "Beyond Tlatelolco: Design, Media and Politics at Mexico '68," *Grey Room* 40 (Summer 2010): 116.

23. Ibid., 23.

24. For more on the graphic design of the Olympiad, see Ana Elena Mallet, "Tlatelolco: Perpetual Past" (http://www.museumashub.org/sites/museumashub.org/files/AnaElena Mallet_Tlatelolco-PerpetualPast.pdf); Eric Zolov, "Showcasing the 'Land of Tomorrow': Mexico and the 1968 Olympics," *The Americas* 61, no. 2 (October 2004): 159–188. For a survey of the graphics of the student movement, see Georges Roque, "La gráfica del 68," *Memorial del 68* (México D.F.: Universidad Nacional Autónoma de México, 2007), 216–233.

25. *The Cultural Olympiad*, 4 (Organizing Committee of the Games of the XIX Olympiad, 1968), 745–746.

26. "Ignoro dónde está lo que filmé el 2 de octubre," *La Jornada*, August 22, 2007. In the early 1970s, González Hernández would be appointed to lead the film department charged with documenting the presidency of Echeverria when he was elevated to the executive office.

27. Alberto del Castillo Troncoso, *La fotografía y la construcción de un imaginario: Ensayo sobre el movimiento estudiantil de 1968* (México, D.F.: Instituto de Investigaciones Dr. José María Luis Mora, 2012).

28. See also José Agustín, *Tragicomedia Mexicana I: La vida en México de 1940–1970* (México, D.F.: Planeta, 1990), 255–270; Enrique Krauze, *La presidencia imperial: Ascenso y caída del sistema politico mexicano, 1940–1996* (Barcelona: Tusquets, 1997), 303–396.

29. Armando Partida Tayzan, "Entrevista con Juan Mora Catlett" *Raúl Kamffer: Soñador del cine de autor* (México, D.F.: UNAM 1994), 131.

30. Álvaro Vázquez Mantecón, "El 68 en el cine mexicano" *Memorial del 68* (México D.F.: Universidad Nacional Autónoma de México, 2007), 192–203.

31. "La juventud combatió con rosas / La juventud se entreró sin flores / Se quemo en los hornos militares / Se castró / Y aun muerta fue violada / Pero no se crea que hemos olvidado / No hemos dejado de morir / No hemos dejado de morir / No hemos dejado de morir!"

32. Antonio Padilla Arroyo, *De Belem a Lecumberri: Pensamiento social y penal en el México decimonónico* (México, D.F.: Archivo General de la Nación, 2001).

33. Jesse Lerner, "Superocheros," *Wide Angle* 21, no. 3 (June 1999): 2–35.

34. Sergio García, "Toward a Fourth Cinema," *Wide Angle* 21, no. 3 (June 1999): 89.

35. Álvaro Vázquez Mantecon, *El Super-8 en México, 1970–1989* (México D.F.: Filmoteca de la UNAM, 2012).

36. Jorge Ayala Blanco, *La búsqueda del cine mexicano* (México, D.F.: Posada, 1986), 350.

37. The first Spanish language translation of Alexander Medvedkin's account on the Soviet Kino-train appeared in 1973 as *El cine como propaganda politico: 294 días sobre ruedas* (Buenos Aires: Siglo XXI, 1973). Another source of inspiration for this practice was the Cuban Cine Móvil.

38. The members of *Cooperativa Cine Marginal* included Gabriel Retes, Ramón Villar, Eduardo Carrasco Zanini, Paco Ignacio Taibo II, and Enrique Escalona.

39. These were regularly screened at the National University and in other noncommercial venues. There are some significant exchanges and intersections between radical Mexican film and the so-called New Latin American Cinema as well. Yucatán's Miguel Barbachano Ponce produced one of Cuba's first postrevolutionary films, *Cuba baile* (1960), Julio García Espinosa's first feature film and symbolically a starting point of the new Cuban cinema. Cine de la Base's Raymundo Gleyzer made a condemnation of the betrayal and corruption, *México: la revolución congeleada*. These connections are worthy of further exploration, along the lines Masha Salazkina develops in her "Moscow-Rome-Havana: A Film-Theory Road Map," *October* 139 (Winter 2012): 97–116.

40. Paco Ignacio Taibo II, *68* (México, D.F.: Planeta, 1991), 18.

41. Luis Camnitzer, "The Sixties," reprinted in *On Art, Artists, Latin America and Other Utopias,* ed. Rachel Weiss (Austin: University of Texas Press, 2009), 17.

42. "el imenso potential que encierre como instrumento de concienzación en manos de obreros organizados." Alfonso Gumucio Dagrón, *Super 8: teoria y práctica de un nuevo cine* (Caracas: Wiphala, 1981).

43. Gilles Deleuze and Felix Guattari, "May 68 Did Not Take Place," *Hatred of Capitalism,* ed. Chris Kraus and Sylvère Lotringer (Los Angeles: Semiotexte, 2001), 210.

8

Tokyo 1969: Revolutionary Image-Thieves in the Disintegrating City

Stephen Barber

Tokyo's urban unrest of the 1960s possesses a cumulative chronology that slowly accumulates into outbreaks of irrepressible violence. It extended across the entire decade, beginning in 1960 with rioting and demonstrations around the Japanese parliament building against the U.S.-Japan Security Treaty, ratified in June, which limited Japan's military capacity and allowed Japanese territory to be used for U.S. military bases and activities. These led to sustained protests and confrontations in Shinjuku and other central spaces, principally between student activists and riot police, intensifying in 1968 and 1969, before disappearing from the city's streets and mutating into other forms and concerns in the 1970s, such as those of terrorist factions whose aims and agendas resonated with similar groups in Europe. The political imperatives of the Tokyo protests were incoherent and contradictory, with student factions ranging from extreme right-wing and militarist groupings, whose aim was to restore the power of Japan's imperial system, to extreme left-wing groupings that intended to instigate a Communist revolution. All were united by hatred of the United States, of its pervasive influence in Japanese political and popular culture since the U.S.-led Allied Occupation of Japan (1945 to 1952), and especially of U.S. military interventions in Vietnam and other parts of Asia.

The preeminent cultural manifestation of protest in 1960s Japan emerged in the medium of film, extending from avant-garde experimentation to feature films made by directors who often perceived themselves as activist artists.

Although Tokyo's culture of riots is often seen as having originated in 1960, William Marotti has traced it further back in time, to the U.S.-led Occupation, arguing that, even in its early stages, Tokyo's riots had a counterpart in artistic activity, with accompanying exhibitions and film screenings:

> The confrontation within which the everyday was embedded, however, simultaneously hearkened back to an earlier moment of conflict and political dis-identification during the early years of the Allied (and predominantly American) Occupation of Japan, one that conditioned the later context and yielded, as one of its fraught products, the Yomiuri Independent exhibition. A surge of labor activism and peaceful protest on the verge of democratically transforming the political landscape was curtailed by Occupation authorities, preserving an old guard and permitting a reassertion of familiar forces of power and authority.[1]

Film constituted a sensitized medium for the exploration of the surge of protest throughout the 1960s. The first part of Koji Wakamatsu's film *United Red Army* (2008), prior to its semifictional retrospective analysis of the transformation of 1960s rioting into terrorist aberrations, provides a kind of chronological archive of film footage of riots in Tokyo's urban landscapes. The riots were extensively filmed, both by police authorities seeking to identify and punish rioters, and by the rioters themselves, during an era in which lightweight Super-8 film cameras became extensively available and affordable. The three-minute duration of Super-8 film cartridges required rioters making films to focus precisely on filming what they saw as most essential and visually arresting. Wakamatsu incorporates both types of footage into his filmic archive of the riots, with a particular emphasis on the chaos and violence of the rioters' experience—for example, in sequences in which film cameras become the targets of riot police assaults, grabbed by police officers' hands and thrown against the ground. In many ways, such footage anticipates contemporary riot footage shot on iPhones and other digital devices—for example, in conflicts in the cities of Egypt, Libya, and Syria, whose ocular dynamics have fueled works by contemporary artist filmmakers such as the Lebanese Rabih Mroué's *The Pixellated Revolution* (2012).

Most of the participants in Tokyo's riots were students or activists associated with the student movement, and many came from art schools. In the 1960s, the Japanese university and art school system was in acute turmoil. In her book *Anti-Academy*, Alice Maude-Roxby analyzes the development of the organized student movement in Tokyo, with its emphasis on individual acts in extreme tension with their encompassing social framework, together with the particular collective grievances of its participants:

> The student movement was at its height in 1968 and a series of struggles between '68 and '69 prompted the emergence of Zenkyoto (All Campus Joint Struggle League), a non-sectarian radical students' group. Zenkyoto was an association of individuals who wanted to join the struggle not as members of particular parties or sects, but on their own terms. It started out as a protest against concrete issues such as tuition fee hikes and misuse of funds, and quickly developed into a struggle against the existing social structure with wider political and philosophical implications. Once students started to question institutions and their structures, they recognized their own systematic exploitation in the name of education.[2]

Films of Riotous Urban Space

A number of feature film directors initiated distinctive stylistic experiments in the representation of urban space in riotous transformation during what seemed to many a potentially revolutionary moment. In particular, Toshio Matsumoto's *Funeral Parade of Roses* (1969) and Nagisa Oshima's *Diary of a Shinjuku Thief* (1969) probed the intimate rapport between Tokyo's urban unrest and the intensive artistic and sexual experimentation then ongoing in the distinctively countercultural Shinjuku district.[3] The remainder of this chapter gives an account of the unique cultural history of riot filmmaking in late-1960s Tokyo and its rapport with both urban street culture and art. It examines the particular challenges faced by filmmakers in creating images of the immense, proliferating space of Tokyo, concentrating on *Funeral Parade of Roses* and *Diary of a Shinjuku Thief* but also counterpointing them with sequences in films by Chris Marker and Andrei Tarkovsky. It then concludes by evaluating the enduring relevance of such urban filmmaking for contemporary Tokyo's visual culture.

Urban filmmaking in Tokyo at the end of the 1960s reflects the very particular dynamics and breadth of filmmaking practices of the era, as well as the wide-ranging architectural expansion that had been taking place in the city during the preceding decade. Although the Japanese studio system appeared ossified and in decline, and many younger filmmakers had no desire to work in it, experimentation in Tokyo-based film was wide-ranging, from the structuralist works of Takahiko Iimura to films funded by independent production collectives such as the Art Theatre Guild, which were often preoccupied with issues of sexuality and dissident politics, as in the films of Shuji Terayama.⁴ Some filmmakers, such as Oshima, oscillated between working within the studio system and beyond it. Many financially fragile studios looking for means to survive, such as the Toei company, explored previously peripheral or despised genres such as horror or pornography, and commissioned series of such films. Hence, as the studios arbitrarily assigned them work, filmmakers working for the Japanese studios had to demonstrate great flexibility in moving between genres and styles. To some extent, the mutability of filmmaking in Tokyo at this time mirrored that in Europe, where there was also a heightened concern with political and sexual issues and with stylistic experimentation. However, the historical and cultural context of Japan in the late 1960s, and its influence on urban life and representations, was distinctly different.

The urban geography of Tokyo that facilitated protests, especially those staged in the district of Shinjuku, with its wide avenues and adjoining narrow alleyways, resulted directly from the calamitous recent history of the city—that is, the large-scale destruction of Tokyo during World War II, and the Occupation by U.S. military forces, which followed that destruction. As with many other industrial cities in Japan, Tokyo was extensively firebombed, resulting in enormous casualties, especially in March 1945. Entire areas of the city vanished. As well as causing human losses, the firebombing also engulfed Tokyo's libraries, film archives, and historical buildings such as temples and shrines, so that much of the city's past was erased. At the same time, among both Japanese observers and those newly arrived from other countries, there was an increasing interest in witnessing and archiving that erasure in photography, writing, and film. The American film historian and filmmaker Donald Richie arrived in the city at the end of December 1946 as a typist and trainee journalist attached to the U.S. military. He wrote in his journal of the visual reconfiguration of the city by its destruction: "I stand at the main crossing on the Ginza, nothing between me and the mountain [Mount Fuji] . . . I stand and watch the mountain fade. From this crossing it had not been seen since Edo times, but now all the buildings between are cinders. Between me and Fuji is a burned wasteland, a vast and blackened plain where a city had once stood."⁵

For many young filmmakers, artists and architects in Tokyo, the erasure of the city that they witnessed as children also entailed the sweeping away of the constrictive militarist and familial structures of the prewar era, so the city's destruction also possessed an exhilarating aspect, with the sense that the city could now be transformed from zero into something entirely new. This was the case for filmmakers such as Oshima and Matsumoto, as well as the architect Arata Isozaki and the theater director Juro Kara, who plays one of the central characters in *Diary of a Shinjuku Thief*. However, the U.S. Occupation had primarily negative impacts. The U.S.-Japan Security Treaty remained in force; American armed forces remained widespread in Japan, and during the Vietnam War air bases close to Tokyo were used extensively for supply and reinforcement; and the American authorities imposed an often idiosyncratic censorship regime on Japanese filmmaking. All of these realities were perceived as subjugating the country to the military and cultural power of the United States. Moreover, after its initial signature in 1960, the treaty needed to be ratified once a decade, and the violent urban protests and street battles that form the key narrative events of *Funeral Parade of Roses* and *Diary of a Shinjuku Thief* were related to the imminent renewal of the treaty in 1970.

Those two films, then, were impelled by a very specific set of cultural and historical traumas, which impacted directly upon their location filming of Tokyo as an urban space inflected by fast-moving riots and protests. Their urban space is in multiple states of turmoil and needs to be captured in a mobile way that accentuates ongoing processes of urban and human mutation. Matsumoto and Oshima responded to those processes by adopting techniques such as handheld camera, blurred images, and rapid cutting to induce disorientation in the spectator's perception and accentuate the speed with which he or she experiences the city's uproar. But whereas *Funeral Parade of Roses* and *Diary of a Shinjuku Thief* were notable as in-depth filmic explorations of Tokyo and Shinjuku by locals, visiting filmmakers Chris Marker and Andrei Tarkovsky emphasized Tokyo as an "excessive" urban space, labyrinthine in structure, impossible to grasp in its entirety, and extending into apparently limitless suburban sprawl. Their work approached the engulfing megalopolis more obliquely, incorporating fragments from it into films composed of trajectories across the city, generated in order to probe issues of memory and representation. It is worth considering these momentarily before more fully analyzing Matsumoto and Oshima.

Trajectories across the City in Marker and Tarkovsky

The French filmmaker Chris Marker visited Tokyo on numerous occasions over an extended period of time, first arriving with a plan to film the Olympic Games of 1964, the preparations for which entailed a wide-ranging transformation of the city, including the construction of many multilevel inner-city highways. The Olympics were eventually filmed by the Japanese director Kon Ichikawa as *Tokyo Olympiad* (1965), but during his visit Marker made the film *The Koumiko Mystery* (1967), which focused on his obsession with a young Japanese woman. However, Marker's most revealing images of Tokyo were in his film *Sans Soleil* (1982), in which he returned to the city after a long absence and filmed the locations in the city in which his memory had concentrated past moments, represented by film sequences. Marker visits sites with particular significance for him, such as the Gotokuji temple, dedicated to the cats of Tokyo, but he also amasses his images on the move, in transit from site to site, and from moment to moment, filming the sleeping inhabitants of subway trains, and interposing the hallucinations and nightmares—drawn from Japanese popular culture and television—which occupy their mental space. In his commentary for the film, Marker evokes the city's unique urban space: "Tokyo is a city criss-crossed by trains, tied together with electric wire, she shows her veins . . . One could get lost in the great architectural masses and the accumulation of details, and that created the cheapest images of Tokyo: overcrowded, megalomaniacal, inhuman. He thought he saw more subtle cycles there, rhythms, clusters of faces caught sight of in passing, as different and precise as groups of instruments."[6] In 1968 and 1969, Marker was preoccupied with events in Europe, and his involvement in Paris in the filmmakers' collectives SLON and ISKRA, but he remained engaged with events in Tokyo, notably the violent protests against the construction of the Narita international airport, which involved the uprooting of numerous farming communities. Marker filmed riot sequences himself and also appropriated others shot by Japanese filmmakers. In *Sans Soleil*, such sequences are processed through computer programs, with the resulting transformed images presented by Marker as inhabiting what he calls the "Zone": a terrain, inspired by Tarkovsky's science fiction film *Stalker* (1979), which propels the human eye futuristically beyond the habitual parameters of both the filmic and the urban.

Andrei Tarkovsky visited Tokyo in September 1971, at a time when the urban protest movement had mutated, with many of its student participants despairing of the possibility of revolution, and entering a kind of internal exile in the ascendant corporate Japan of the 1970s. Tarkovsky perceived Tokyo as a salutary urban space, writing in his diary: "Japan is a wonderful country, of course. Nothing in common with Europe or America. Tokyo is an amazing city. There's not a single factory chimney, not a single house that looks like any other."[7] In this sense, Tarkovsky's perception of Tokyo differs from those of Marker and Richie, who saw it as a site enduringly imprinted with the residues of its U.S. Occupation, and who noted an extreme homogeneity in its architecture, especially in the suburbs. Tarkovsky reconfigured the city for his own distinctive purpose, coming to Tokyo to shoot a sequence for his film *Solaris*, also science fiction, in which an astronaut, Berton, inhabits what Tarkovsky calls "a town of the future": an unnamed megalopolis entirely composed of highway underpasses and overpasses, bordered by immense towers. In a notable sequence, Berton has an argument with another astronaut, Kelvin, who is shortly to leave on a mission to the planet Solaris. Berton abruptly leaves Kelvin's house, which is in the countryside, and an extended five-minute sequence shows Berton driving at speed into and through the city, in the dense network of highways that had been constructed in advance of the Tokyo Olympic Games. Finally, the camera ascends, away from Berton's car, viewing the chaos of intersecting highway junctions from above. Once the sequence is over, Tokyo, which is never identified by name, vanishes from the film, existing in isolation in the film only in that autonomous sequence.

Funeral Parade of Roses and *Diary of a Shinjuku Thief*

Marker and Tarkovsky, as short-term visitors, reinvent Tokyo in fragmentary apparitions in which memory, imagination, and duration are probed by transits across the face of the city, using the camera to examine urban facades while unleashing multiple sensations. *Funeral Parade of Roses* and *Diary of a Shinjuku Thief*, by contrast, are wholly centered on Tokyo's inner-city unrest, its culture of riots, and the intensity of participating in them at a very specific moment in time. The exterior sequences of both films were shot in Shinjuku, a district focused upon a wide plaza adjoining a commuter-hub railway station that became intimately associated in the 1960s with both riots and experimentation in visual arts and media. As Peter Eckersall emphasizes in his book *Performativity and Event in 1960s Japan*, Shinjuku is a pivotal urban location because it forms

> a window onto the wider protest movement at the end of the 1960s. The gathering at Shinjuku saw thousands of people meeting at the plaza and occupying the large open space on the lower-level west exit to sing protest songs, debate politics, and agitate against the perceived political order of capitalism and the revival of military state hegemony. The gatherings began in February 1969 and continued until May, when they were officially banned. The protesters subsequently ignored the prohibition, and accounts suggest that making the gatherings illegal in fact attracted wider attention. Subsequently, through May and June the protests grew in size and intensity. Newspaper reports suggest that at the gathering on 28 June 1969, protestors' attendance peaked

at around 7,000 people. Revolutionary dictums were combined with performative approaches to fostering political resistance . . . There were also regular clashes with riot police, confrontations that bled out from the station to include nearby roads and neighborhoods in the scene of activity.[8]

Shinjuku also formed the primary location of nightclubs and bars for the city's gay and lesbian cultures, in the "Golden Gai" area (where Marker also opened a bar). Its plaza became a pivotal gathering place for the city's sexual outcasts—notably, its transvestites and transsexuals—as well as for demonstrators. It also formed an impromptu space for spectacles by performance artists—both Matsumoto's *Funeral Parade of Roses* and Oshima's *Diary of a Shinjuku Thief* document performances in that location, either as a central focus of the narrative or as a background element. In the late 1960s, the vast department stores and business towers surrounding the plaza were already illuminated with immense neon billboards advertising technology corporations, although by the end of the following decade those billboards had been replaced by moving-image screens. The Shinjuku district had a heavy police presence, and Matsumoto, as he explains in his DVD commentary to the film, was unable to obtain official permission to film there. As a result, the exterior sequences of the film were done covertly, usually in one take, before the police arrived to break up the filmmaking process.[9] That enforced urgency and spontaneity in part determines the stylistic form of *Funeral Parade of Roses*, as it does with *Diary of a Shinjuku Thief*, shot with similar rapidity. The film image is infused with a sense of immediacy, with urban space caught by handheld cameras in single takes, which focus primarily on the faces and bodies of the characters in their juxtaposition with the surrounding buildings' facades. In his DVD commentary, Matsumoto evokes Jean-Luc Godard's filming of the streets, neon signs, and billboards of Paris in the early 1960s as an inspiration for his own filming of Tokyo. The film's approach to interior spaces is inflected by similar spatial dynamics. Matsumoto shot the film in small rooms and crowded nightclubs, often dense with figures dancing or engaged in sexual acts, so that the camera has to maneuver and negotiate its way through tight space, evoking a perpetual sense of mobility.

Young directors such as Matsumoto and Oshima had to be flexible not only in their filmmaking but in the ways in which their films were financed and distributed. This was evident in Oshima's ability to work both within the studio system and at its periphery. The Art Theatre Guild, which began its work in 1961 and existed entirely outside the studio system, distributed and cofinanced films, including *Funeral Parade of Roses* and *Diary of a Shinjuku Thief*, as well as the films of Shuji Terayama. It formed only one of many "collective" organizations of autonomous film production operating in the city. Although such organizations possessed relatively small budgets, their networks of affiliated movie theaters (separate from the chain theaters controlled by the studio system) allowed the films that they produced to be widely seen. Filmmakers operating within them also worked as theater directors, choreographers, or musicians, or taught in art schools, and had little inclination to pursue linear careers or to confine themselves to one medium. For example, *Funeral Parade of Roses* was Matsumoto's first feature film, but rather than pursuing work in that format, his later projects (alongside art school teaching) extended into experimental forms, short films—and later, digital works—which analyzed issues of camera movement and the manipulation or multiplication of visual images.

The narrative of *Funeral Parade of Roses*, drawn from a range of sources in Greek tragedy and myth, concerns a young transvestite named Eddie who has previously murdered his mother and now works as a prostitute in a gay bar in Shinjuku, the "Bar Genet." He also pursues friendships with other transvestites and with a group of young would-be revolutionaries who are preoccupied with the ongoing riots. (See Figure 8.1.) Eddie has an affair with the bar's drug-dealing proprietor, but when the proprietor discovers that he is actually Eddie's father, he stabs himself to death in their apartment, leading Eddie to pierce his own eyes with the same knife, before going out onto the street, clutching the knife and attracting a crowd of onlookers. The final shot of the film circles through the crowd before focusing on the knife, poised against the facade of a nearby building.

Funeral Parade of Roses evokes the gay subcultures of Tokyo, which are located below street level, especially in subterranean bars, night clubs, and art galleries. It is in the subterranean sequences of the film that the camera must infiltrate itself between amassed bodies in order to isolate the sequence's significant action. Similarly, once the action shifts to street level, the camera follows the film's characters through the movements of pedestrians, who often obstruct or assault them. The filming of Tokyo's urban space in Matsumoto's film demands an exceptional mobility from the bodies of the protagonists as they attempt to penetrate its space. Urban space only opens out when the camera ascends to viewing positions above the city such as those of buildings overlooking the Shinjuku plaza, or the summit of the Tokyo Tower.

In *Funeral Parade of Roses*, the urban space of Tokyo is seen by its characters as if in a process of irreparable disintegration, reflecting the growing

Figure 8.1 The fragmented urban space of Tokyo in *Funeral Parade of Roses* (Matsumoto, 1969)

perception of the time in Japan that rapid urban expansion, together with pollution and the exhausting of natural resources, had radically destabilized the environment, whose precarious existence was also communicated by the violent protests against U.S. military power. That precarity was manifested notably in the medium of photography, in such seminal projects as the photographing of the bodies of the mercury-poisoned citizens of the fishing community of Minamata begun by W. Eugene Smith in 1963.[10] Many young Japanese photographers of the 1960s, such as Eikoh Hosoe and Kikuji Kawada, were also concerned with the ongoing ecological devastation of Japan and sought to evoke it in images of corporeal and landscape contamination. At the same time, Japan was being reinvented as a utopian urban environment through its immense architectural projects, such as those undertaken in advance of the Tokyo Olympic Games and the construction of an entire subcity of technological innovation on the edge of Osaka for the "Expo '70" world's fair. The tension between urban contamination and urban utopia produced exceptionally volatile urban environments, whether rendered in still photography or in films. Eckersall emphasizes the uniqueness of the 1960s in Japan's cultural and social history, with its population "under the mass sway of the energetic events of Japan's most dynamic decade—an era of perhaps greater agitation and change than any other in its history."[11]

In depicting such seismic events, the urban space depicted in *Funeral Parade of Roses* constantly fragments. One sequence shows the funeral of another suicide, the Bar Genet's manager, who had ended his life due to his jealousy of Eddie's relationship with the bar's proprietor. After the funeral, Eddie notices with horror that much of the vast, decrepit cemetery has become waterlogged, and that many tombs have subsided, vanishing below the water. Matsumoto parallels the disintegration of the cemetery with that of Tokyo. Eddie exclaims that he wishes that not only the city, but the entirety of Japan, would sink below water and disappear.

The title of Terayama's film *Throw Away Your Books, Rally in the Streets* (1971) incites its spectators to explore the city and stage confrontations with its figures of authority. However, the young revolutionaries depicted in *Funeral Parade of Roses* are never seen in Tokyo's streets, and they decline to participate in the demonstrations taking place at the moment in which the film is set. Instead, in company with Eddie, they remain enclosed in interior spaces, engaged in wild sex parties and watching television news broadcasts that show the confrontations between protesters and riot police. They also make films of the television news and then project those films to themselves, in the same room. Hence, filmic images are distorted by technological processes of replication in a way that anticipates those Marker would later include as the contents of the "Zone" in his film *Sans Soleil*, in which any riot, anywhere in the world, is equivalent to any other. Matsumoto anticipates a global obsession with media images of conflict, and an accompanying loss of direct physical contact with urban protest. Revolution has been abstracted and transformed into ever-diminishing representations, which form a source of excitation for sexual acts or for the filmmaking process, but not for social activism.

Matsumoto also devotes sequences of *Funeral Parade of Roses* to demonstrating the ways in which the filmic medium can oscillate between familiarizing and defamiliarizing urban space for its viewers. He does this by including a number of interviews, resonant of those in mid-1960s films by Godard. They possess an insurgent and disruptive presence in the film, as documentary elements, intentionally fracturing the consistency of its linear narrative fiction. In particular, Matsumoto conducts dialogues with young transvestites in the Shinjuku plaza, filming them at night against the background of the district's illuminated buildings. Most of the interviews follow a repetitive framework in which the same questions are posed and the same answers given, so that they provide a sense of stability in the disintegration and furor expressed by the film's narrative as a whole. In part, although the city may be eroding and submerged in uncontrollable riots, and the film's characters

Figure 8.2 The performative space of Tokyo's Shinjuku district in *Diary of a Shinjuku Thief* (Oshima, 1969); frame top right shows the book thief, Birdey (Tadanori Yokoo) with the salesgirl, Umeko (Rie Yokoyama)

are all heading toward death, a sense of stability is also provided by the recognizable urban presence of the familiar plaza and billboards of Shinjuku.

Oshima's film *Diary of a Shinjuku Thief*, filmed around the same time as *Funeral Parade of Roses*, opens with a sequence set in the same Tokyo location: the plaza alongside the Shinjuku railway station, where a theater company is staging an open-air performance. (See Figure 8.2.) The film never leaves the Shinjuku district, focusing on a narrow terrain, which the film relates to the mental journey of its central character, Birdey, a young book thief who steals from the shelves at the huge Kinokuniya bookshop. The film generates much of its narrative from the particular resonances of that urban location and its reputation as a site for countercultures and sexual experimentation, in the same way that filmmakers in other cities of the late 1960s sometimes shot on location—for example, in San Francisco's Haight-Ashbury or West Berlin's Kreuzberg district—in order to evoke a similar sense of riotous urban exploration. Oshima's film is concerned more explicitly than *Funeral Parade of Roses* with making connections between sexual acts and revolution, cutting directly between sex scenes and shots of the street riots in Shinjuku. The film ends with an extended sequence of rioting, its narrative

Figure 8.3 Street riots at the Shinjuku train station at night near the end of *Diary of a Shinjuku Thief* (Oshima, 1969)

open-ended, as though prised apart by the engulfing violent uproar of the period. (See Figure 8.3.)

Another factor that unites the two films is their obsession with the work of the French writer and filmmaker Jean Genet. Just as the title of Matsumoto's *Funeral Parade of Roses* alludes to Genet's novel *Pompes funèbres* (1947), Oshima's *Diary of a Shinjuku Thief* refers to Genet's novel *Journal du voleur* (1949). Genet's film *Un Chant d'amour* (1950) had been distributed internationally via filmmakers' cooperatives and seen widely by filmmakers in Japan. It exerts an especially strong stylistic influence on the filming of gay sexual acts in *Funeral Parade of Roses*. The naming of the nightclub where Eddie works in that film is an homage to Genet, and when Birdie steals books from the Kinokuniya bookshop he heads directly for the works of Genet, who had himself been a book thief and was imprisoned several times for his thefts. Genet was at the height of his international reputation in 1969, actively supporting the Palestinian struggle, the Black Panther Party in the United States, and the rights of immigrant workers in France. All of his novels had been translated into Japanese, and he was a seminal figure for many of Tokyo's experimental artists, choreographers, and theater directors, as he remains in Tokyo today. Indeed, Genet spent part of 1969 in Tokyo, where he visited his friend Jackie Maglia and took part in several of the largest and most violent confrontations between the student movement and riot police in November and December of that year. Maglia recalled Genet's participation in the demonstrations: "People hooked up to one another . . . so they'd be harder to arrest. Genet pretended to be 'reviewing' the masked soldiers who'd come to control the crowd. He looked each soldier squarely in the eye (many of them were handsome)."[12] However, Genet declined to meet filmmakers and artists while in Tokyo as he was interested only in political involvements at this time.

Even more than Matsumoto's film, *Diary of a Shinjuku Thief* is a film of urban fragments, in which narrative elements are disconnected and subordinated to the exploration of urban space. The film is composed of a set of momentary encounters, transits, and pursuits between the book thief and a salesgirl at the bookshop, Umeko, who arrests him in the act of theft, and between them and the theater director played by Juro Kara. Like Matsumoto, Oshima also focuses on the ability of the mobile camera to scan the surfaces and subterranean spaces of the city, in order to collect traces and residues, including those imprinted upon exterior walls and buildings in the form of graffiti and advertising billboards, which then amass to create an image of the city in crisis, akin to that of Italian neorealist films. Although the exploration of urban space is largely accorded the work of defining and carrying the film—to the point at which, in *Diary of a Shinjuku Thief*, the characters occasionally appear peripheral to the film's preoccupations—the urban space is disintegrating, subject to perpetual amendment, a sequence of fragments that will never cohere.

An Ambivalent Relationship to Activism

In both *Funeral Parade of Roses* and *Diary of a Shinjuku Thief*, the revolutionary aspirations of the protesters are treated by the filmmakers with a degree of irony and linked to the idea of revolution as an art of performance, a notion that Genet had developed in his theatrical work, as in his play *The Balcony* (1957). The revolutionary "cell" in Matsumoto's film never leave their room, and become consumed by the media images of the riots taking place in the avenues outside. The sexual imperatives around the relationship between the two characters in *Diary of a Shinjuku Thief* also render them largely oblivious to the riots that surround them and finally engulf the entire film. This oblique, ambivalent relationship to activism and revolutionary commitment is also present in Koji Wakamatsu's films of that era—for example, *Violated Angels* (1967) or *Go, Go, Second Time Virgin* (1969). Wakamatsu analyzed the philosophical rapport between sexual and revolutionary acts in works structured in the form of exploitation or pornographic films. He was also preoccupied with the connections between the protest culture of late-1960s Tokyo and the terrorist cells that emerged, directly or indirectly, from that culture. His wide-ranging engagement with terrorism, rioting, and violence had an international dimension, especially focused on events in the Middle East. Alongside its retrospective archiving of the 1960s Tokyo riots, his more recent film *United Red Army* also looks back at the terrorist cells of the 1970s with their implosive internal dynamics. In this light, both *Funeral*

Parade of Roses and *Diary of a Shinjuku Thief* appear prescient in their depictions both of an all-consuming apathy and of forms of terrorism whose imageries and definitions could be endlessly manipulated and distorted.

Also at the end of the 1960s, Donald Richie made the last of his many films, *Cybele* (1968), which, like *Funeral Parade of Roses*, adopts a mythic narrative structure and uses a cemetery location—that of the vast Yanaka cemetery in eastern Tokyo—to explore its concern with urban and cultural disintegration. In the final sequence, Richie depicts a group of naked figures, performed by the Zero Jigen performance art group, who appear to have been slaughtered and piled up on top of each other. As Richie notes in his DVD commentary to the film, those images led to the censorship and banning of the film in numerous countries.[13] But they also serve to intimate an overturning of the sense of exhilaration and often-playful experimentation that had characterized Tokyo-based filmmakers' work during the second half of the 1960s. Richie's vision resonates, even against the filmmaker's intentions, with the images of piled-up bodies filmed by Soviet cinematographers as they arrived at the Auschwitz concentration camp in February 1945 or those photographed in Tokyo's streets following the U.S. firebombing of the city the following month.

Such unexpected transits across time are as revealing as the perpetual movements through urban space that propelled the narratives and determined the distinctive stylistic texture of films of Tokyo such as those I have discussed. Their images of urban space in a state of violent turmoil have remained resonant ones for filmmaking and for digital arts in Tokyo—evident, for example, in the work of the director Shinya Tsukamoto and the mutating megalopolis of his films, such as *Tokyo Fist* (1995). The films of Takashi Miike carry a preoccupation with the city's Shinjuku district akin to that of *Funeral Parade of Roses* and *Diary of a Shinjuku Thief*, as a unique urban environment in which events habitually occur that would otherwise be impossible and inconceivable and that need to be seized at speed. The particular ethos of late-1960s film-production and distribution structures in Japan, exemplified by the Art Theatre Guild, still survives in Tokyo through institutions such as Image Forum. After being rarely seen for many years, *Funeral Parade of Roses* and *Diary of a Shinjuku Thief* were, in many ways, resuscitated by the DVD medium, which allowed viewers the opportunity to reconstruct the time and space of their fast-moving urban transits. Even though the urban space of Tokyo, notably that of Shinjuku, is now largely unrecognizable from its late-1960s documentation by Matsumoto and Oshima, it still presents an open environment for filmmakers and digital artists preoccupied with the scanning of urban mutations and with the exploration of pivotal moments of disquiet and unease with the forms of the city.

The filmic exploration of Tokyo's late-1960s era of riots often took the form of intimate examinations of urban surfaces and their interaction with the human figures poised against them. Those riven surfaces formed apertures and held contents, always precarious and unstable, ready to unleash volatile memory, conflict, and sexual energy. As such, they had to be captured with both urgency and flexibility in lithe movements across the face of the city, thereby generating films that enduringly appear as vital archives, revealing the forms of urban space in states of uproar and transformation.

NOTES

1. William Marotti, *Money, Trains, and Guillotines: Art and Revolution in 1960s Japan* (Durham NC: Duke University Press, 2013), 4. Marotti also provides a comprehensive chronology of Tokyo's culture of riots, and its interconnections with the city's art culture, across the 1960s, on pages xii to xxi.

2. Alice Maude-Roxby, *Anti-Academy* (Southampton, U.K.: John Hansard Gallery, 2014), 14. Maude-Roxby emphasizes how crucial art schools were for film in late-1960s Japan, notably through a form of erasing and reinventing their established curriculum, as in the case of the Bigakko art school in central Tokyo, which ran workshops for urban exploration in a range of media.

3. According to imdb.com, *Diary of a Shinjuku Thief* was released in Japan on February 15, 1969, and in western Europe and the United States on various dates in 1970–1973; *Funeral Parade of Roses* was released in Japan on September 13, 1969, and in the United States in October 1970.

4. Iimura also collaborated extensively with artists, musicians, and choreographers in 1960s Tokyo, such as Yoko Ono and Tatsumi Hijikata. His conception of "Cine-Dance," in which he physically entered the performance space of choreographers such as Hijikata with his camera and intentionally disrupted their work through his filming of it, forms a pivotal experimental film technique, resonating with the approach of Kurt Kren in filming the work of the Viennese Actionists during the same era. In his pamphlet *Media and Performance* (Tokyo: self-pub., 2007), 21, Iimura allies his experimental filmmaking techniques to those of "expanded cinema" in the United States and comments: "One example of 'expanded cinema' is the experimental combining of film and performance to arrive at a 'film performance.' I was creating 'Cine-Dance,' a rare combination of media and dance." Terayama also worked in the media of dance, theater, and performance art, and his films, such as *Throw Away Your Books, Rally in the Streets* (1971), demonstrate the intimate interconnections between film, performance, and street culture in the art scene of late-1960s Tokyo.

5. Donald Richie, *Tokyo: A View of the City* (London: Reaktion Books, 1999), 27. In this book, Richie incorporates his original journal account of 1947 into his 1990s memories of Tokyo in its era of devastation.

6. Chris Marker, voice-over commentary within the film *Sans Soleil* (Criterion Collection DVD, 2003).

7. Andrei Tarkovsky, *Time within Time: The Diaries 1970–1986* (London: Faber and Faber, 1994), 43–44. In contrast to Marker's experience of Tokyo, Tarkovsky's visit to the city was a brief, concentrated one.

8. Peter Eckersall, *Performativity and Event in 1960s Japan: City, Body, Memory* (Palgrave Macmillan, Basingstoke, 2013), 82. Eckersall provides a nuanced commentary on the relationship between the Shinjuku riots and the art experimentations that accompanied them, in such areas as dance, photography, music, and performance art, as well as film.

9. Toshio Matsumoto, commentary to the film *Funeral Parade of Roses* (Eureka Collection DVD, 2007).

10. See W. Eugene Smith, Enrica Viganò, and Britt Salvesen, *W. Eugene Smith: More Real Than Reality* (New York: Distributed Art Publishers, 2011).

11. Eckersall, *Performativity and Event*, 164.

12. Edmund White, *Genet* (London: Chatto and Windus, 1993), 596. White's research and extensive interviews with Genet's friends and associates generate rare traces of Genet's stay in Japan and of his participation in the Shinjuku riots of 1969; his time in Japan is otherwise largely undocumented.

13. Donald Richie, commentary to the film *Cybele* (Image Forum DVD, 2004). Richie shot his film extremely rapidly, in exterior locations and across the span of one afternoon, improvising as he went along. His film is one of the most extensive documentations of the work of the Zero Jigen performance art group, whose work was notable in late-1960s Japan for its disruptive interventions in urban space. As Eckersall writes in *Performativity and Event in 1960s Japan* (17): "Zero Jigen's ritual performances (called *gishiki*) included absurd and uncanny processions, naked acts of sensual arousal, and scandalous confrontations with the public. Zero Jigen performances caused consternation and reveled in conflict with state authorities and institutions, defiling urban spaces and outraging social decorum."

Contributors

Stephen Barber is a professor in the Faculty of Art, Design and Architecture at Kingston University, London. His books include *Abandoned Images: Film and Film's End* (Reaktion Books, 2010); *The Walls of Berlin: Urban Surfaces: Art: Film* (Solar Books, 2011); *Muybridge, The Eye in Motion: Tracing Cinema's Origins* (Solar Books, 2012); *Performance Projections: Film and the Body in Action* (Reaktion Books, 2014); and, most recently, *Berlin Bodies* (Reaktion/University of Chicago Press, 2017). He is currently writing a book on the film projects of the Japanese artist Tatsumi Hijikata.

Stanley Corkin is a professor of English and History, and Niehoff Professor and co-chair of the Program in Film and Media Studies, at the University of Cincinnati. Corkin is author of four books: *Realism and the Birth of the Modern United States: Cinema, Literature, and Culture* (University of Georgia Press, 1996); *Cowboys as Cold Warriors: The Western and United States History* (Temple University Press, 2004); *Starring New York: Filming the Grime and Glamor of the Long 1970s* (Oxford University Press, 2010); and *Connecting the Wire: Race, Space, and Postindustrial Baltimore* (University of Texas Press, 2017).

Jesse Lerner is a professor of Media Studies at Pitzer College. His short films and feature-length experimental documentaries have won numerous prizes at film festivals in the United States, Latin America, and Japan. His books include: *F Is for Phony: Fake Documentary and Truth's Undoing* (with Alexandra Juhasz, University of Minnesota Press, 2000); *The Shock of Modernity: Crime Photography in Mexico City* (Turner/INAH, 2007); *The Maya of Modernism: Art, Architecture, and Film* (University of New Mexico Press, 2011); *Ismo Ismo Ismo: Experimental Cinema in Latin America* (with Luciano Piazza,

University of California Press, 2017); and *The Catherwood Project: Incidents of Visual Reconstructions and Other Matters* (with Leandro Katz, University of New Mexico Press, 2017).

Jon Lewis is the Distinguished Professor of Film Studies at Oregon State University. He has published twelve books, including *Whom God Wishes to Destroy . . . Francis Coppola and the New Hollywood* (Duke University Press, 1995); *Hollywood v. Hard Core: How the Struggle over Censorship Saved the Modern Film Industry* (New York University Press, 2000); and *Hard-Boiled Hollywood: Crime and Punishment in Postwar Los Angeles* (University of California Press, 2017).

Gaetana Marrone is a professor of Italian at Princeton University. Her principal publications include: *La drammatica di Ugo Betti* (Novecento, 1988); *New Landscapes in Contemporary Italian Cinema* (Annali d'Italianistica, 1999); *The Gaze and the Labyrinth: The Cinema of Liliana Cavani* (Princeton University Press, 2000); a critical edition of Ugo Betti's *Delitto all'isola delle capre* (Pacini Fazzi Editore, 2006); and the two-volume *Encyclopedia of Italian Literary Studies* (2007), of which she was general editor. She has also produced award-winning films, including *Woman in the Wind* (1988) and the documentaries *Images of a University* (1996) and *Zefirino: The Voice of a Castrato* (2007). She is currently finishing a monograph on the director Francesco Rosi.

Mark Shiel is Reader in Film Studies and Urbanism in the Department of Film Studies at King's College London. He is the author of *The Real Los Angeles: Hollywood Cinema, and the City of Angels* (Reaktion Books, 2012) and *Italian Neorealism: Rebuilding the Cinematic City after World War Two* (Wallflower Press/Columbia University Press, 2006) and the co-editor of *Cinema and the City: Film and Urban Societies in a Global Context* (Blackwell, 2001) and *Screening the City* (Verso, 2003), both with Tony Fitzmaurice. He is currently writing a third monograph, which is a study of Los Angeles film, media, and the built environment in the 1960s.

Jennifer Stob is an assistant professor of Art History at Texas State University, San Marcos. Her scholarship combines the study of aesthetic theory, experimental film and video, and transnational cinema. Her writing has appeared in *Moving Image Review and Art Journal (MIRAJ)*, *Philosophy of Photography*, *Studies in French Cinema*, and *Film Criticism*; she coprograms Experimental Response Cinema, a microcinema based in Austin, Texas; and she is currently finishing a book on social space and the film theory of the Situationist International.

Andrew J. Webber is professor of Modern German and Comparative Culture at the University of Cambridge. He has published widely on German and European film, literature, and other media. His most recent books are *The European Avant-Garde, 1900–1940* (Polity, 2004); *Berlin in the Twentieth Century: A Cultural Topography* (Cambridge University Press, 2008); as coeditor, *Cities in Transition: The Moving Image and the Modern Metropolis* (Wallflower Press/Columbia University Press, 2008), and as editor, *The Cambridge Companion to the Literature of Berlin* (Cambridge University Press, 2017).

Film Title Index

Acapulco 68 (Salomón Laiter, 1968), 197
Accattone (Pier Paolo Pasolini, 1961), 71
A dónde van nuestros hijos (Benito Alazraki, 1958), 193
Ah, verda'? (Sergio García, 1973), 206
Angry Breed, The, (David Commons, 1968), 169
Anticlimax (Gelsen Gas, 1969–1973), 206
Architecture of Mexico (Spencer Moore, Prod. Allen-Moore Productions, 1952), 190
Atecingo (Grupo Cine Testimonial, 1973), 207
August 29, 1970 (Francisco Martinez, 1971), 169

Baader Meinhof Komplex, The, (Uli Edel, 2008), 111n51
Batallón Olimpia: documento abierto (Canal 6 de Julio, 1998), 201
Beat Generation, The, (Charles F. Haas, 1959), 177
Billy Liar (John Schlesinger, 1963), 142, 144, 172, 182, 186, 224
Bob and Carol and Ted and Alice (Paul Mazursky, 1969), 168

Bonnie and Clyde (Arthur Penn, 1967), 8, 178
Breathless (Jean-Luc Godard, 1960), 135
Brecht die Macht der Manipulateure (Break the Power of the Manipulators, Helke Sander, 1968), 93, 104, 106
Brucemas (Dan McLaughlin, 1968), 177
Bucket of Blood, A, (Roger Corman, 1959), 177
Bush Mama (Haile Gerima, 1976), 169

Cactus Flower (Gene Saks, 1969), 146
Campeones de la cultura (Julio Pliego, 1968), 197
Canoa (Felipe Cazal, 1976), 198
Caprice (Frank Tashlin, 1967), 170
Ce n'est qu'un debut (États généraux du cinéma, 1968), 45
Chase, The, (Arthur Penn, 1966), 8
Chicano Moratorium (Thomas Myrdahl, 1970), 169
Click, fotógrafo de modelos (René Cardona Jr., 1967), 195
Colpire al cuore (Gianni Amelio, 1982), 68
Columbia Revolt (Newsreel, 1968), 26, 141–143, 146–156, 160

Comunicados (film series, 1968), 201
Contempt (Jean-Luc Godard, 1963), 135
Coogan's Bluff (Don Siegel, 1968), 146
Critique de la séparation (Critique of Separation, Guy Debord, 1961), 41

Darling (John Schlesinger, 1965), 142
Demonstration, Century Plaza, 1967 (LAPD, 1967), 171
Departamento de soltero (René Cardona Jr., 1969), 195
Despedida de casada (Juan de Orduña, 1966), 195
Diary of a Shinjuku Thief (Nagisa Oshima, 1969), 214, 216–227
Domingos (Manuel Michel, 1968), 197
Don Juan '67 (Carlos Velo, 1966), 195

Easy Rider (Dennis Hopper, 1969), 8, 19, 137n11, 139n34
El año de la rata (Cooperativa Cine Marginal, 1971), 206
El brazo fuerte (Giovanni Korporaal, 1958), 197
El bulto (Gabriel Retes, 1991), 206
El cambio (Alfred Joskowicz, 1971), 206
El fin (Sergio García, 1970), 206
El grito (López Aretche, 1969), 199–202
El topo (Alejandro Jodorowsky, 1970), 197
En el balcón vacío (Jomi García Ascot, 1961), 194
Eva (Manuel Michel, 1968), 197
Explotados y explotadores (The Exploited and the Exploiters, Grupo Cine Octubre, 1974), 207

Fall of the Romanov Dynasty, The, (Esfir Shub, 1927), 42
Fando y Lis (Alejandro Jodorowsky, 1968), 197
400 mil años de deportes (Juan Guerrero, 1968), 197
Funeral Parade of Roses (Toshio Matsumoto, 1969), 214, 216, 218–227
Funny Girl (William Wyler, 1968), 145

Go, Go, Second Time Virgin (Koji Wakamatsu, 1969), 225
Graduate, The, (Mike Nichols, 1967), 8, 149, 168
Greetings (Brian De Palma, 1968), 26, 141–143, 147–150, 153–160
Guadalajara 68 (Angel Bilbatúa, 1968), 197
Guanajuato 68 (Nacho López, 1968), 197
Guide for the Married Man, A, (Gene Kelly, 1967), 170

Hells Angels on Wheels (Richard Rush, 1967), 169
Herstellung eines Molotow-Cocktails (Making of a Molotow Cocktail, Holger Meins, 1968), 91, 97–99
He Walked by Night (Alfred L. Werker, 1948), 176
Historia de un documento (Oscar Menéndez, 1970), 204
Hurlements en faveur de Sade (Howls for Sade, Guy Debord, 1952), 41

I cannibali (Liliana Cavani, 1969), 26, 77–82, 84, 86
Il posto (The Sound of Trumpets or The Job, Ermanno Olmi, 1961), 70
Imágen 68 (Julio Pliego, 1968), 197
It's a Bikini World (Stephanie Rothman, 1967), 168

Killer of Sheep (Charles Burnett, 1977), 169
Kind of Loving, A, (John Schlesinger, 1962), 142
Koumiko Mystery, The, (Chris Marker, 1967), 217
Kuhle Wampe (Slatan Dudow, 1932), 105

La battaglia de Algeri (The Battle of Algiers, Gillo Pontecorvo, 1966), 207
La Chinoise (Jean-Luc Godard, 1967), 21, 53, 164, 167
La dolce vita (Federico Fellini, 1960), 66
La Jetée (Chris Marker, 1962), 49
La libertad es un hombre chiquito con ganas de darle en la madre a todo el mundo, la

soledad es el mismo hombre un poco menos politizado (Rafael Montero, 1973), 206
La montaña sagrada (Alejandro Jodorowsky, 1973), 197, 199
La notte (Michelangelo Antonioni, 1961), 70
La otra virginidad (Juan Manuel Torres, 1975), 204
Lecumberri, el palacio negro (Arturo Ripstein, 1976), 204
Le Gai Savoir (Jean-Luc Godard, 1968), 53
Les Carabiniers (Jean-Luc Godard, 1963), 167
Lions Love . . . and Lies (Varda, 1969), 167, 178
Live a Little, Love a Little (Norman Taurog, 1968), 170
Lola (Jacques Demy, 1961), 177
Los albaniles (Grupo Cine Octubre, 1974), 207
Los escuincles (Antonio Reynoso, 1968), 197
Los olvidados (Luis Buñuel, 1950), 192–193

Mamma Roma (Pier Paolo Pasolini, 1962), 71
Man and a Woman, A, (Claude Lelouch, 1966), 177
Medium Cool (Haskell Wexler, 1969), 7, 26, 112–136
Me gustan los estudiantes (Mario Handler, 1968), 201
México 68 (Rafael Corkidi, 1968), 197
Midnight Cowboy (John Schlesinger, 1969), 141–143, 146–160
Model Shop (Jacques Demy, 1968), 26, 177–184
Mondo Mod (Peter Perry, 1967), 175
Monterrey 68 (Salomón Leiter, 1968), 197
Mujeres, mujeres, mujeres (José Díaz Morales, 1967), 195
Mural efímero (Raul Kamffer, 1968–1971), 203

Nantes—Sud-Aviation (États généraux du cinéma, 1968), 45
Napoletani a Milano (Neapolitans in Milan, Eduardo De Filippo, 1953), 68
NICHT löschbares Feuer (Inextinguishable Fire, Harun Farocki, 1969), 91, 99
Night Tide (Curtis Harrington, 1961), 177
1960 (Gabriele Salvatores, 2010), 66, 68, 86
Ni olvido, no perdón (Richard Dindo, 2012), 199

Olimpia 68 (Giovanni Korporaal, 1968), 197
Olimpiada en México (Alberto Isaac, 1968), 197, 199
Olympia (Leni Riefenstahl, 1938), 197
Oskar Langenfeld: 12 Mal (*Oskar Langenfeld: 12 Times*, Holger Meins, 1966), 98
Outside Man, The, (Un homme est mort, Jacques Deray, 1972), 178

Pixellated Revolution, The, (Rabih Mroué, 2012), 213
Playtime (Jacques Tati, 1967), 206
Point Blank (John Boorman, 1967), 169
Popi (Arthur Hiller, 1969), 145
Powers of Ten (Charles and Ray Eames, two versions, 1968, 1977), 9
Puebla 68 (Rafael Corkidi, 1968), 197

Ralph Story's Los Angeles (KNXT TV, Los Angeles, 1964–1970), 176
Rebel without a Cause (Nicholas Ray, 1955), 174
Reprise du travail aux usines Wonder (États généraux du cinéma, 1968), 45
Requiem 29 (David Garcia, 1970), 169
Riot on Sunset Strip (Arthur Dreifus, 1967), 174–175
Rocco e i suoi fratelli (Rocco and His Brothers, Luchino Visconti, 1960), 69
Rojo amanecer (Jorge Fons, 1989), 199, 203
Romanzo popolare (Come Home and Meet My Wife, Mario Monicelli, 1974), 88n27
Rosemary's Baby (Roman Polanski, 1968), 145

Sans soleil (Chris Marker, 1982), 217, 222
Sixth Side of the Pentagon, The, (Chris Marker, François Reichenbach, 1968), 9
Solaris (Andrei Tarkovsky, 1972), 218
Stalker (Andrei Tarkovsky, 1979), 217

Star is Born, A, (William Wellman, 1937), 173
Street Scenes (Martin Scorsese, 1970), 19
Strip, The, (László Kardos, 1951), 173
Sur le passage de quelques personnes à travers une assez courte unité de temps (On the Passage of Several Persons through a Rather Brief Unity of Time, Guy Debord, 1959), 41
Sweet Sweetback's Baadasssss Song (Melvin Van Peebles, 1971), 169

Tajimara (Juan José Gurrola, 1965), 195
Targets (Peter Bogdanovich, 1968), 169
Taxi Driver (Martin Scorsese, 1976), 178
Teorema (Pier Paolo Pasolini, 1968), 8, 26, 70–77, 85–86
Throw Away Your Books, Rally in the Streets (Shuji Terayama, 1971), 222
Tlatetlolco, verano de 68 (Carlos Bolado, 2012), 199
Tokyo Olympiad (Kon Ichikawa, 1965), 197, 216
Totò, Peppino e la . . . malafemmina (Totò, Peppino and the . . . Bad Woman, Camillo Mastrocinque, 1954), 68
Touch of Evil (Orson Welles, 1958), 176
Trabajo olimpico (Felipe Cazals, 1968), 197
24 horas de placer (René Cardona Jr., 1968), 195
2. Juni 1967 (Thomas Giefer und Hans-Rüdiger Minow, 1967), 96
Two or Three Things I Know about Her (Deux ou trois choses que je sais d'elle, Jean-Luc Godard, 1967), 167

2001: A Space Odyssey (Stanley Kubrick, 1968), 96

Uccellacci e uccellini (Pier Paolo Pasolini, 1966), 71
Umbrellas of Cherbourg, The, (Les Parapluies de Cherbourg, Jacques Demy, 1964), 177
Una y otra vez (Grupo Cine Testimonial, 1972–1975), 207
Un Chant d'amour (Jean Genet, 1950), 224
Un Chien andalou (Luis Buñuel and Salvador Dalí, 1929), 101–2
United Red Army (Koji Wakamatsu, 2008), 213, 225
Un toque de roc (Sergio García, 1988), 206

Violated Angels (Koji Wakamatsu, 1967), 225

Weekend (Jean-Luc Godard, 1967), 92, 179
Where Were You When the Lights Went Out (Hy Averback, 1968), 145
Wild in the Streets (Barry Shear, 1968), 132
Worte des Vorsitzenden (Words of the Chairman, Harun Farocki, 1967), 102

Young Girls of Rochefort, The, (Les Demoiselles de Rochefort, Jacques Demy, 1967), 177
Y si platicamos de agosto? (Maryse Sistache, 1980), 199

Zabriskie Point (Michelangelo Antonioni, 1969), 172–173, 178

Subject Index

Academy Awards, 5, 142, 149–150, 197
Acapulco, 195, 197
actionism, 91, 104
advertising, 20, 42, 67, 219, 225
Africa, 144
African American(s), 10, 123–127, 129, 133, 145, 151, 153–154, 169
agitprop, 2, 19, 26, 38, 43, 91, 93, 95, 98, 105, 108n12
Ailes, Roger, 143
Aimee, Anouk, 177, 187n40
Alberca Olímpica (Mexico City), 195
Albonico, Giulio, 82
Albrecht, Donald, 11
Alfaro Siqueiros, David, 203
Algerian War, 52–53, 182, 207
Allied Occupation of Japan (1945–1952), 212
Amelio, Gianni, 68
American Civil Liberties Union (ACLU), 171
American Institute of Architects, 22
Anger, Kenneth, 150
"anni di piombo" (years of lead), 67
Antigone (play), 77, 89n41

antiwar (movement), 21–22, 112–114, 145, 155, 170, 172, 186n28
Antonioni, Michelangelo, 18, 21, 32n61, 68, 70, 172–173, 178, 182
Apostolides, Alex, 176
Arab Spring, 58n9, 64n93
Arc de Triomphe (Paris), 51
Archigram, 4
Architectural Association, 9
architectural preservation, 4, 24
Aristotle, 131
Arrau, Claudio, 196
art, 17, 19, 25, 40–41, 53, 63n62, 73, 91, 107, 139n28, 156, 165, 183, 191, 195–197, 203, 213, 226
art cinema, 3, 18, 168, 170, 178
art deco, 4, 11, 165
art nouveau, 4
arts and crafts movement, 4
Art Theatre Guild (Japan), 214, 219, 226
Asia, 5, 10, 17, 144, 182
Atack, Margaret, 18
Atelier de recherche cinématographique, 43
Atlanta, 150

audiences, 2, 17, 19, 43, 47–48, 55, 59n14, 75, 100, 150–151, 167–168, 178, 196, 205
Außerparlamentarische Opposition (Extraparliamentary Opposition or APO), 95
Auther, Elissa, 17
automobiles, 6, 9, 51, 88n27, 164, 179
avant-garde, 2, 4, 16–18, 25, 40, 43, 151, 159, 168, 194, 212
Ayala, Leopoldo, 205

Baader, Andreas, 109n15
Bach, Johann Sebastian, 180
Baltimore, 13
Banham, Reyner, 4, 9, 176, 180–182
Barbey, Bruno, 46
Barragán, Luis, 191
Barthes, Roland, 50
Bartlett, Hall, 194
Baudrillard, Jean, 182–183
Baumgärtel, Tilman, 97
BBC (British Broadcasting Corporation), 9, 74, 180
beatniks, 176–177
beaux-arts style, 4
Beckett, Welton, 170
Beheiran movement (Japan), 186n28
Bentham, Jeremy, 204
Bergdoll, Barry, 12
Berkeley (California), 12, 16, 22, 144
Berlin, 1, 8, 12, 16, 26, 91–111, 144, 186n28, 223
Berlinale. *See* Berlin International Film Festival
Berlin International Film Festival, 92, 107nn4–5
Berlin Wall, 93, 110n45
Berlusconi, Silvio, 67
Berman, Marshall, 164
Bertolucci, Bernardo, 18
Betti, Laura, 71
Beverly Hills (Los Angeles), 170, 174, 187n37
Beyer, Herbert, 196
Bilbatúa, Ángel, 197, 199
billboards, 41, 180–181, 219, 223, 225
Black Lives Matter, 64n93

Black Panther Party, 126
Black Panthers. *See* Black Panther Party
Black Power, 153, 170, 164
black studies, 169
Bleecker Street Cinema (New York), 151
Bocca, Giorgio, 67–68
body (human), 18, 75–78, 148
Bogdanovich, Peter, 167, 169
bohemians, 4, 146, 159, 173, 195
Bolivia, 14, 206
Bonerz, Peter, 124–125
Bordes Mangel, Enrique, 199
Borromini, Francesco, 78
Boston, 144, 150
Boulevard Saint Michel (Paris), 26
bourgeoisie, 26, 51, 55, 70–72, 74–76, 78, 80, 84, 133, 151
Braester, Yomi, 9
Brecht, 105, 109n29
Brechtian staging, 97, 99–100, 102, 105–106
Breda Tower (Milan), 81, 89n55
Broadway (New York), 152, 156, 159
Bronzeville (Chicago), 124–125
Brunetta, Gian Piero, 67
Bruno, Giuliano, 11
Brunsdon, Charlotte, 10
Buhler, Alain, 40–41
built environment, 1–2, 4, 11, 16, 19, 31n52, 131, 134, 142, 146–149, 180–182
Bunker Hill (Los Angeles), 165
Buñuel, Luis, 101, 192–193
Burnett, Charles, 169
Butler, Judith, 55

Cahiers du cinéma (journal), 3
Calabresi, Luigi, 68, 87n4, 87n6
Calder, Alexander, 196
California, 168–169, 172, 182
Canby, Vincent, 117, 181
Candela, Felix, 195
Cannato, Vincent, 145
Cannes Film Festival, 2, 18, 20, 44, 92, 193
Capanna, Mario, 68
capitalism, 5, 20, 53, 67, 71, 92, 95, 99, 148, 183, 218
Caracas, 17, 207

Carter, Bunchy, 172
Casabella (journal), 9, 19
Casetti, Francesco, 3
Cassavetes, John, 151
Casteñeda, Luis, 196
Castanedo, Rafael, 197
Castro, Fidel, 14
Catholicism, 73, 74, 86
Cavani, Liliana, 26, 77–86, 89n54
CBS (Columbia Broadcasting System), 6
Cecchi d'Amico, Suso, 69
censorship, 2, 8, 37, 143, 168, 193, 198, 205, 216, 226
Central Park (New York), 149, 155–56
Centro Universitario de Estudios Cinematográficos (CUEC), 201, 206–207
Century City (Los Angeles), 169–171
Century Plaza Hotel (Los Angeles), 170–172
Chabrol, Claude, 44
Champlin, Charles, 180
Champs Elysées (Paris), 36, 51
Chapultepec Park (Mexico City), 191
Chatman, Seymour, 70
Chávez Morado, José, 203
Chávez, Oscar, 201
Chicago, 1, 7, 13, 17, 26, 112–136, 137n17, 138n21, 144, 164
Chicago Police Department, 118
Chicago Reader (newspaper), 124
Chicago Seven, 113, 136n2
Chicago Sun-Times (newspaper), 114
Chicago Tribune (newspaper), 124
Chicano Moratorium, 165, 169, 186n28
China, 7, 182
Church, Frank, 112
Cineaste (journal), 3
Cinema Novo (Brazil), 206
Cinémathèque française, 2, 5, 44
cinematographers, 46, 82, 113–114, 122–123, 197, 199, 226
Cineteca Nacional (Mexico), 205
Cinétracts, 19, 26, 35–58, 62n53
Ciudad Satélite (1957), 191, 200, 203, 206
Ciudad Universitaria. *See* UNAM
Civil Rights Act (U.S.), 132
Clarke, David, 9
Clarke, Shirley, 167

class, 5, 11, 15, 19, 24, 43, 52, 66–67, 70–76, 82, 105, 135, 141–145, 149–151, 153–155, 169, 174, 191–193, 199, 207
classical cinema, 3, 178
Clementi, Pierre, 78
Clermont-Ferrand, 16
Clouzot, Claire, 80
Cohn-Bendit, Daniel, 16
Cold War, 94, 99, 176
Colombia, 14
Colomina, Beatriz, 193
Colonia del Valle (Mexico City), 195
Columbian Exposition, 130
Columbia Pictures, 8, 15–16, 21–22, 144, 146, 151, 154, 160
Columbia University, 8, 15–16, 21, 146–147, 151–153. *See also* Morningside Park
Combat (newspaper), 54
communism, 16, 40, 42, 92
Compagnies Républicaines de Sécurité (CRS), 48–49, 55, 63n69
comparative urbanism, 10, 16
Congress of Industrial Organizations (U.S.), 144–145, 155
consumerism, 20, 40, 56
Contra Costa College, 172–173
Contropiano (journal), 9
Cook, Peter, 4
Coppola, Francis Ford, 137n11
Corman, Roger, 167, 171
corporate power, 2, 8, 94, 131, 217
Cosgrove, Denis, 7
Costard, Hellmuth, 97
counterculture, 17, 21, 131–132, 134, 136n2, 154–155, 159, 170, 173, 190, 197, 205, 223
COunter INTELligence PROgram (COINTELPRO), 126, 132, 138n27. *See also* Federal Bureau of Investigation, FBI
Cowie, Peter, 18
Cronkite, Walter, 6
Cuba, 14, 62n53, 182, 189–190, 205–207
Cuevas, José Luis, 203
Cultural Revolution (China), 7
Czechoslovakia, 5, 133–134

Daley, Richard J., 113, 124, 131–133
Dalí, Salvador, 101

Dancigers, Oscar, 193
Dars, Jean-François, 45
Davis, Angela, 172, 182
Davis, Rennie, 112–113
Death Valley, 172
Debord, Guy, 26, 39–40, 44–45, 61n47, 134
Debray, Régis, 14
De Filippo, Eduardo, 68
de Gaulle, Charles, 2, 16, 20, 44, 51, 182
deindustrialization, 145
Deleuze, Gilles, 178, 207
del Moral, Enrique, 203
Democratic National Convention, 7, 112, 115, 117, 124, 128, 144
Democratic Party (U.S.), 13, 112, 145
demonstrations, 22, 25, 35–36, 38–39, 41, 44, 47, 51, 81, 95, 112, 115–118, 129, 132–134, 144, 165, 169, 170–172, 183, 212, 222, 224
Demy, Jacques, 167, 177–183, 188n53
Denfert-Rochereau (Paris), 36
De Niro, Robert, 149, 155–156
Denmark, 40
De Palma, Brian, 26, 141–142, 149, 151
department stores, 109n15, 109n22, 219
détournement, 39, 41–47, 53–57
Detroit, 150
Deutsche Film- und Fernsehakademie Berlin (DFFB, the German Film and Television Academy), 93, 95–98, 101, 104
Diaz Ordaz, Gustavo, 17
Díaz, Porfirio, 204
Die Welt (newspaper), 105
Die Zeit (newspaper), 107n4
digital images, 57, 213, 220, 226
direct action, 37, 39, 104
Disneyland, 183
documentary film, 2, 18–19, 26, 43, 45, 66, 82, 85–86, 96, 98–99, 104, 114–115, 117–118, 122–123, 127–130, 135, 139n29, 141, 143, 150–153, 156, 169–170, 175, 190, 197, 199, 201–207
Doel, Marcus A., 11
Donald, James, 10
Dow Chemical, 99, 103–104, 106
downtown, 78, 81, 85, 155, 159, 164, 172

Drew, Robert, 139n29
drugs, 122, 159, 181
Ducasse, Isidore, 54
Dumage, Eric, 46, 48
Dutschke, Rudi, 17, 95, 105, 144
Dziga Vertov, 95, 135
Dziga Vertov Group, 38

Eames, Charles and Ray, 9
Ebert, Roger, 114–115, 117, 123, 130
Echeverría, Luis, 199, 205
Eckersall, Peter, 218, 221
École des Beaux-Arts (Paris), 12, 24, 41
École technique de photographie et cinématographie (Paris), 19
economic miracle (Italy), 66–67, 70, 74; (Mexico), 194
editing, 47, 48, 118–119. *See also* montage
8mm film, 27, 185n11. *See also* Super 8
Eisenstein, Sergei, 42
Ekland, Britt, 78, 80
Ellington, Duke, 196
El Lissitzky, 107
Elsaesser, Thomas, 3, 101
Empire State Building (New York), 147
Ensslin, Gudrun, 109n15
equality, 25
eroticism, 40, 73
Espinosa, Julio García, 190, 208n3
Estadio Azteca (Mexico City), 196
États généraux du cinéma, 17, 19, 44
Europe, 2, 3, 5, 16, 26, 144, 170, 193, 212, 215, 217
everyday life, 7, 20–21, 55. *See also* Henri Lefebvre
experimental film, 2, 47, 108n7, 168, 194, 227n4
exploitation film, 168, 170, 177, 225
Expo '70 (World's Fair, Osaka), 221
expressionist movement, 11
expressways, 24, 124. *See also* freeways; highways

factories, 26, 50, 61n42, 67, 69, 71, 74, 76–77, 88nn27–28, 99, 104, 217
The Factory (Andy Warhol), 159

Subject Index

Fanon, Frantz, 15
Farocki, Harun, 26, 91, 93, 97–110
Fascism, 3, 17, 52, 85, 89n54, 94
Fava, Alberto, 85
Federal Bureau of Investigation (FBI), 119, 126
Federal Republic of Germany, 91, 94, 105
Felguérez, Manuel, 203
Fellini, Federico, 21, 32n61, 66, 68
feminism, 3, 64n82, 107, 207
Field Museum of Natural History (Chicago), 115, 123, 130
Fifth Republic (France), 20
Film and Photo League (U.S.), 143
film noir, 168, 173, 176
film studios, 8, 46–48, 67, 170, 177–178, 184n3, 214–215, 219–220
Filmtract(s), 53–55
firebombing (Tokyo), 215, 226
Fischer, Lucy, 11
Florence, 4, 17
Fonseca, Gonzalo, 196
formalism, 13, 135, 156
Forman, Milos, 18
Forster, Robert, 119
Fosada, Victor, 205
Foster, Norman, 25
Foucault, Michel, 78, 83
Fox News, 143
Frampton, Hollis, 19
France, 9, 11–12, 18, 20, 35, 39–40, 44, 46, 52, 63n75, 64n82, 134–135, 178, 182, 224
Frankfurt, 64n80, 96, 109n15
Fraser, Ronald, 7
Free University (Berlin), 95
Free Venice Beachhead (newspaper), 37n187
freeways, 17, 164, 170, 177, 181, 187n37. *See also* expressways; highways
French New Wave, 44, 135, 167, 194. *See also* nouvelle vague
Fuller, Samuel, 167
functionalism, 4, 192, 199, 208n9

Gaines, Jane, 55
Gallant, Mavis, 35–37, 39, 48, 54
Gans, Curtis, 112

Garboli, Cesare, 74
Garcés, Mauricio, 195
Garcia, David, 169
García, Héctor, 199
García, María, 199
García, Sergio, 206
Gardner, Fred, 172
Gare d'Orsay, 24
Gaullism, 36, 52
gay rights movement, 146. *See also* Stonewall Rebellion
gaze (cinema), 43, 47, 79, 83, 85, 102–103
Genet, Jean, 224–225
gentrification, 138n21, 155, 158
geographers, 7, 10, 13, 51
geography, 9, 26, 179–180, 182, 215
Germany, 91–93, 95–96
Gervais, Marc, 75
Gestapo, 108n13
Getino, Octavio, 190
ghetto, 15, 123–124, 131, 133, 166
Girotti, Massimo, 72, 77
Gitlin, Todd, 114, 134
globalization, 6, 10
Gobille, Boris, 38
Godard, Jean-Luc, 20–21, 38, 45, 53, 61n47, 61n51, 62n59, 92–93, 129, 135, 164, 167–168, 179, 182, 219, 222
Goeritz, Mathias, 196
González Hernández, Servando, 199
Gorin, Jean-Pierre, 38, 135
Gower, Terence, 209n19
Gramsci, Antonio, 69
Grant Park (Chicago), 26, 115–117, 130
Great Britain, 40
Great Migration, 124
Greenwich Village, New York, 146, 148, 156
Griffith Park (Los Angeles), 182
Grosvenor Square (London), 144
Groupe Medvedkine, 43, 45
Grupo Cine de la Base (Argentina), 206
Grupo Cine Liberación (Argentina), 206
Gruppo 1999 (Italy), 17
Grupo Ukamau (Bolivia), 206
Guattari, Felix, 207
guerilla warfare, 14–15

Guevara, Che, 14
Gumucio Dagrón, Alfonso, 207

Haight-Ashbury district (San Francisco), 223
Hamburg, 97
handheld camera, 74, 79, 117, 174, 216, 219
Hanoi, 93, 96
happenings, 17, 92
haptic effect, 101, 103
Harlem, 15, 151, 153–154
Harvey, David, 13, 51
Harvey, Sylvia, 18
Haussmann, Georges-Eugène, 13, 190
Havana, 207, 210n39
Hayden, Tom, 113, 144
Hays, K. Michael, 8, 12
highways, 124, 216, 218. *See also* freeways; expressways
hippies, 7, 117–118, 130, 149, 167, 170–172, 176–177, 182
Hoffman, Abbie, 113, 115, 131–132, 146
Hoffman, Dustin, 149
Hollywood, 2, 8, 18, 20, 143, 151, 165–168, 170, 172–173, 177–178, 184n3. *See also* New Hollywood
homosexuals, 4, 72, 155
Hopper, Dennis, 8
Hosoe, Eikoh, 221
House Un-American Activities Committee (HUAC), 15
housing, 19, 22, 72, 98, 166, 191, 195
Huggins, John, 172
Huillet, Danièle, 92
Huxtable, Ada Louise, 24

ideology, 3, 39, 81, 183
Iimura, Takahiko, 214
Illinois, 113, 118, 132–133
Imperfect Cinema, 190, 206, 208n3
imperialism, 5
independent filmmaking, 18, 151, 167, 169, 175, 194, 198, 207
industrial cinema, 2–3, 16, 18, 114, 151
Instituto Cubano del Arte e Industria Cinematográficos (ICAIC, Cuba), 206–207

Internationale Situationniste (journal), 134. *See also* Situationist International
International Movement for an Imaginist Bauhaus, 40
ISKRA, 62n61, 217
Italy, 8, 9, 19, 40, 66–67, 70, 76–77, 82, 86

Jacobs, Jane, 22–23
James, David, 18–19, 153–154, 168
Jameson, Fredric, 31n52, 169
Japan, 2, 212–218, 221–222, 224, 226
Jardines de Pedregal (Mexico City), 190–191
Jarr, Víctor, 201
Johnson, Lyndon Baines, 112, 148, 155, 157, 170, 201
Joskowicz, Alfredo, 203, 206
Joyce, James, 21

Kara, Juro, 216, 225
Kast, Pierre, 43
Katsifiacas, George, 16
Kawada, Kikuji, 221
KCET Television (Los Angeles), 172
Kellner, Douglas, 25
Kennedy, John Fitzgerald, 66, 127, 133, 155, 171
Kennedy, Robert Francis, 5, 127–128, 142
Kent State University, 19
Kienholz, Edward, 183
King, Martin Luther, Jr., 5, 112, 142
Kinokuniya bookshop (Tokyo), 223–224
Kirk, Grayson, 146–147
Klonsky, Mike, 132
Kluge, Alexander, 92, 96
Koeck, Richard, 11
Koolhaas, Rem, 9
Korporaal, Giovanni, 197
Kotanyi, Attila, 134
Krassner, Paul, 132
Krause, Linda, 10
Kreuzberg district (Berlin), 223

labor unions, 14, 35–36, 189, 192, 194, 205
Labro, Philippe, 13, 37
Lambrate (Milan), 74

landscape, 1–2, 26, 71, 73, 78, 91, 114, 170, 176, 180, 190, 193, 196, 213, 221
Langlois, Henri, 2, 5, 44
l'Architecture d'aujourd'hui (journal), 9
L.A. Rebellion filmmakers, 169
Latin America, 5, 14, 144, 197, 201, 207
Latino, 154, 165, 169
Latin Quarter (Paris), 36, 40, 47, 49
Lavin, Sylvia, 170
Layerle, Sebastien, 43, 47
Leacock, Richard, 139n29
Lebel, Jean-Jacques, 165
Le Corbusier, 4, 190
Leduc, Paul, 197
Lefaivre, Liane, 8, 12, 25
Lefebvre, Henri, 20–21, 32n52, 47. *See also* everyday life
Le monde (newspaper), 25, 181
Lenin, Vladimir Ilyich, 15
Le Querrec, Guy, 46
Lerner, Adam, 17
Les Halles (Paris), 40
Lester, Richard, 18
Lettrist International, 40
Levinas, Emmanuel, 55
Lewis, Oscar, 193
Leyda, Jay, 42
Libya, 213
Liebknecht, Karl, 93
Lincoln Park (Chicago), 115, 130
Lindsay, John, 145
Lipton, Lawrence, 176
Lison, Andrew, 17
Little Appalachia (Chicago), 120–123, 138n21
locations (filming), 1, 10, 20, 98, 104, 114–119, 124, 127–130, 145, 151, 160, 167, 169–170, 172–177, 193, 195, 204, 216–219, 223, 226
Lockwood, Gary, 177
Lombardy (Italy), 69, 71, 76, 78, 86
London, 4, 9, 10, 14, 25, 40, 144, 164, 193
London Psychogeographical Committee, 40
López Mateos, Adolfo, 195
Lopez, Nacho (Ignacio López Bocanegra), 193, 197

Los Angeles, 1, 5, 9, 13, 17, 19, 26, 150, 164–84
Los Angeles Department of City Planning, 166
Los Angeles Free Press (newspaper), 165–168, 171, 176, 182
Los Angeles Police Department (LAPD), 168, 171–173
Los Angeles Times (newspaper), 165, 172, 178
Lotta Continua, 4, 68
Lowenstein, Allard, 112
LSD, 132, 174
Lu, Andong, 11
Luxemburg, Rosa, 15, 93
Lynch, Kevin, 181
Lyotard, Jean-François, 182–183

Macedo, Miguel, 204
Macherey, Pierre, 169
Madrid, 16
Maglia, Jackie, 224
Mahler, Horst, 99
Mailer, Norman, 13–14, 113
Malle, Louis, 20
Mallgrave, Harry Francis, 8, 12
Malraux, André, 44
Mangano, Silvana, 71–72
Manhattan, 15, 24, 26, 146–148, 154, 156, 159
Manila, 17
Margulies, Michael D., 119, 129
Marine Midland Bank (New York), 156
Marin, Louis, 182–183
Marker, Chris, 9, 43–46, 49, 61n42, 214, 216–219, 222
Marotti, William, 213
Martinez, Francisco, 169
Marxism, 3, 9, 13, 18, 42, 47, 71, 107, 143, 182
Marx, Karl, 42, 143
Maspéro, François, 38
mass media, 4, 7, 38, 192–193
Massood, Paula, 10
Mastrocinque, Camillo, 68
Matsumoto, Toshio, 27, 214–216, 219–226
Mattioni, Luigi, 79

Maude-Roxby, Alice, 213
Maysles, David and Albert, 137n16
McCarthy, Eugene, 112
McGovern, George, 112
Meany, George, 145, 155
media, 3, 6–8, 11, 13, 20, 25, 35–38, 41, 45–47, 51, 57, 67, 78, 84, 93–94, 96–97, 100, 104, 127, 131, 135, 144, 150, 192–195, 218, 225
Mediaset Group (Italy), 67
Medvedkin, Alexander, 43, 45
Meinhof, Ulrike, 98
Meins, Holger, 26, 91, 93, 96–100, 107
Mekas, Adolfas, 150–151
Mekas, Jonas, 150–151, 194
Memphis, Tennessee, 5
Menéndez, Oscar, 204–205
Metinides, Enrique, 199
Metz, Christian, 3
Mexiac, Adolfo, 203
Mexican Revolution, 191
Mexico, 1, 17, 144, 189–208
Mexico City, 1, 17, 19, 26–27, 144, 189–208
MGM (Metro Goldwyn Mayer), 172–173
Miami, 13, 113, 159
Michigan Avenue (Chicago), 117
middle class, 5, 67, 70, 145, 174, 191–193, 195, 199
Middle East, 225
migration, 69, 124, 157, 191
Milan, 1, 8–9, 24, 26, 66–86
Milan Triennale, 9, 24
Mitchell, W.J.T., 65n94
Mobil Oil, 172
modern architecture, 11, 74, 190–193. *See also* modernism
modernism, 3, 25, 147, 170, 206
Mojave Desert, 172
Monaco, Paul, 17
montage, 39, 45–47, 53, 84, 101, 104–105, 127, 158. *See also* editing
Montevideo, 17
Montoya Pérez, Jesús, 195
Moravia, Alberto, 73
Morin, Edgar, 182
Mormon Tabernacle Choir, 196
Morningside Heights, 15

Morningside Park, 8, 21, 151–152. *See also* Columbia University
Morricone, Ennio, 74, 79
Moscow, 94
Motion Picture Association of America (MPAA), 8
Motion Picture Herald (newspaper), 180
Mount Etna, 73, 77
Mouvement du 22 mars (22 March Movement), 61n51
movie sets, 11, 114, 177
Moya, Rodrigo, 199
Mozart, Wolfgang Amadeus, 76
multiculturalism, 25
multifamiliares (housing), 193, 199, 203, 206
Mumford, Lewis, 115
murals, 203, 209n19, 59n26
Murri, Serafino, 73
Museum of Modern Art (Mexico City), 191
music, 7, 18, 41, 74, 76, 131, 159, 173–174, 196, 201, 220
Mussolini, Benito, 88n28
Muzio, Giovanni, 79
Myrdahl, Thomas, 169

Nairn, Tom, 49
Nanterre, 5, 16, 20–21, 35, 40, 55
Nantes, 16, 45
Narita international airport (Tokyo), 217
narrative, 2, 10, 19–20, 26, 36, 43–44, 46, 57, 72, 83, 114–119, 123, 129–130, 141–143, 146, 149–153, 155–159, 168–170, 174–178, 194, 199, 216, 219, 222–226
narrative fiction film, 2, 19–20, 26, 146, 168–170, 194, 199
Narvarte (Mexico City), 195
National Anthropology Museum (1964), 191, 195
National Autonomous University of Mexico (officially, the Universidad Nacional Autónoma de México, or UNAM), 190, 196, 200–201, 203, 207
National Commission on the Causes and Prevention of Violence (U.S.), 133
National Conference for a New Politics (U.S.), 112

Subject Index

National Mobilization Committee to End the War in Vietnam (Mobe), 112
National Polytechnic Institute (Instituto Politécnico Nacional, Mexico), 203
National Socialism (Germany). See Nazism
National Student Association (U.S.), 112
Nazism, 55, 91, 94–95, 108n13
neighborhoods, 4, 13, 17, 69, 123–125, 127, 138n21, 146, 151–152, 166–167, 174, 179, 189–190, 192–193, 195, 219
neo-avant garde, 194
neocapitalism, 67
neo-classical architecture, 4, 22, 74, 130, 146, 152
neon lights, 181, 219
neorealism, 31n52, 119, 137n11
Nestler, Peter, 92
Netherlands, 9, 40
New Cinema Group (Grupo Nuevo Cine), 194–195
New Hollywood, 8, 151, 168. See also Hollywood
New Jersey, 164
New Jersey Turnpike, 147
New Left, 4–5, 16, 112–113, 132, 135, 142, 153, 165, 170
Newman, Chris, 129
New Objectivity, 11
newspapers, 38, 46, 80, 94–95, 104, 113, 131, 201
Newsreel, 19–20, 26, 141–151
New York, 1, 3, 7, 13, 16–17, 19, 22, 26, 112, 123, 127, 141–160, 167, 193, 196
New York Cinetracts Collective, 19
New York Times (newspaper), 22, 24, 117, 144, 150, 181
Nichols, Mike, 8, 168
Nilsson, Harry, 148, 161n16
Nixon, Richard Milhous, 26, 133, 141, 143, 173
Noguchi, Isamu, 156
North America, 5
Northrop Frye, 73
North Vietnam, 5, 133, 167
Nouel, Thierry, 56

nouvelle vague, 26, 38, 92. See also French New Wave
Nowell-Smith, Geoffrey, 18

Oberhausen Manifesto, 91–92, 96
occupation (military), 96, 99, 203, 212–217
occupation (students), 5, 8–9, 12, 16, 21–24, 35–37, 40–41, 52, 56, 59n26, 65n94, 134, 152
Occupy movement, 64n93
Ockman, Joan, 25
Office of Film, Theatre, and Broadcasting (New York), 145
O'Gorman, Juan, 203
Ohio, 19
Ohnesorg, Benno, 96
Oldenburg, Claes, 22
Olmi, Ermanno, 68, 70
Olympic Games (1960, Rome), 66
Olympic Games (1964, Tokyo), 27, 216, 218, 221
Olympic Games (1968, Mexico City), 189, 194–197, 199, 206
O'Neill, William, 133
Op Art, 197
Open Theater, 172
Oppenheimer, Martin, 14–15
Orfila, Arnaldo, 193
Ortega Flores, Salvador, 195, 203
Ortese, Anna Maria, 85
ORTF (Office de Radiodiffusion Télévision Française), 38, 205
Oshima, Nagisa, 27, 214–215, 219, 223–226

Palacio de Lecumberri (Mexico City), 190, 204
Palacio de los Deportes (Mexico City), 195
Palestinian territories, 224
Pan-Am Building, 158
Pan American Union, 193
Pani, Mario, 191, 193, 195, 199, 203
Paramount Pictures, 120, 123, 129
Paris, 1–3, 5, 7, 12–13, 16–17, 19–20, 24, 26, 35–58, 92, 95, 133–135, 144, 164–166, 177–178, 182–183, 193, 217, 219
Paris Commune, 13, 53

Parra, Ángel, 201
Parra, Violeta, 201
Partido Comunista Mexicano (Mexican Communist Party), 192
Partido Obrero-Campesino Mexicano (Mexican Workers' and Peasants' Party), 192
Partido Revolucionario Institucional (Mexico), 205
Pasolini, Pier Paolo, 8, 18, 26, 68, 70–77, 85–86
Paviot, Paul, 43
peasant (society), 14–15, 43, 72, 76, 198, 208
Peck, Abe, 132, 134
pedestrians, 36, 79, 148, 176, 180, 220
Penn, Arthur, 8
Pennebaker, D. A., 123, 139n29
Pentagon, The, 9, 112–113
Penz, Francois, 11
Peoples' Park, Berkeley, California, 22
performance, 17, 81, 96–97, 100–102, 106, 121, 219, 223, 225–226, 227n4, 228n13
Petro, Patrice, 10
Philadelphia, 13
Phillips Jr., Alex, 199
photography, 38–39, 44, 47, 50, 81, 199, 215, 221
Piano, Renzo, 25
Piazza della Repubblica (Milan), 26, 79, 81
Piazza Duca d'Aosta (Milan), 76
Piazza Fontana bombing (Milan), 8, 67–68, 86
piazzas (architecture of), 79, 85, 90n62
Pinelli, Giuseppe, 67–68
Pirámide de Ehécatl (Mexico City), 191
Place de la République (Paris), 26, 36
Plaza de las tres culturas (Mexico City), 17, 191–192, 199
poetry (poetic), 13, 56, 106, 176, 196
Polanski, Roman, 20, 167
police, 4, 16, 20–22, 24, 26, 35, 38, 48–51, 53, 55, 67–68, 78, 81–85, 96–97, 118, 129–130, 132–133, 144, 146, 151, 153, 165, 168–174, 176, 183, 205, 212–213, 219, 222, 224
pollution, 12, 166, 221
Pompidou, Georges, 182

Pop art, 177, 183
pornography, 55, 155, 165, 215, 225
posters, 41–42, 51, 80–81, 92, 97, 104, 197
post-Fordism, 164
postindustrial city, 25
postmodernism, 4, 11, 24, 164
post-structuralism, 3, 13
Prague, 7, 12, 133
Prague Spring, 133
Pratt Institute (New York), 22
Production Code (U.S.), 143
progressive movements, 14, 18, 73, 77, 112, 126, 145, 168
prostitution, 148, 150, 157, 159, 165, 220
psychedelia, 159, 174, 197, 206
psychoanalysis, 3, 13

Quattrocchi, Angelo, 49
Quinson, Christian, 46, 48

race, 4, 5, 11, 123–127, 137n17, 151–155, 169
racial inequality, 145
racial integration, 22
radicalism, 143–144
radicalization, 15–16, 19, 57, 120, 154
radio, 9, 25, 36–38, 41, 136, 180
Rai (Italy), 66
Ramírez Vázquez, Pedro, 191, 195–196
rationalist architecture, 2, 4, 21, 170
Raymond, Marc, 19
Red Army Faction (Rote Armee Fraktion), 26, 91
Reinickendorf (Berlin), 98
Reisz, Karel, 21
Reitz, Edgar, 92, 96
religion, 72, 75, 182
Renov, Michael, 150
Republican Party (U.S.), 13, 145
Resnais, Alain, 20–21, 43, 45
Restivo, Angelo, 18
Retes, Gabriel, 206
Riboud, Marc, 46
Rimsky-Korsakov, Nikolai, 180
Ripa, Ornella, 81
Ripstein, Arturo, 204
River Po, 71
Rivette, Jacques, 44

rock music, 7, 148, 159, 174, 177, 195
Rogosin, Lionel, 150
Rome, 16, 24, 66–67, 78, 144, 183
Roosevelt, Theodore, 145
Rossen Morrison, Manuel, 195
Rossi, Aldo, 4
Ross, Kristin, 7
Rouch, Jean, 43, 207
Rubin, Jerry, 113, 115, 130–132, 146
Rudd, Mark, 15–17, 154
rural society, 14–15, 43, 173, 191, 207
Ruta de la Amistad (Route of Friendship) (Mexico City), 196, 206

Saint German (Paris), 40
Salazar, Ruben, 165
Sánchez, Aaron, 199
Sander, Helke, 93, 104–107
San Francisco, 7, 19, 144, 146, 150, 159, 172, 178, 223
San Siro (Milan), 74
Sarris, Andrew, 8, 130
Saura, Carlos, 20
Schilling, Derek, 20
Schleier, Merrill, 11
Schlesinger, John, 26, 141–142, 151, 157
Schlondorff, Volker, 18
Schneider, Peter, 105
Schumann, Robert, 180
Scorsese, Martin, 19, 151
Scott Brown, Denise, 4, 8–9
Scott Brown, Timothy, 17
semiotics, 3, 13, 180
sex, 13, 55, 71, 75–76, 142–143, 195, 214–215, 219, 222–225
sexuality, 155, 215
Sharits, Paul, 19
Shinjuku district, Tokyo, 17, 212–227
Shub, Esfir, 42
Simon, John, 127, 131
Sindicato de Trabajadores de la Industria Cinematográfica (Cinema Industry Workers Union), 194
Sindicato de Trabajadores Ferrocarrileros de la República Mexicana (Union of Railroad Workers of the Republic of Mexico), 192

Singer, Daniel, 39
Situationist International (SI), 26, 39–42, 45, 47, 57, 61n47. *See also* Internationale situationniste
16mm film, 20, 38, 43, 46, 49–50, 52–54, 142, 171, 201, 205–206
SLON (Société pour le Lancement des Oeuvres Nouvelles), 45, 56, 217
Slonecker, Blake, 21
slums, 138n21, 193
Smith, Jack, 165
Smith, W. Eugene, 221
Snow, Michael, 18, 92
social justice, 25, 45
social media, 57
Society of Afro-American Students (Columbia University), 21
Soja, Edward, 170
Solanas, Fernando, 190
Soldier Field (Chicago), 115
Sophocles, 77, 146
Sorbonne, 26, 36, 46, 203
Sordo Madaleno, Juan, 195
Sosa, Mercedes, 201
sound, 20, 37, 57, 73–74, 80, 82, 118, 125, 129, 149
soundtrack, 82, 149, 174–175, 185n26, 201
South Central Los Angeles, 165, 169
South Side (Chicago), 123–128, 131, 133
Soviet film, 42–43, 47, 95, 205
Soviet Union, invasion of Czechoslovakia, 5; cinematographers at Auschwitz, 226
Sozialistischer Deutscher Studentenbund (SDS, the League of German Socialist Students), 95, 105
Spock, Benjamin, 112
Springer, Axel, 105
Springer Building, 8, 26, 93–95
Springer Group (newspapers), 99, 104–107
Stacconi, Ulisse, 85
Stamp, Terence, 71–72, 75
Stanek, Lukasz, 21
Starr, Harrison, 172
State Street (Chicago), 124–125
Stazione Centrale (Milan), 76, 79, 85
Stern, Robert A. M., 22
Stevenson, Adlai, 133

Stirling, James, 25
Stockholm, 100
Stonewall rebellion, 146. See also Gays rights movement
Strasbourg, 16
Straub, Jean-Marie, 92
streamlined modern architecture, 11, 165
street film (Straßenfilm), 98
strikes, 9, 15, 21–22, 35–38, 40–41, 44, 53, 134, 144, 151–154, 192, 206
structuralism, 3, 214
Strum Group, 19
students, 2–3, 9, 17–22, 24, 26, 35–36, 40, 44–46, 49, 51, 67, 74, 79, 92, 95–96, 105, 127–128, 134, 141, 144, 151–155, 165–167, 183, 189, 193, 198, 201–203, 207, 213–214
Students for a Democratic Society (SDS), 15, 21, 113, 126, 132, 144, 150, 154
suburbanization, 6
suburbs, 40, 51, 56, 70, 123, 169, 217
Sullerot, Évelyne, 37, 39, 52
Sunset Boulevard, 173
Sunset Strip (Los Angeles), 26, 165, 168–169, 173–176
Super 8 (film), 204–207, 213
superocheros movement (Mexico), 19, 190, 205
Superstudio, 4
Suri, Jeremy, 16
Surrealism, 101, 197
Syria, 213

Tafuri, Manfredo, 4, 9
Tarkovsky, Andrei, 214, 216–218
Tautin, Gilles, 50
Teague, Lewis, 168
Technical University Berlin, 92, 95–96
technology, 11, 21, 164, 219
Tehran, 93–96
television, 6, 20, 37–38, 41, 66–67, 74, 84, 96–97, 100–104, 119, 134, 148, 172, 176, 197, 201, 205, 217, 222
Temple of Augustus (Rome), 78
Terayama, Shuji, 215, 220, 222
Tet offensive, 5, 148, 155
Texas, 154, 157

theory, 39, 45, 57, 97, 153; in architecture, 9, 12; critical theory, 64n80; film theory, 42–43, 47
Third Cinema, 190, 206
Third World, 5, 14
35mm film, 142, 205–206
Thomine, Alice, 12
Thompson, Hunter S., 133
Times Square (New York), 147–148, 154, 158
Tlatelolco (Mexico City), 26, 189–193, 199, 203–204, 206, 208
Toei Company (film studios, Japan), 215
Tokyo, 1, 7, 16–17, 27, 197, 212–227
Tokyo Tower (Tokyo), 220
Tolstoy, Leo, 76
Torres Torija, Antonio, 204
Tour Montparnasse (1969–1973), 3, 8
Touraine, Alain, 182–183
trade unions. See labor unions
transportation, 166
Tribune Tower (Chicago), 131
Trueblood, Beatrice, 196
Truffaut, Francois, 20, 92
Tschumi, Bernard, 12
Tse-tung, Mao, 7, 15
Tula (Hidalgo, Mexico), 196
Tweedie, James, 9
Twentieth Century Fox, 170
Tzonis, Alexander, 8, 12, 25

UNAM. See National Autonomous University of Mexico
underground film, 18, 150
underground newspapers, 6, 132, 165, 177
United States of America, 2, 11, 15, 19, 24–25, 99, 132–133, 141–144, 150, 153, 159, 167, 178, 183, 194, 212, 216, 224
universities, 14–15, 40, 68, 92, 95, 146–147, 149, 182, 213
University of California Los Angeles (UCLA), 167, 169, 172, 183
University of Nanterre, 5, 16, 20–21, 35, 40, 55, 182
University of Rome, 24

University of Southern California (USC), 167–168, 179
University of the Sacred Heart (Milan), 86
urbanism, 10, 16, 20, 134, 192, 194
urbanization, 10, 70
Urban League, 22
urban planning, 2–4, 9, 21, 40, 42, 49, 190–193
urban renewal, 24, 192
Uruchurtu, Ernesto, 191
U.S. Army, 118
U.S. Department of Justice, 173
U.S.-Japan Security Treaty, 212, 215
U.S. National Guard, 19, 117–118, 132–133
U.S. Secret Service, 172
U.S. State Department, 17
utopia, 1, 3–4, 12, 54, 183, 190, 221

Vallejo, Demetrio, 192
Vallotton, Félix, 54
Valpreda, Pietro, 67
Van Cliburn, 196
van der Rohe, Mies, 4
Vaneigem, Raoul, 55, 134
Varda, Agnes, 167, 178
Venice (Italy), 9
Venice (Los Angeles), 26, 169, 173, 176–178, 180, 182
Venice Beach. *See* Venice (Los Angeles)
Venturi, Robert, 4, 8–9
Victorian, 130, 156, 160, 165
video, 20, 57, 201
Vidler, Anthony, 8
Vidor, King, 167
Viénet, René, 41–43, 45, 53, 56
Vietnam, 5, 14, 91, 95, 99, 100, 103–105, 133, 156, 167, 177, 181–183, 212
Vietnam War, 5, 27, 35, 99, 144, 148, 155–157, 174, 183, 216
Viglietti, Daniel, 201
violence, 2, 5, 11, 13–15, 27, 48, 55, 73, 80–81, 97, 101, 103, 117, 119, 133, 144, 146, 152, 164, 169, 171–176, 182–183, 206, 212–213, 225

Visconti, Luchino, 68–69, 85
Vitti, Monica, 20
von Humboldt, Alexander, 204

Walker, Dan, 133
Wallace, George, 142–143
Warhol, Andy, 159, 167, 194
Warren Commission (The President's Commission on the Assassination of President Kennedy), 155
Warsaw, 16
Warsaw Pact, 132
Washington, DC, 13, 94, 122, 193, 198
Watts (Los Angeles), 165, 169, 171, 182
Weatherman (aka the Weathermen), 15, 154
Webb, Lawrence, 10, 25
Weimar Germany, 11
West Berlin, 92, 93–96, 99, 186n28, 223
West Village (New York), 146
Wexler, Haskell, 7, 26, 112–136, 164
Whiting, Cecile, 177
Williams, Raymond, 143
Wojcik, Pamela Robertson, 10–11
Wood, Robin, 25
working class, 5, 15, 43, 70–71, 74, 105, 141, 153, 169, 193
World Trade Center (1966–1973), 3, 8
World War II, 3, 5, 13, 43, 157, 164, 191, 215
Wrigley Building (Chicago), 130
Wyman, Lance, 196

Yale University, 8, 22, 25
Yamasaki, Minoru, 170
Yippies, 113, 130–132, 146
Yokoo, Tadanori, 223
Yokoyama, Rie, 223
Youngblood, Gene, 167
Young, Whitney M., Jr., 22
Yupanqui, Atahualpa, 201

Zavattini, Cesare, 194
Zenkyoto (All Campus Joint Struggle League) (Japan), 214

Also in the series *Urban Life, Landscape, and Policy*

Scott Larson, *"Building Like Moses with Jacobs in Mind": Contemporary Planning in New York City*

Gary Rivlin, *Fire on the Prairie: Harold Washington, Chicago Politics, and the Roots of the Obama Presidency*

William Issel, *Church and State in the City: Catholics and Politics in Twentieth-Century San Francisco*

Jerome Hodos, *Second Cities: Globalization and Local Politics in Manchester and Philadelphia*

Julia L. Foulkes, *To the City: Urban Photographs of the New Deal*

William Issel, *For Both Cross and Flag: Catholic Action, Anti-Catholicism, and National Security Politics in World War II San Francisco*

Lisa Hoffman, *Patriotic Professionalism in Urban China: Fostering Talent*

John D. Fairfield, *The Public and Its Possibilities: Triumphs and Tragedies in the American City*

Andrew Hurley, *Beyond Preservation: Using Public History to Revitalize Inner Cities*

www.ingramcontent.com/pod-product-compliance
Lightning Source LLC
Chambersburg PA
CBHW042248240426
43672CB00020BA/2991